HAMLET

HAMLET
FOLD ON FOLD

GABRIEL JOSIPOVICI

YALE UNIVERSITY PRESS
NEW HAVEN AND LONDON

For information about this and other Yale University Press publications, please contact:

U.S. office: sales.press@yale.edu   www.yalebooks.com
Europe Office: sales@yaleup.co.uk   www.yalebooks.co.uk

Typeset in Adobe Garamond Pro by IDSUK (DataConnection) Ltd
Printed in Great Britain by TJ International Ltd, Padstow, Cornwall

Library of Congress Cataloging-in-Publication Data

Names: Josipovici, Gabriel, 1940– author.
Title: Hamlet : fold on fold / Gabriel Josipovici.
Description: New Haven : Yale University Press, [2016]
Identifiers: LCCN 2015039587 | ISBN 9780300218329 (hardback)
Subjects: LCSH: Shakespeare, William, 1564–1616. Hamlet. | Shakespeare,
    William, 1564–1616—Characters—Hamlet. | BISAC: DRAMA /
    Shakespeare. | LITERARY CRITICISM / Drama.
Classification: LCC PR2807 .J75 2016 | DDC 822.3/3—dc23
LC record available at http://lccn.loc.gov/2015039587

A catalogue record for this book is available from the British Library.

10 9 8 7 6 5 4 3 2 1

To Bernard Sharratt and Marion O'Connor

About anyone so great as Shakespeare, it is probable that we can never be right; and if we can never be right, it is better that we should from time to time change our way of being wrong.

T.S. Eliot

I take it as some kind of criterion for an understanding of *Hamlet* that one understands the special fascination this play famously exerts upon us.

Stanley Cavell

CONTENTS

PREFACE

M any years ago, when I was writing plays for the students at the University of Sussex, I wrote a play called *Comedy*. I had long been fascinated by an image in D. W. Robertson's *A Preface to Chaucer* from a medieval psalter from Reims, now in Cambridge. The page is divided horizontally in two; in the top portion a group of men are playing the psaltery and bells and decorously singing from choirbooks, while in the bottom half a sort of ape-devil beats on a drum slung round his shoulders while around him men whirl in dance, turn somersaults and stand on their heads. I was seized with the notion of writing a play in which an ape-devil would shout out instructions, such as 'Comedy!', 'Tragedy!', 'Melodrama!', and a small group of performers would leap into words and action. The ape-devil would stop them, start them, move them into the positions on the stage he wished them to adopt and generally control them – until, towards the end, the mechanism of his control would start to break down and they would eventually turn against him and destroy him.

In this way, I thought, I would be able to write a series of short plays without being at the mercy of a single plot to which I would be bound for the duration of the evening. But I soon found that I could not both introduce an audience to wholly new plays (or playlets) and then play (yes!) with them as I wished without making the performance intolerably long. I needed instead to make use of plays with which the audience was already familiar. I thus decided to use *Hamlet*, *The Importance of Being Earnest* and a hybrid Victorian melodrama to provide the elements of my own drama. Among other things I discovered, while working with my brilliant cast, that it is possible to condense *Hamlet* into 12 minutes, not just because it is so well known that it only needs a phrase or two to remind the audience of a whole scene, but also because, despite its complexity, it drives forward with great pace from the first moment to the last. Comedy does not work like that. It all depends on timing, on detail, and Wilde's masterpiece emerged as a meaningless rush if given the 12-minute treatment. I had to find another way of conveying its essence in a brief compass.

I don't know if my fascination with *Hamlet* dates from that time or if I chose it as my quintessential tragedy because it already exerted its hold upon me. In my introduction I try to suggest reasons for our belief that we all know and in a sense have always known *Hamlet*. And because we all feel we know *Hamlet*, we all have views upon it, and probably all have unfinished business with it. It was that sense of unfinished business which drove me to write this book. And having previously written a book on the Bible I felt that I was inured to the criticism or condescension that would naturally come my way from scholars who have made Shakespeare or even just *Hamlet* their life-study. This does not mean that I have paid no attention to recent (and not so recent) scholarship on and criticism of the play. I have, but not in any thorough or systematic fashion. Rather, I have picked my way through it, reading what seemed illuminating to me and ignoring the rest. I cannot see a way round that, since I would never have been able to write my book had I attempted to read the bulk of what has been written on *Hamlet*, and it was a book I felt I needed to write. If I have blundered or merely repeated a well-known argument as though it were my own, I ask forgiveness.

Many people have given me their support. Brian Cummings first suggested I write on *Hamlet*. Bernard Sharratt read an earlier draft and gave me encouragement and twenty closely typed pages of his comments, which made me feel he ought to be writing it, not I. George Craig and Charles Nicholl too were enormously encouraging and gave me the confidence to go on in my own way. Steve Mitchelmore, Giglia Sprigge and Victoria Harding all read early drafts and responded with warmth and detailed criticism, which is what one expects of friends. At Yale I have benefited from the support and encouragement of Robert Baldock for close on thirty and Candida Brazil for close on twenty years. Such long-term links not just with a publisher but with individual editors is of vital importance for any writer and is, alas, becoming the exception rather than the rule. I am aware how lucky I have been. At a crucial moment in the writing I was encouraged to continue by attending a Jewish funeral and hearing the son, at the climax of his eulogy to his father, turn to the coffin and quote Horatio's dirge on Hamlet: 'Good night, sweet Prince, and flights of angels sing thee to thy rest.' Tamar Miller was, as always, more than supportive. Needless to say, all the faults that remain are my own.

NOTE ON SOURCES

For ease of reference, all *Hamlet* quotations are from the best-known and most used modern edition of the play, that in the Arden Shakespeare, Second Series, ed. Harold Jenkins, 1982. Line references in the headings to the subsections of each fold also refer to Jenkins's edition as do references in brackets in the text. References to other Shakespeare plays are to the one-volume Pelican Shakespeare, ed. Alfred Harbage, 1969.

INTRODUCTION

S cene 3 of Heiner Müller's 1977 play *Hamletmachine* goes like this:

SCHERZO

The university of the dead. Whispering and muttering. From their gravestones (lecterns) the dead philosophers throw their books at Hamlet. Gallery (ballet) of the dead women. The woman dangling from the rope. The woman with her arteries cut open, etc. . . . Hamlet views them with the attitude of a visitor in a museum (theatre). The dead women tear his clothes off his body. Out of an upended coffin, labelled HAMLET I, step Claudius and Ophelia, the latter dressed and made up like a whore. Striptease by Ophelia.

OPHELIA: Do you want my heart, Hamlet? *Laughs.*

HAMLET: *Face in his hands.* I want to be a woman.

Hamlet dresses in Ophelia's clothes. Ophelia puts the make-up of a whore on his face. Claudius — now Hamlet's father — laughs without uttering a sound. Ophelia blows Hamlet a kiss and steps with Claudius/HamletFather back into the coffin. Hamlet poses as a whore. An angel, his face at the back of his head: Horatio. He dances with Hamlet.

VOICES: *From the coffin.* What thou hast killed thou shalt love.

The dance grows faster and wilder. Laughter from the coffin. On a swing, the Madonna with breast cancer. Horatio opens an umbrella, embraces Hamlet. They freeze under the umbrella, embracing. The breast cancer radiates like a sun.

At a first reading or viewing we might be inclined to treat this as typical German directors' theatre – a form of theatre which could be summed up as: Take a piece of classic drama and do with it what you will, the more outrageous the better. But a little reflection should lead us to revise this view. For does not Müller catch something profound about *Hamlet*, the way that, in our recollection, the play loses any shape it might have had in the theatre and fragments instead into a series of vivid but confusing impressions? We do not remember its climactic scenes as we remember Lear on the heath or Macbeth at bay, but rather an ever-proliferating jumble of phrases and of episodes whose meaning and *raison d'être* seem to have almost disappeared – a ghost, a joke at the expense of an old man, a mime, a mad young woman distributing flowers, the solemn sound of a military funeral, etc., etc.

Everything in this play seems to find an echo somewhere else, but, as Müller brings out, the echoes are imperfect and lead us up alleyways without exit or else with exits into quite different universes. Sex and death are everywhere, but how exactly are they related? Theatricality and histrionics colour almost every scene, but to what end? Everything seems to mean something and to relate to everything else, but what it means and how it relates never quite comes into focus. Of course every great work of art is full of cross-references, of echoes which gradually create something that is not so much a narrative or a play or a painting or a piece of music as an entire and resonant *world*. This is as true of Dante's *Commedia* as of Poussin's *Landscape with a Snake*, of *Crime and Punishment* as of Beethoven's Opus 109 piano sonata. But in *Hamlet* the echoes are somehow *too* insistent, the parallels *too* close, the springs of action excessively overdetermined, while when one comes to examine them closely they evaporate into thin air.

To begin with, as the American lady is supposed to have said, the play is rather too full of quotations: 'I have that within which passes show', 'The time is out of joint', 'To be or not to be', 'Very like a whale', 'O what a noble mind is here o'erthrown', 'The lady doth protest too much', 'The readiness is all.' Partly because the play is so famous, partly because so many of its lines are so memorable, but partly too, perhaps, for a deeper, more secret reason, it feels as if we had always known it, even when we see or read it for the first time.

And then, as I've said, there are the internal parallels or echoes which are thrust into our consciousness. There is not one family at the centre of the action, as in *Othello*, or even two, as in *Macbeth* and *Lear*, but three: Hamlet, his dead father (with the same name), and his uncle-stepfather, Claudius; Laertes, his (soon-to-be) dead father, and his sister; Fortinbras, his father (with the same name) and his bed-ridden uncle – not to speak of Priam, Hecuba and their dead son, the subject of the Player's speech in Act II. Hamlet, we learn, was born the day his father, Old Hamlet, defeated the Norwegians, in the form of Old Fortinbras, thereby taking possession of some Norwegian land, and he dies just as Young Fortinbras invades Denmark, blessing the conquest with his dying words. The parallels are too insistent to ignore, but what are we to make of them? Again, what Old Hamlet tells his son about his murder is then at Young Hamlet's instigation acted out, first in a dumb-show and then in a play, yet Lucianus, the murderer in the play, is not, as in Old Hamlet's account, the king's brother, but his nephew – not, in other words, Claudius, if this is meant to echo the situation as Hamlet conceives it, but Hamlet himself – and the victim Claudius – or is the victim actually the father he professes to adore? Insistent, yes, but, again, strangely resistant to interpretation (though a gift to those psychoanalytically inclined, some of whom, and not the most foolish, even claim that it is really Gertrude asleep in the orchard and Hamlet is not slaying his father but sleeping with his mother). Again, Old Hamlet, in the crucial fifth scene of the first act, explains to his son what has befallen him, but Young Hamlet is not sure whether the apparition is telling him the truth or pouring poison into his ear in order to drag him to perdition – no, hold on, the murder is said to consist of the *literal* pouring of poison into Old Hamlet's ear by his treacherous brother . . . It seems as if every image, every word, sends us off to other scenes, images and words in a desperate attempt to get the play under control, to make clear to ourselves exactly what is going on – yet every such attempt seems to make things more rather than less confusing.

Moreover, in no other play of Shakespeare's – probably no other major literary work – are so many key episodes shrouded in mist. Has Claudius been legally elected according to Danish custom or has he usurped the throne? Is his marriage to his brother's wife seen as perfectly natural by everyone but Hamlet, or do others share his feeling that it should not have happened at all and was in any case over-hasty? Did Claudius commit adultery with his brother's wife or merely woo his widow? Why does Claudius not react to the mime, which is meant to reflect his murder back at him? Does Ophelia drown by accident or is it suicide? What exactly is the nature of the wager that Claudius enters into with Laertes over the duel?

Scholars have fretted over these and a host of other issues for centuries, but despite their best efforts the problems remain unresolved. Could it not be, then, that the proliferation of such puzzles points to something in the play itself? Eliot famously thought the reason for much of the confusion was that Shakespeare had failed in some way, perhaps by not finding the proper 'objective correlative' for what he was trying to say. But that is a counsel of despair, typical of Eliot's perpetual unease with Shakespeare, which contrasts strikingly with his lifelong trust of Dante. Cannot these puzzles and confusions be seen as part of the *fabric* of the play, part of what the play is *about*, rather than as so many problems to be explained away?

Curiously, several contingent facts associated with the play also contribute to our sense of it as oddly confused and confusing. We know, for instance, that there was an original *Hamlet* circulating in England in the 1590s, but it has not survived as has the original *King Lear* (a play called *King Leir*), and we do not know if it was by Shakespeare himself (unlikely) or by Kyd or by some other, unknown, playwright. Then again, for many of Shakespeare's plays we have two versions, a small format or quarto version, published in his lifetime, and a version in the large format of the noble Folio, published not long after his death by his fellow actors and stakeholders in the company, John Heminge and Henry Condell. For *Hamlet*, though, we have three versions: a so-called Bad Quarto of 1603 (Q1), possibly a pirated version produced from memory by an actor or actors who had taken part in the play (this standard explanation has been questioned in recent years); a Good Quarto of 1605 (Q2), nearly twice as long as Q1 and probably Shakespeare's working script, rushed into circulation in response to the Bad Quarto; and the Folio of 1623 (F), almost as long as Q2, and including some lines not in that version, while removing rather more lines that are. This, many scholars believe, represents the acting version finally decided on by the playwright and the company. Most editors and directors combine the Good Quarto and the Folio, feeling that if they stuck to one or the other they would be leaving out some of the best-loved bits and generally weakening the play. And, finally, the play in both Q2 and F is so long (one of the longest of his plays) that practically all performances of *Hamlet*, as well as being an amalgam of Q2 and F, are cut in some way or other. This means that no two productions of *Hamlet* will use exactly the same text. (In line with recent developments in the approach to older texts, the recent (2006) edition of the play in the Third Series of Arden texts runs to two volumes, the first consisting of the Second Quarto text and the second of the First Quarto and the Folio, thus allowing readers to make up their own minds. A few little theatres have tried putting on Q1 or Q2 or F in the same spirit of purity, but this seems unlikely to catch on at Stratford or in any other major playhouse.)

Then of course there are the cruxes which bedevil most of Shakespeare's plays: words or phrases that editors feel they have to emend because as they stand they seem to make no sense, or words and phrases that belong to one text but not the other (leaving Q1 out of the discussion), forcing editors to make decisions about which to use and which to drop. 'O that this too too solid flesh would melt,/ Thaw and resolve itself into a dew,' Hamlet begins his first soliloquy (I. 2. 129ff.). Or so the Folio tells us. The Quarto has 'sallied', which editors emend to 'sullied', made dirty, polluted. An important difference, though perhaps in the theatre whichever the actor says can be heard either way, and perhaps Shakespeare never made up his mind about which he wanted. Later (III. 4. 180–1), when Hamlet confronts his mother in her closet, he briefly refers to the corpse of Polonius, whom he has just killed by mistake, then rounds on her once more, chiding her for her behaviour. He ends with a couplet: 'I must be cruel to be kind. This bad begins, and worse remains behind.' That is the Quarto reading. The Folio has: 'Thus bad begins . . .' Harold Jenkins, in his Arden edition (Second Series, 1982), insists the correct reading has to be the Quarto (he is partial to it), and that 'this' refers to the killing of Polonius. 'Thus', on the other hand, would be vaguer and more ominous, and refer more generally to all that has been happening, and seems to me to fit better with the sententious quality of such couplets. Though there is only the difference of a single letter, there is, in this instance, no way that an audience could mistake 'this' for 'thus' and no way for us to determine which was the word Shakespeare wished to use.

One final example. As Claudius seeks to persuade Laertes to take part in the plot he has devised to do away with Hamlet once and for all, he mentions a 'gentleman of Normandy, one Lamord', who recently visited Elsinore. Some critics have seized on this as a hint of apocalypse, the personification, so near the bloody climax, of death, La Mort. The Folio, however, has the innocent 'Lamound', which might suggest, if the Folio does indeed incorporate Shakespeare's revisions, that he spotted the dangers of over-emphasis on the name he had chosen for the Norman gentleman and so changed it to something *without* those connotations. Again, we have no way of knowing.

There is a further problem with the text, though again it is not unique to *Hamlet*. Modern editions of Shakespeare present the plays as neatly divided into acts and scenes, but such divisions were first introduced systematically by Nicholas Rowe in his edition of the plays in 1709, a full century after Shakespeare. 'Rowe worked on the neoclassical assumption that the division of the plays into five acts was the correct and natural scheme of things,' Emrys Jones points out in his important *Scenic Form in Shakespeare*. However, he goes on to say, Rowe had a kind of authority for what he did in the First Folio, which already divides the comedies into five acts and some of them into scenes as well – but then the First Folio was itself making a bid to monumentalise Shakespeare, to turn him into a classic almost at the instant of his death. In the Folio some of the histories and tragedies are also divided into acts and scenes, but others only into acts, while yet others have nothing marked after the initial 'Actus Primus. Scoena Prima'. For *Hamlet* Acts I and II are marked, and the first three scenes of Act I as well as the first scene of Act II, but after that, nothing. This does not affect us in the theatre, because every director has in any case to find his or her own way through the play and to decide where the interval should occur. (Elizabethan productions probably ran without intervals.) But it does make the text, whichever edition we read the play in, seem much more clearly organised and laid out than it ever was in Shakespeare's time.

So what *is Hamlet* if its textual basis is so uncertain, and do we ever see the play as Shakespeare would have wanted it done? Does it exist at all? And what does 'wanted' mean here? These are real questions, but perhaps less troubling today than they were fifty years ago. Textual work on Proust and Joyce, for example, has shown us that we are pursuing a myth if we think we can ever get to 'what the author really wrote' – a myth, in fact, which has its origins in the Renaissance and the Reformation, with their desire to get back to the pure, unsullied text of Plato or the Gospels by removing the encrustation of later times. Art, we are now starting to understand, has never come into being in this way, especially not in the world of the theatre, particularly the ad hoc and largely improvisatory world of the Elizabethan theatre.

The really peculiar thing about *Hamlet*, though, is that this myth of the truth being inherent in a text (or a person) turns out to be one of its central themes. Claudius and the court try to get to the heart of Hamlet, to find out what he is 'really up to', something he is well aware of and strenuously resists. At the same time he himself is engaged in precisely the same endeavour, asking himself obsessively (as Othello, Lear and Macbeth never do) who he is and why he is acting as he does. All of which reinforces the strange sense of the play as being both inside and outside us, always known and familiar and also largely unknown and unknowable – very like our sense of ourselves, in fact.

Given all this, Heiner Müller's *Hamletmachine* emerges less as an exercise in self-indulgence and more as one (East German) playwright's account of his experience/memory of the play. And it suggests that all attempts to get at 'what *Hamlet* is really about' are setting about things in the wrong way. The play has so many mirrors, so many internal echoes, that it is difficult to get a grip on what is going on and in precisely what order. We may emerge into the street at the end of a performance, or put down the book, but we never really emerge from the play, just as we never really emerge from ourselves. Yet while we are watching or reading we are carried along by the sheer exuberant inventiveness of the play. In the theatre in fact it seems far more seamless, far more of a finely tuned engine, than, say, *Measure for Measure* or *Lear*. Partly this is because it is at once so painful and so funny, and the humour is not confined to a subplot or even to a minor character like the Fool – for Hamlet, as we will see, is himself both the hero and the Fool, and he is on stage nearly the whole time. But partly it is that, although the play is extremely difficult to reconstruct after the event, it is brilliantly constructed moment by moment to convey a sense at once of a hopeless stasis, of endless talk and nothing decisive happening, and of a machine hurtling helplessly towards a conclusion at once longed for and fought against.

This doubleness is felt by every viewer and reader, but it is very difficult to hold on to. For if we try to understand the play, to fathom its deepest springs, we lose the sense of its unfolding in time, while if we focus on its relentless forward motion we feel ourselves being carried not towards understanding but away from it. And all the while this double movement precisely mirrors Hamlet's own experience.

So how to marry what we might call the vertical dimension of understanding with the horizontal dimension of unfolding? (Roman Jakobson would have called this the metaphorical and the metonymic axes.) How, at a practical level, to marry discussion of what the play is 'about', the kind of discussion that forms the staple of literary criticism, with discussion of how the play unfolds in time? The trouble with undue emphasis on the former is that the unfolding aspect is lost; the trouble with the latter is that it can descend into mere commentary and paraphrase ('and then . . . and then . . . and then') and lose sight of the play's deeper meanings.

The answer should be obvious: if this dilemma is mirrored in Hamlet himself then we must pay attention to how and why this is the case. In other words, we must accept that we will have to court the danger of mere paraphrase and commentary, and counter it by an awareness of how every moment, as well as leading to the next moment, is also filled with the weight of all the other moments that make up the play.

Emrys Jones, in the quietly profound book I have already referred to, *Scenic Form in Shakespeare*, suggests that by concentrating on the *scene* in the first instance, we can get an understanding of the way Shakespeare's plays as experienced in the theatre are comparable to musical works as experienced in a concert hall or opera house: 'When we see them performed,' he says, 'what we enjoy is, in part, the process of "going through" the work, taking pleasure in its texture and structure in a way which critical accounts which limit themselves to interpretation can hardly do justice to.'

Remember that the division of the plays into acts and scenes is not Shakespeare's. We can all recognise a 'scene', as Jones asserts, but not an 'act'. A scene may be subdivided, made up of an infinite number of smaller bits, but it still has a unity, and it is this he tries to bring out. This is true of some of the acts as well, notably Act I, but not of all. I wonder, though, if even the idea of a scene does not make us think too much of a play as being made of these rather as a necklace is made up of beads strung on a string. Is there not some other way of talking about such units, one that will stress their dynamic interrelation rather than their discreteness?

I would suggest that there is, and that it lies in a word I have been using, the word 'unfolding'. Here we can do no better than to turn to a poet who spent his life meditating on the nature of folding and unfolding: Mallarmé.

Mallarmé was very fond of fans. He wrote several poems about them and thought deeply about their magic and their mystery. He wrote a sonnet to his wife about them:

Eventail (de Madame Mallarmé)

Avec comme pour langage
Rien qu'un battement aux cieux
Le futur vers se dégage
Du logis très précieux

Aile tout bas la courrière
Cet éventail si c'est lui
Le même par qui derrière
Toi quelque miroir a lui

Limpide (où va redescendre
Pourchassée en chaque grain
Un peu d'invisible cendre
Seule à me rendre chagrin)

Toujours tel il apparaisse
Entre tes mains sans paresse.

In George Craig's fine, strictly literal – insofar as Mallarmé can ever be translated literally – translation:

Fan (for Madame Mallarmé)

With, by way of language,
No more than a flutter in the skies,
The future line slips out
Of its most precious resting place

Wing, far below, bearing
This fan if it is indeed
That same by which behind
You some looking glass has gleamed

Limpid (down into which will fall
Its every grain driven
A little invisible ash
Alone a grief for me)

May it always so appear
Between your tireless hands.

He also wrote a poem to his daughter about fans, at the end of which he speaks of 'Ce blanc vol fermé que tu poses/ Contre le feu d'un bracelet' ('This white shut flight you lay/ Against a bangle's fire'), and this image of a white shut flight brings out the ideal state towards which the fan gestures. For a fan is not simply vertical when shut and horizontal when open, it allows us to imagine (allows Mallarmé to imagine) an *absolute* verticality and an *absolute* horizontality united in one object so small and light it almost does not exist – the very model of Mallarmé's ideal poem. It is static on the page and flies away in the imagination; it is spread out, word after word, each taking up space on the page, and it takes up no space at all in the imagination: *ce blanc vol fermé*.

Indeed, the fan is for Mallarmé what the compass was for Donne and the phoenix for Shakespeare, an object or mythical beast turned into a conceit, and therefore replaceable by similar objects or beasts. He can, in another poem, find the same effect in a different object, as when he describes how the cathedral of Bruges emerges from the mist 'pli selon pli', fold on fold, as the mist disperses around it, a phrase Pierre Boulez used as the title for his great setting of and musical meditation on Mallarmé. And though there might seem to be not just a gap but a veritable chasm between the hyper-refined poetry of Mallarmé and Shakespeare's robust theatre, the notion of the fan, which can be both shut tight and opened up wide, catches precisely what I feel is characteristic of *Hamlet*, the way that, as the play unfolds, each moment seems to carry vertically on top of it all the other moments in the play, and how any attempt to talk about it must be alert to both this and to the way it unfolds. For unlike the word 'scene', the word 'fold' has a physical quality to it, it is palpable, not abstract. As if to alert us to this, the play opens with the words: 'Who's there?' uttered by one of the soldiers on the battlements of Elsinore, and back comes the riposte: 'Nay, answer me. Stand and *unfold* yourself.' The word can be translated here as 'reveal', a word Shakespeare could have used but chose not to, going instead for a word with primarily physical connotations and only a secondary metaphorical meaning, perhaps in order to stress the physical and gradual nature of such revelation. He uses the word again in Q2 towards the end of the play. Hamlet is explaining to Horatio how he found out, on the ship taking him to England, about the King's plot to have him killed. He steals a letter the King has entrusted to Rosencrantz and Guildenstern, and then 'withdrew/ To mine own room again, making so bold,/ My fears forgetting manners, to unfold/ Their grand commission' (V. 2. 15–18). Here the word simply means to 'make manifest', that is, to unseal the envelope. And, indeed, the Folio has replaced it with 'unseale', perhaps because of the awkward rhyme with 'bold', but perhaps also because Shakespeare did not want to debase a word he found, for whatever reason, significant, by using it in this more abstract sense.

In the introduction to his remarkable study of the complex concatenation of events that led up to the outbreak of the First World War, *The Sleepwalkers*, Christopher Clark remarks:

> A Bulgarian historian of the Balkan Wars recently observed that 'once we pose the question "why", guilt becomes the focal point.' Questions of guilt and responsibility in the outbreak of war entered the story even before war had begun. The entire source record is full of ascriptions of blame (this was a world in which aggressive intentions were always assigned to opponents and defensive intentions to oneself) and the judgement

delivered by Article 231 of the Treaty of Versailles has ensured the continuing prominence of the 'war guilt' question. Here, too, the focus on *how* suggests an alternative approach: a journey through the events that is not driven by the need to draw up a charge sheet against this or that state or individual, but aims to identify the decisions that brought war about and to understand the reasoning or emotions behind them. This does not mean excluding questions of responsibility entirely from the discussion – the aim is rather to let the why answers grow, as it were, out of the how answers, rather than the other way about.

There could not be a better description of my aim in this book. By examining *Hamlet* fold on fold I want to take a journey through the events that is not driven by the need to draw up a charge sheet against this or that individual, but aims to identify the decisions taken in the course of the play and to understand the reasoning or emotions behind them. I want to let the why answers grow out of the how – not '*Why* does Hamlet act as he does?' but '*How* does Hamlet act?' In so doing, I believe, we will achieve a better understanding of this extraordinary and mysterious play.

While writing what follows I have listened constantly to the wonderful commentaries on Beethoven's piano sonatas given by András Schiff at the Wigmore Hall in the course of 2013 to accompany his performance of the complete Beethoven cycle, and available on the Wigmore Hall website. The freedom the form of a lecture-recital gives him to stop at any point and go back to some earlier passage or work of Beethoven's, or to the work of Bach or Haydn, or to follow some other related train of thought and to demonstrate before his audience how a passage should, in his opinion, be played, and why, more than makes up for what might be felt as the dangers of a mere commentary or paraphrase. Alas, I am no Schiff, and my audience consists of readers, not listeners, but I think we can take his approach to heart, reminding ourselves of Emrys Jones's remark that our experience of Shakespeare in the theatre is much more like that of listening to music in the concert hall than of deciphering a difficult text. I have also learned a great deal from Edward Snow's remarkable book on Bruegel's *Children's Games*, another teeming, confusing, overdetermined early modern masterpiece which consistently denies us the satisfaction of reducing it to a single 'story' while never allowing us to forget that it is a highly wrought artefact.

FOLD ONE

1.1 (I. 1. 1–19)

We begin where, in the theatre, we always begin: waiting for something to get under way. Shakespeare is often content to start in leisurely fashion and only gradually turn the comic or tragic screw – but not here:

> *Barn.* Who's there?
> *Fran.* Nay, answer me. Stand and unfold yourself.
> *Barn.* Long live the King!
> *Fran.* Barnardo?
> *Barn.* He.
> *Fran.* You come most carefully upon your hour.
> *Barn.* 'Tis now struck twelve. Get thee to bed, Francisco.
> *Fran.* For this relief much thanks. 'Tis bitter cold,
>   And I am sick at heart. (1–9)

'Who's there?' Never has such a mighty edifice rested on two such small and simple words (Dante's 'Nel mezzo' and Proust's 'Longtemps' run them close). Who's there, indeed, becomes the leitmotif of the play. Who is it we see on the stage before us, an actor or a 'character'? Who is the ghost whose appearance sets the whole

action going, Hamlet's father come back from the dead or a malignant spirit come to trick him into perdition? Who is Claudius, a
murderous and incestuous usurper or a loving uncle and husband?
Who is Gertrude, a conniving adulteress or a loving widow and
mother? Who is Ophelia, a demure daughter or a tormented spirit?
Who, for that matter, does Hamlet see when he looks in the glass?
None of these questions is fully answered by the end of the play, but
what we come to understand is that they are far less straightforward
than they seem.

At the same time the question functions in a perfectly straightforward and transparent way at the start of this fold, as, in 45
commonplace words, Shakespeare gives us all the information we
need. Two sentries meet at midnight, one come to relieve the
other, and the next few lines will inform us that this is the battle-
ment of the castle of the Danish king at Elsinore. Commonplace,
but carefully chosen. As I argued in the introduction, Shakespeare
could have used the word 'reveal', but he chose to use the word
'unfold' instead, a word whose metaphorical meaning is, precisely,
'reveal yourself', but whose primary meaning suggests a physical,
gradual process: even in the dark, only dimly perceived, the act of
recognition follows the same course as it would in full daylight: a
body is seen and then a voice is heard and a name is uttered, and
all these together allow the person to be recognised.

We are of course likely to see the play in a dark, closed audito-
rium; Shakespeare was writing for the Globe, open to the skies,
and the performances would have taken place in the afternoon.
Thus Shakespeare has to work that much harder to get us to
imagine a midnight scene. Yet in this play, which delights in
drawing attention to itself, there is none of that winking at
the audience which we find in the famous Dover cliffs scene in
King Lear. Precisely because there will be so much metatheatrical
reference later on, Shakespeare is here at the start concerned to
get across as simply and efficiently as possible where we are in
the fiction of the play: on the battlements of Elsinore at the
changing of the guard (a moment of transition) in the middle
of the night.

And yet in the theatre, as this opening scene unfolds before us, we are beset by a sense of confusion. For one thing, the exchanges are so brief we have little time to sort out just who is who; all we can do is get a general idea of what is going on. For another – and this is the first of those oddities I mentioned in the introduction with which the text is beset – it seems to be the *incoming* sentry who asks what we might expect the outgoing one to ask ('Who's there?'), and though this seems not to matter, it must register as a slight jolt as we watch and listen. And then there are Francisco's last lines in the passage quoted, ''Tis bitter cold/ And I am sick at heart'. Surprisingly, this is not taken up by Barnardo, who asks instead: 'Have you had quiet guard?', to which Francisco responds: 'Not a mouse stirring.' Nevertheless, this adds to our sense of foreboding and disorientation.

Horatio and Marcellus enter, whereupon Francisco asks what we would have expected him to ask at the very start: 'Stand, ho! Who is there?' to be answered by Horatio's 'Friends to this ground' and Marcellus's 'And liegemen to the Dane.' Both phrases will come to resonate for us as the 'ground' on which they stand is discovered to be contested territory, to be defended both from Norway and from Poland, as well as being the ground on which the Globe is built and on which the actors stand to deliver their lines, while the title 'the Dane', here referring to Claudius, the incumbent King of Denmark, will, at a climax in the action, be taken over by Hamlet: 'This is I,/ Hamlet the Dane' (V. 1. 250–1). However, in the present moment they are answers which satisfy Francisco, who then takes his leave: the guard has been changed, the play is under way.

1.2 (I. 1. 20–146)

The new arrival, Horatio, asks at once: 'What, has this thing appeared again tonight?' and is told by Barnardo that it has not, whereupon Marcellus explains what they are talking about and why they are there:

> Horatio says 'tis but our fantasy,
> And will not let belief take hold of him,
> Touching this dreaded sight twice seen of us.
> Therefore I have entreated him along. (26–9)

Something has come to disrupt the forward continuity of life: the eruption of the unnatural into the natural world, and, as we will see, of the past into the present. Whether because we know *Hamlet* or because we know the genre of the ghost story, we intuit that this 'thing' is a ghost of sorts. And it seems that Horatio, recognised by the others as a 'scholar', must be the one to speak to the Ghost, should it appear again this night.

As befits a more learned man, he is sceptical: 'Tush,' he says, ''twill not appear'. Nevertheless, Barnardo is determined to fill him (and, of course, us) in on the details of the Ghost's previous appearance to them:

> Last night of all,
> When yond same star that's westward from the pole,
> Had made his course t'illume that part of heaven
> Where now it burns, Marcellus and myself,
> The bell then beating one – (38–42)

At this point *last night* and *now* are suddenly elided as the Ghost makes its entry. Now we finally see what this 'thing' looks like. But it's worth noting before we do so that Barnardo is not simply using a long-winded and 'poetic' way of saying: 'It was almost one in the morning when . . .' Today we tell the time by looking at our watches but Barnardo and his comrades did so by looking at the heavens and listening to the chiming of church bells. This places them – and us as we listen – within an ordered universe in which we live out our little lives always aware that we are part of a bigger picture – the universe and the Christian dispensation within which churches function. This is strangely soothing, setting the ordered cosmos against what, from the anxious first 'Who's there?', we have felt to be the fevered atmosphere of the Danish king's castle.

And it is against this ordered backdrop that the Ghost makes his entry.

All scholars are agreed that *Hamlet* was written in 1600/1, and that its immediate source is a lost play, known to us from a number of contemporary references, that prominently featured a ghost, and which was ridiculed at the time both for this and for its bombast. Thomas Lodge, for example, in 1596, describes a 'ghost which cried so miserably at the Theatre, like an oyster-wife, *Hamlet, revenge*'. The phrase 'Hamlet, revenge', Jenkins tells us, 'became a by-word', to be found in works by Dekker and Rowlands among others (p. 83). Shakespeare's primary task, once he decided to work with this material, was thus in some way to defuse the laughter that would be likely to greet the appearance of a ghost crying revenge. In typical fashion he manages this by a mixture of doing better what had been crudely done by his predecessor and by the simple but radical expedient of not taking the Ghost for granted, as a stage prop, but making the question of its reality and its nature a central *theme* of his play. Here we see him at work on both fronts. The audience is so gradually introduced to the Ghost that we are hardly aware of the minute incremental steps whereby it has been prepared for it. First of all there has been Francisco's 'I am sick at heart' (1. 9), and now we hear first of a 'thing' and then of a 'dreaded sight', while Shakespeare draws us into his web by placing at the centre a figure of sturdy common sense whose initial reaction, like ours, is scepticism. Yet Jenkins is surely wrong to describe Horatio as a 'sceptic'; nothing in his subsequent words and actions in this play suggest he is a full-blown sceptic, only someone with his feet firmly on the ground who naturally doubts what his friends have told him and what Barnardo starts to repeat to him for the benefit of the audience. In other words Horatio plays the sort of role in the play that the chorus did in Greek tragedy: he speaks for us, the audience, as we would like – and feel ourselves – to be. So when Barnardo greets the sight of the Ghost with: 'In the same figure like the King that's dead' and Horatio responds: 'Most like. It harrows me with fear and wonder' (a harrow is a heavy frame of wood or iron set with iron nails which is dragged over ploughed land to break up any hard lumps that remain, so that the image, though in a sense conventional, would have been physically felt by most members of the audience), two things happen to us: we believe him, and we half recall the ritual words uttered by Barnardo at the very start: 'Long live the King!' and thus sense that the play is going to revolve around the question: Who really is 'the King'? The one who is dead or the one who is living?

Horatio is enjoined, as a learned man, to speak to the Ghost, and he promptly does so with a mixture of horror at its coming and awe at its appearance, thus leaving us with a powerful sense of the ambiguity inherent in what we are witnessing: it is something unnatural and should not be happening, but on the other hand it evokes not simply horror but, as Horatio says, 'fear and wonder':

> What art thou that usurp'st this time of night,
> Together with that fair and warlike form
> In which the majesty of buried Denmark
> Did sometimes march? By heaven, I charge thee speak. (49–52)

But the Ghost says nothing, and when charged again to speak vanishes without a word. Yet its presence has been established beyond doubt. Horatio, our 'eyes', speaks for us when he says:

> Before my God, I might not this believe
> Without the sensible and true avouch
> Of mine own eyes. (59–61)

That it is the dead King too is no longer in doubt. Horatio suddenly broadens the canvas and sets the castle we have been cooped up in since the start in the larger context of Baltic geopolitics: it is, he explains, the Old King dressed in the very armour with which he fought both the Norwegians and the Poles. 'This,' he pronounces, 'bodes some strange eruption to our state' (72). Here, in a cunning transition, Shakespeare brings the geopolitical into the present. Marcellus asks why it seems that the whole of Denmark is currently on war alert, and Horatio explains. 'Our last King,/ Whose image even but now appear'd to us' (83–4) was, it seems, challenged to single combat by Fortinbras, King of Norway, and, defeating him, took as his spoil all the land Fortinbras had hitherto conquered. (The land, presumably, that of Denmark: this is one of the many places in the play – the most famous or infamous being the terms of the duel between Hamlet and Laertes at the end – where the language is so full of legal and other terms that it is difficult for an audience to follow precisely.) Young Fortinbras, his son, a Hotspur-like figure as he is here described, has got together a band of hotheads to try and recover this land, whence the present unease in Denmark. Could it be, then, that the appearance of Old Hamlet has to do with this? Is he come, in a sense, to call on the Danes to make sure his hard-fought conquests are not dissipated?

The question is left in the air as Horatio evokes the strange and unnatural events that preceded Julius Caesar's murder in the streets of Rome, a passage that recalls Shakespeare's own recently performed *Julius Caesar* and which, like the accounts in that play, Shakespeare derived from Plutarch and a variety of Roman historians and poets. It's a powerful passage, yet, unlike everything that has gone before, it feels perhaps a little too 'literary' and 'dramatic':

> In the most high and palmy state of Rome,
> A little ere the mightiest Julius fell,
> The graves stood tenantless and the sheeted dead
> Did squeak and gibber in the Roman streets . . . (116–19)

That Shakespeare himself did not feel comfortable with this is shown by the fact that he cut the speech down in the Folio text, but even more, as we will see, by the way he goes on to handle such 'literary' speeches as the play unfolds.

In the midst of this, the Ghost suddenly reappears. Horatio adjures it once more to speak and say 'If there be any good thing to be done/ That may to thee do ease', and 'If thou art privy to thy country's fate,/ Which, happily, foreknowing may avoid' (133–7). When the Ghost still does not answer Marcellus offers to strike it with his spear, but at this point the cock crows and the Ghost, seen first in one part of the stage, then in another, disappears altogether.

1.3 (l. 1. 147–80)

The remainder of this amazing scene consists of the discussion between the men of the significance of the Ghost and Horatio's assertion that they must inform 'young Hamlet' (175) of what they have seen.

The effect of the conversation is to define the nature of the Ghost that now we, as well as they, have seen. Like all traditional ghosts it fled on hearing the cock crow, fled, moreover, 'like a guilty thing/ Upon a fearful summons' (153–4). Once again we are not simply being informed but having a world shaped for us that is both ordered and coherent. 'I have heard,' says Horatio, helping place the Ghost in that twilit world we most of us inhabit, where a whole variety of things are neither wholly believed nor wholly disbelieved:

> I have heard
> The cock, that is the trumpet to the morn,
> Doth with his lofty and shrill-sounding throat
> Awake the god of day, and at his warning,
> Whether in sea or fire, in earth or air,
> Th'extravagant and erring spirit hies
> To his confine; (153–60)

To which Marcellus adds some words which secure the appearance of the Ghost within the realm not only of folklore, but of the Christian dispensation:

> Some say that ever 'gainst that season comes
> Wherein our Saviour's birth is celebrated,

This bird of dawning singeth all night long;
And then, they say, no spirit dare stir abroad,
The nights are wholesome, then no planets strike,
No fairy takes, nor witch hath power to charm,
So hallow'd and so gracious is that time. (163–9)

'So have I heard and do in part believe it,' responds Horatio. 'In part' is a stroke of genius. Though referring specifically to the relations of ghosts and evil spirits to the Christian dispensation, it nevertheless helps maintain the ambiguities which have entered the play with the Ghost: dressed in his armour he comes with all the majesty and power of the old King, yet he is also only a spirit who dare not tarry when day comes, not so very different from witches with their power to harm.

As if to exorcise such malignancy, Horatio, in some of the most beautiful lines in the play, alerts us to the coming of day. Once again, this is very far from being simply a fancy way to say that the night, with all its terrors and confusions, is over:

But look, the morn in russet mantle clad
Walks o'er the dew of yon high eastward hill.

These lines are often highlighted as an example of Shakespeare's lyrical skills, but it cannot be overemphasised that it is passages like this and the description of the midnight hour earlier that establish the prism through which we view the dangerous and corrupt place which is the Denmark, and particularly the Elsinore, of the play. They establish that quality of normality which, as Emrys Jones rightly says, is the ground-bass of Shakespeare's plays. But they do more. As another Oxford scholar, John Jones, has pointed out in relation to Sophocles, they establish for the audience a profound sense of man's place in a universe which moves according to profounder rhythms than any human being can ever fathom, but whose intuition by us at certain moments, such as this, is strangely soothing in the midst of the torments and horrors men inflict on themselves and on one another.

And when Horatio goes on to say that what they have seen must be reported to Young Hamlet at once, for he alone will have the power to make the Ghost speak, we are prepared for what is to come. Never departing from the most down-to-earth realism (except perhaps in Horatio's *Julius Caesar*-like speech), Shakespeare has, in a mere 180 lines, both set the scene and touched on most of the major themes of the entire play.

FOLD TWO

2.1 (I. 2. 1–63)

We have now seen the ghost of Old Hamlet and we have heard of Old and Young Fortinbras of Norway, and, right at the end of the last fold, of Young Hamlet, and perhaps we wonder if he is going to turn out to be a hothead like Young Fortinbras. Shakespeare has prepared us for the entry of the hero – we are after all attending a play called *The Tragedy of Hamlet, Prince of Denmark* (so the Quarto; the Folio omits the second phrase) – as assiduously and with as much cunning stagecraft as he had earlier prepared us for the appearance of the Ghost. And what we have to bear in mind first of all is that while everything we are now to see and hear will come to us filtered through the prism of that first fold, Claudius, Gertrude, Hamlet and the rest have not had that experience. So far as we know, they have no idea that a ghost is stalking the battlements of Elsinore.

With a flourish of trumpets the King and Queen and assembled courtiers, including Hamlet, take up their places. And before a word is spoken we are aware of Hamlet. Amidst the assembled courtiers and the King and Queen he is as conspicuous by his black clothes as the Ghost of Old Hamlet was on the dark battlements by his gleaming armour.

Shakespeare does not as a rule play much on the clothes his characters wear, though as actor and author involved with the production of his plays he would no doubt have had his views on how his characters should dress. If a character's clothes are mentioned it is usually in the comedies, in order for the audience to laugh at them – most notably when Malvolio is tricked into appearing before Olivia in outrageous garments; in *The Merchant of Venice*, on the other hand, it is up to the director to make Shylock as different from or as similar to the other Venetians as he wishes. But in this scene Hamlet's garb is not simply commented on, it becomes the focus of attention. 'Good Hamlet,' admonishes his mother,

>   cast thy nighted colour off,
> And let thine eye look like a friend on Denmark.
> Do not for ever with thy vailed lids
> Seek for thy noble father in the dust.
> Thou know'st, 'tis common: all that lives must die,
> Passing through nature to eternity. (I. 2. 68–73)

Hamlet picks this up:

> 'Tis not alone my inky cloak, good mother,
> Nor customary suits of solemn black . . . (77–8)

Hamlet, it appears, is still in mourning for his father when the rest of the court have reverted to their normal clothes; this, both Claudius and his mother suggest, is excessive and even insulting – a silent criticism, especially of his mother for shedding *her* mourning garments too soon.

We will return to this exchange. Here it is important to note that to an Elizabethan audience a suit of black would have suggested something else as well as mourning. Three decades later Milton could still write:

> But hail thou Goddess, sage and holy,
> Hail divinest Melancholy,

Whose saintly visage is too bright
To hit the Sense of human sight;
And therefore to our weaker view,
O'erlaid with black staid Wisdom's hue.
                    ('Il Penseroso', ll. 11–16)

Black is the colour of melancholy, and while of course melancholy is associated with mourning ('Turn melancholy forth to funerals;/ The pale companion is not for our pomp,' admonishes Theseus at the start of *A Midsummer Night's Dream*, when he announces his forthcoming wedding to Hippolyta), it is not exclusively so. For the Elizabethans melancholy (black bile) was one of the four humours into which they divided human temperaments. It was associated with sorrow, and this they thought could be caused by love, loss or ill health. 'The grossest part of our blood is the melancholy humour,' writes Nashe in *The Terrors of the Night* (1593):

> which in the spleen congealed whose office is to disperse it, with his thick steaming fenny vapours casteth a mist over the spirit and clean bemasketh the fantasy. And even as slime and dirt in a standing puddle engender toads and frogs and many other unsightly creatures, so this slimy melancholy humour, still thickening as it stands still, engendreth many misshapen objects in our imaginations.

As this might suggest, it was, of all the humours, the one that had the greatest vogue at the time, a source of endless fascination to the age, culminating in Robert Burton's enormous *Anatomy of Melancholy* (1621), a veritable encyclopedia of the condition, written as much in the spirit of Rabelais as in that of Galen. In fact, while the other three humours, the choleric, the phlegmatic and the sanguine, remained firmly in the realm of medicine and physiology (the choleric person was deemed to have a red face etc.), melancholy transcended this and became rather a condition of the times.

As such, it was often seen as a fad. Just as the dandy defined a later age, so the melancholic, alone, apart, dressed in dark clothes and nursing a grievance against himself and the world, defined the Elizabethan age, and Shakespeare, like many dramatists, avails himself of this type, most notably in Jaques in *As You Like It*, written shortly before *Hamlet*. 'I can suck melancholy out of a song,' he says, 'as a weasel sucks eggs' (II. 5. 10–11). But, like the dandy, the melancholic is not simply a figure of fashion. The roots of fashion go deeper than many an Elizabethan melancholic or Regency dandy realised. Hamlet's melancholy, in fact, can only be fully understood when set in the larger European context. And by that I mean not only its German and Italian contexts, but its context in the cultural lifeblood of a society in transition from the relative stability of the Middle Ages to something new and exciting, but also profoundly disturbing. (Hamlet, we will shortly learn, is a student at the University of Wittenberg, the very place where Luther in 1517 nailed his theses to the church door, the act which historians commonly take to herald the start of the Reformation; and he later quotes the great fifteenth-century Florentine philosopher Pico della Mirandola on the dignity of man.)

It was Victor Hugo, in his great essay on Shakespeare, who first made the connection between Hamlet and Dürer's *Melancholia*: 'Like the baleful spirit of Albrecht Dürer,' he writes, 'Hamlet might be called "Melancholia". Over his head, too, there flies the disembowelled bat, and at his feet are science, the sphere, the compass, the hourglass, love, while behind him, on the horizon, a great and terrible sun which only seems to make the sky more dark.'

Dürer was one of Luther's staunchest supporters. But it was actually in 1514, three years before Luther nailed his theses to the church door in Wittenberg, that he produced his remarkable engraving. In fact it was one of two, which he obviously saw as a pair because, as Erwin Panofsky tells us, in every instance but one he gave them away together. The first was entitled *St Jerome in his Study* and the second, more mysteriously, *Melencolia I*. I don't think it's fanciful to see them as Dürer's response to the crisis many thinking people felt was engulfing their world. The *St Jerome*

depicts the saint, who gave the Christian West its Latin Bible, as a
man at ease within the tradition, quietly translating Scripture,
with his sleeping lion and dog at his feet. A skull and hourglass
remind him of his mortality, but he accepts that as a natural part
of being human: as we were born so must we die. *Melencolia I*
depicts what happens when that sense of tradition has vanished. A
large woman sits in the open, next to a ruined house, with her
head on her hand, in the other a compass – but she is not working.
Her eyes are wide open but she looks not out at the world but
inwards, into herself. From her belt hang a bunch of keys and an
open purse. Round her, in disarray, lie various measuring instruments and tools, behind her an hourglass and a magic square.
Sitting above her is a putto, visibly scribbling. An eerie moonlight
blankets the scene and, on the left, above a sheet of water, a bat
spreads its wings, on which the mysterious title is displayed. The
two figures of the giant brooding woman and the putto convey an
overwhelming impression of tension and anxiety.

Panofsky, the foremost student of the artist in the first half of
the twentieth century, relates Dürer's image to Neoplatonic
notions of genius, in particular to Ficino's theory that 'the creative,
Saturnian melancholy is the prerogative of theologians, poets and
philosophers', and to his disciple Cornelius Agrippa's notion that
the *furor melancholicus* can stimulate both reason and imagination
to superhuman activity. But this, it seems to me, is far too upbeat
a reading, and one that sits oddly with the image he has just
described so forcefully. More to the point is a passage from Dürer's
own writings which Panofsky cites just a page earlier: 'The lie is in
our understanding, and darkness is so firmly entrenched in our
minds that even our groping will fail' – a powerful expression of
the sense of solitude and desolation which, Luther would suggest
a few years after the engraving was made, can only be overcome by
an awareness of the saving grace of Christ.

Dürer's vision of melancholy, far from depicting the rapture of
genius, presents us, I feel, with what happens when the authority of
tradition no longer has a hold on us. Far from being liberated, we
grow incapable of action, marooned in a sea of conflicting choices.

There are many ways of seeing this transition. The historian of philosophy Robert Pippin, in his discussion of an essay of Max Weber's, puts it like this:

> Tolstoy had noted that in pre-modern times or times oriented around the centrality of nature and not historical time, the prospect of death was much easier to bear. The cycle of life and death had (or was experienced as having) a regular and predictable pattern. After some stretch of time, if one were fortunate enough to have lived into middle age, one could console oneself with the thought that one had basically seen all that life had to offer. The cycle of birth, growth, work, love, reproduction and death had run its course. What more there was to see would likely be only a repetition. Even the great events on the world stage, wars, famine and so forth, were themselves the return of the eternal troubles of the human heart, were themselves repetitions. With the advent of a historical consciousness, though, and so some belief in the uniqueness of historical events, especially the unrepeat-ability of historical moments, it was impossible to avoid the crushing sense that death was completely meaningless, occupied no place in any natural cycle; was an event without possible consolation . . . One's death became a mere ending at some arbitrary point; there would always be something, probably an infinity of distinct and unprecedented events, to 'miss'.

It is the sense that our lives are unique to us and that we need to make something of them, according to this account, that leads to the modern condition of melancholy. It is a new condition in that it is the result of the transition from a settled, agrarian society to a rootless urban one.

It would of course be possible to put much flesh on these bones and show in detail the nature of this transition in different areas of Europe at different points in the early modern period. Shakespeare scholars, notably Robert Weimann, have been doing just that in recent decades for Elizabethan society and drama. But to see the crisis that beset Western Europe in the early modern period as a purely social one, though it comes naturally to our secular age, leaves out of account a central component of the transition, which is the loss of confidence at the end of the Middle Ages in the Christian world picture which had underpinned society for a thousand years (it is not a coincidence that Weimann, like Heiner Müller, is an East German, raised in the Marxist fold, who only later moved to the West). That world picture consists of a set of interlocking views which rest on the belief that God created the universe and man, and that he maintains a benign interest in them. Dante, at the start of his great cathedral-like poem, may be lost in a dark wood, but assistance comes in the form of Virgil, sent by a kind of divine relay race that has its source in the Virgin Mary herself. Virgil takes him in hand and leads him as far as he is able, to the earthly paradise, when his place is taken by Beatrice, who takes him up to Heaven before, at the very end, handing him over to St Bernard. What he could never have achieved by himself he achieves with the help of others, who know better and more than he does, and who appear for him in his moment of need.

Dante has his own personification of melancholy, though, significantly, it is not called that but Sloth or Laziness, what the Church called *acedia* and codified as the fourth cardinal sin. In Canto 4 of *Purgatorio* Dante and Virgil come across the figure of Belacqua:

We drew near; and there were persons in the shade behind the rock, in postures people take for negligence. And one of them, who seemed weary, was sitting embracing his knees, holding his face down low between them. 'O my sweet lord,' said I, 'look at that fellow: he appears more negligent than if Laziness were his sister.' Then he turned to us and gave us his attention, shifting his face up a bit along his thigh, and said: 'Now you go on up, you are so vigorous!' (*Purgatorio*, 4.103–14)

Dante suddenly recognises him as an old acquaintance. Delighted that Belacqua is in this place and not in Hell, Dante exclaims: 'Belacqua, now I do not grieve for you any longer; but tell me: why are you sitting just here? Are you waiting for a guide, or have your old habits claimed you again?'

> And he: 'O brother, what good would climbing do? For the angel of God sitting on the threshold would not let me go in to the torments. First it is necessary for the heavens to turn around me outside here as long as they did in my life, since I delayed my good sighs until the end, unless prayer help me first, which must rise up from a heart that lives in grace . . .' And already the poet was climbing ahead of me and saying: 'Come along now: see, the meridian is touched by the sun, and on the shore of ocean night already covers Morocco with its foot.' (*ibid.*, 127–39)

The law of Dante's medieval Christian universe decrees that those who never repented pass the remainder of time locked in their respective circles of Hell, but that those who, even if only at the last moment, cast themselves on God's mercy will be consigned to the mountain of Purgatory, whose lower slopes are hard indeed to climb but which gets easier as one goes up. The intriguing thing about Belacqua is that he is an infernal figure in his inability and unwillingness to move, and yet, as he explains, he will slowly and in due time find redemption. Beckett seized on him with delight and named the melancholy hero of his first collection of stories, a Dublin layabout who sees no point in doing one thing rather than another since all in the end amounts to the same thing, Belacqua Shua. For our purposes what is important is that Dante's Belacqua is 'placed', given a precise location in an ordered universe, one in which the law of the heavens keeps him in his place even as it bids Dante and Virgil move on (the last, astronomical, reflections in this canto, as the pilgrims leave Belacqua behind, remind one of the equivalent passages in the first fold of *Hamlet*, to which I have drawn attention as forming a frame for the confusions and corruptions of Elsinore – albeit a much weaker frame than Dante's). Dürer's Melancholy, by contrast, seems lost in a sea of possibilities; we know she will never move.

Everything in Dante's world holds together and each strand – the cosmology, the theology, the history, the psychology – reinforces all the others. Even (the Latin) language seemed to reflect God's truth, and world history could be summed up – and was – by the medieval anagram, *Eva/Ave*, the sin of Eve reversed by the angel's greeting to Mary. By the middle of the seventeenth century this set of interlocking images was in tatters. The notion of authority had everywhere been thrown into question: the authority of kings, of the Pope, of bishops, of Luther himself – since if one's interpretation of the Bible depended on oneself alone, as he taught, and not on the authority of the Church and tradition, who was to say that his reading was right and another man's, equally filled with the spirit of God, wrong? When the deeply traditional Anglican clergyman and poet George Herbert came to write his own version of the *Eva/Ave* ditty the wit was no longer underpinned by absolute certainty but held together only by its own conceit:

$$Ana\text{-} \begin{cases} \text{MARY} \\ \text{ARMY} \end{cases} gram$$

How well her name an Army doth present
In whom the Lord of Hosts did pitch his tent!

The medieval anagram gave a compressed account of universal history, which was felt to be inscribed in language itself; Herbert merely invites us to delight in his ingenious use of the English language.

What does it mean to live in a world in which the anagram *Eva/Ave* is felt to underlie, comfortingly, the entire fabric of the cosmos and of each individual life? A little English poem dating from the thirteenth century probably conveys this better than any analysis of Dante or the medieval cathedrals could do:

Now goth sonne under wod:
Me reweth, Marye, thy faire rode. [*rood*, cross]
Now goth sonne under Tre:
Me reweth, Marie, thy sone and thee. [*me reweth*, I feel
pity for]

The poet sees the sun going down behind the trees, as it does every evening, and meditates on the crucifixion, the 'setting', as it were, of the Son of God. He expresses his sense of pity for both Mary and her child, but that pity is tempered for him and the listener/reader by the knowledge that just as the sun will rise again the following morning, so the Son of God will rise, and, by so doing, save the world and us. The poem effortlessly brings together the natural world, with its cyclical pattern of recurrence, and the unique Christian story. In twenty-three simple words it manages to lament, praise and reaffirm.

What we need is to understand what it feels like to live in a world that, for all its brutality, made sense, and, in one's lifetime, see it transformed into one in which nothing seemed any longer to make any sense and where all attempts to impose meaning were immediately subject to suspicion. And though a new kind of sense, running under the twin banners of Reason and Progress, seemed to emerge in the eighteenth century, by the end of that century this too had come to be regarded with suspicion. It is as if, try as the intelligentsia might to banish it, Dürer's image just would not go away. Which is why if we want to understand what it feels like to be melancholic, in the sixteenth as in the nineteenth century, there is no better guide than the nineteenth-century Danish philosopher, Søren Kierkegaard. In his first major work, *Either/Or*, Kierkegaard presents us with two figures, a melancholy young man and a mature older man. We get to know the young man through a variety of essays, stories and aphorisms, while the older man, a judge, comes to us through a series of letters he writes to the young man. As all commentators on Kierkegaard have noted, the young man of 'Either', who clearly represents Kierkegaard's youthful self, is a great deal more persuasive than the older man of

'Or' – yet we would badly misread the book if we did not see that the young man himself is all too keenly aware that the judge may be right – but aware too that he cannot follow his prescriptions.

The young man is a typical melancholic, and, like all melancholics, he is better at writing than at acting. In the collection of his jottings called *Diapsalmata* he explores his condition. 'I do not care for anything,' he says; and, My melancholy is my most faithful mistress . . .

> Time flows, time is a stream, people say, and so on. I do not notice it. Time stands still, and I with it . . .
>
> I . . . am bound in a chain formed of dark imaginings, of unquiet dreams, or restless thoughts, of dread presentiments, of inexplicable anxieties.

His life is meaningless, and as a result it is utterly boring.

> How terrible tedium is . . . I lie stretched out, inactive, the only thing I see is emptiness, the only thing I move about in is emptiness . . . I do not even suffer pain . . .
>
> If you marry you will regret it; if you do not marry you will regret it . . . Laugh at the world's follies, you will regret it; weep over them, you will also regret that . . . Believe a woman, you will regret it, believe her not, you will also regret that . . . Hang yourself, you will regret it; do not hang yourself you will regret it . . . This, gentlemen, is the sum and substance of all my philosophy.

What such an attitude brings with it is a deep revulsion at the way most people lead their lives:

> Of all the ridiculous things, it seems to me the most ridiculous is to be a busy man of affairs, prompt to meals and prompt to work . . .
>
> Is there anything that could divert me? Aye, if I might behold a constancy that could withstand every trial, an

enthusiasm that endured everything, a faith that could remove mountains, a thought that could unite the finite and the infinite. But my soul's poisonous doubt is all-consuming.

In the face of such corrosive doubt all that is left is to embrace the fact that no one thing seems any more worth doing than any other. In a remarkable essay later in the book, entitled 'The Rotation Method', the young man returns to the theme of boredom. 'Boredom depends on the nothingness which pervades reality; it causes a dizziness like that produced by looking down into a yawning chasm.' Most people who experience this think what they need is change. Bored with the city? Move to the country. Bored with the country? Move to the city. But of course neither move abolishes the boredom. To the connoisseur of boredom, which is what the melancholic is, however, a mode of living suggests itself. Since everything is pointless, make a point of pointlessness. 'You go to see the middle of a play, you read the third part of a book. By this means you ensure yourself a very different kind of enjoyment from that which the author has been so kind as to plan for you.' And if this sounds like Wilde, or Barthes at his most precious, then that is not accidental: they too were struggling to keep going in a world which had become thoroughly emptied of all meaning and value.

The older man, the judge, will have none of this. My dear young man, he says in effect, you exhibit the typical symptoms of the adolescent. What you need is not a grand passion but simply to get married. Take this decision and you will see that all will fall into place. But, we can hear the young man responding, how can I know *who* to marry? That is not important, says the judge, just marry and you will see that your life will suddenly acquire meaning.

Kierkegaard was clearly not satisfied with the judge's response and he comes back to the issue in his next great work, *Fear and Trembling*. Here the stakes have shot up. It is no longer a matter of happiness or otherwise, but of salvation and damnation. Kierkegaard chooses as his parable the story of Abraham and Isaac as recounted in Genesis 22. God asks the man he has chosen, the man to whom he has, in extreme old age, vouchsafed a son to carry on his line, to kill

this very son. How is that possible? Is it a joke? Is it perhaps a temptation by the Devil? We have moved beyond the realm of the aesthetic
and the ethical into the realm of the religious, argues Kierkegaard. If
Abraham is to obey he has to go beyond ethics, blindly trusting a
God who makes no sense. But if he made sense (such is Kierkegaard's
extreme Protestant position) he would not be God; or rather, if we
lived in a world of sense we would not need God.

So Abraham goes ahead and, as we know, is reprieved at the last
minute – but Kierkegaard imagines him broken by the experience,
as Dostoevsky was broken by *his* last-minute reprieve when,
condemned to death for anti-Tsarist activities, he was facing the
firing squad.

Abraham could do it but I am not Abraham – this is
Kierkegaard's constant refrain. He had given up his fiancée the
better to serve God, but wonders for the rest of his life whether he
has done the right thing, has even done what God wanted. He can
see a steeliness of purpose in Abraham which he finds absent in
himself; he can imagine Abraham, but not emulate him.

Auden was a great reader of Kierkegaard, and late in his life he
would write a little clerihew which nicely captures Kierkegaard's
lifelong dilemma:

> Søren Kierkegaard
> Tried awfully hard
> To take The Leap
> But fell in a heap.

Yet Kierkegaard provides the link between Dürer – and Hamlet –
and the modern era, where first Baudelaire and then Freud, Mann
and Kafka were to develop many of the themes he touches on here.
Mann's *Doktor Faustus* in particular is worth bearing in mind as we
return to Hamlet in his black suit alone in the midst of Claudius's
court. For what Mann's Faustus, his modern composer Adrian
Leverkühn, is prepared to sell his soul for is not wealth or love or
fame but freedom from the corrosive sense of suspicion that blights
his life and makes composition impossible – suspicion that

everything he does is second-hand and has been done before and better by others, suspicion that what he takes as invention is merely cliché, suspicion that the one thing for which he lives is of no value or interest to anyone else and of no intrinsic worth. To be free of this spirit of suspicion he is even prepared to make a pact with the Devil. And who is to say, Mann concludes, that his tragic life was a mistaken one?

To return to *Hamlet* and to the opening of the second Fold.
    The King speaks:

> Though yet of Hamlet our dear brother's death
> The memory be green, and that it us befitted
> To bear our hearts in grief, and our whole kingdom
> To be contracted in one brow of woe,
> Yet so far hath discretion fought with nature
> That we with wisest sorrow think on him
> Together with remembrance of ourselves.
> Therefore our sometime sister, now our queen,
> Th'imperial jointress to this warlike state,
> Have we, as 'twere with a defeated joy,
> With an auspicious and a dropping eye,
> With mirth in funeral and with dirge in marriage,
> In equal scale weighing delight and dole,
> Taken to wife. (I. 2. 1–14)

Long before we grasp the meaning of the passage we note – as we immediately noted the colour of Hamlet's clothes – an enormous change in register. Scene 1 had consisted (apart from the brief *Julius Caesar*-like passage about omens) either of short everyday words and phrases – 'Who's there?', 'Speak to me' – or of sudden yet natural lyrical evocations of night and dawn. Here – in a shift as abrupt as the one Proust achieves between the lyrical innocence of Combray and the self-serving hypocrisies of the Verdurin salon at the start of 'Un Amour de Swann' – Shakespeare assails our ears with an interminable speech which, even before we fully grasp its import, strikes us as a rhetorical exercise. It immediately conveys Claudius's character, a character he himself no doubt conceives as 'statesmanlike', but which we experience as hollow, smug and self-serving.

How does Shakespeare achieve this? Margaret Ferguson, in a splendid article, points out that the central rhetorical device deployed by Claudius is that known as isocolon, that is, balanced clauses joined by 'and'. 'Claudius's isocolonic style', she points out, 'is also characteristically oxymoronic: opposites are smoothly joined by syntax and sound.' In this manner Claudius introduces us to all we need to know about recent events at the Court of Denmark: the death of his brother, Old Hamlet, and his marriage to the widow. Yet, while complex pieces of information seem to be offered to us, the precise details are strangely clouded. Succession in Denmark, as scholars point out, was not hereditary but elective, so that the notion that Claudius has somehow 'stolen' Hamlet's birthright, though often later suggested by Hamlet, is certainly not one shared by the court. On the other hand (a phrase we are all too often reduced to using in our dealings with this play) there is the suggestion ('th'imperial jointress to this warlike state') that Gertrude is somehow joint ruler with him, a point made nowhere else in the play, but which floats the idea that his marriage to the widow of the King *may* have been a way of cementing his position.

Our sense, too, that Claudius, though speaking very openly about what has happened, is also curiously opaque to us (while, as we will see, Hamlet, who stresses his own deviousness and silence throughout, is curiously open to us), is reinforced by the almost automatic way he piles oxymorons upon each other, their very number leading to our growing sense of unease and even a desire to laugh:

> Have we, as 'twere with a defeated joy,
> With an auspicious and a dropping eye,
> With mirth in funeral and with dirge in marriage . . .

However, he is the King and for the moment he holds sway, so that nothing on the stage allows us to test our unease. Having thanked the court for its support of him in his new role as Old Hamlet's successor, he goes on to report that Young Fortinbras, taking advantage of Old Hamlet's death and his uncle's old age, is threatening to take over the lands his father lost. To stop this nonsense he is sending two ambassadors, Cornelius and Voltemand, to apprise Old Fortinbras of this and ask him to restrain his impetuous son.

Then, turning to Laertes, he asks him what his suit is, insisting that 'You cannot speak of reason to the Dane/ And lose your voice' (44–5). (We recall Marcellus's 'And liegeman to the Dane'.) Moreover, he insists, Laertes's father, Polonius, his trusted counsellor, is so close to him that he would not dream of refusing whatever the son might ask. Laertes explains that he wishes to return to Paris, which he left only to attend the coronation, and, since Polonius gives his blessing to his desire to return, Claudius does likewise:

> Take thy fair hour, Laertes, time be thine,
> And thy best graces spend it at thy will. (62–3)

A royal way of speaking, perhaps, though, as we will see, in this play time is neither his nor any man's but plays its tricks on all.

It is only now, after all the affairs of state and court have been dealt with, that Claudius turns to the figure in black. Until this moment the scene has been full of incident, totally gripping, yet strangely static. Now, we sense, it starts to move.

2.2 (I. 2. 64–128)

'But now,' Claudius says, pursuing his rhetorical mannerism of isocola,

> But now, my cousin Hamlet, and my son

– and Hamlet speaks his first words:

> A little more than kin, and less than kind.

'Hamlet,' says Ferguson, 'not only refuses to be defined or possessed by Claudius's epithets, the second of which confuses the legal relation of stepson with the "natural" one of son; he also refuses to accept the principle of similarity that governs Claudius's syntax'. Hamlet's words, suddenly creating a counter to what had been the one-way traffic of Claudius's way of speaking, 'unbalances', Ferguson goes on,

> the scale Claudius has created through his rhetoric – a scale in which opposites like 'delight' and 'dole' are blandly equated. Hamlet's sentence disjoins what Claudius has linked; it does so through its comparative 'more' and 'less', and also through the play on 'kin' and 'kind' which points, by the difference of a single letter, to a radical difference between what Claudius seems or claims to be, and what he is. The pun on the word 'kind' itself, moreover, works, as Hamlet's puns so often do, to disrupt the smooth surface of another person's discourse. Hamlet's pun, suggesting that Claudius is neither natural nor kindly, is like a pebble thrown into the oily pool of Claudius's rhetoric.

Brilliant and perceptive as Ferguson's analysis is, it passes over a key factor in this opening exchange: our delight at Hamlet's way with language. Anyone who can do what he has just done in nine short words immediately engages our sympathy. Not only does this phrase provide wit where until now we had been bludgeoned by rhetoric, but suddenly it gives us a point of reference whereby we can feel at ease in our unease with Claudius's mode of discourse. This will become a decisive factor in our response to the play.

Ferguson goes on to make the intriguing point that, by puncturing Claudius's attempt to turn opposites into the same, Hamlet's words reflect 'his (at this point) obscure and certainly overdetermined desire to separate his uncle from his mother'. This shows how difficult it is to read this play 'afresh', without the sense, that is, of all our previous viewings and readings. For what, if anything, have we made of Gertrude so far? She has been present, but silent. We have heard Claudius refer to her as 'our sometime sister, now our queen', have heard him refer to the 'mirth in funeral and . . . dirge in marriage' – but we have heard nothing from her. Is her silence then like that of the courtiers, politic acquiescence, or is it wifely love and pride, or, like Hamlet's, smouldering resentment?

After another exchange between Claudius and Hamlet, which repeats and enriches the play of words and feelings that sparks between them:

> *King.* How is it that the clouds still hang on you?
> *Ham.* Not so, my lord, I am too much in the sun (66–7)

– an exchange that will be picked up in a later verbal duel between Hamlet and the sister of that Laertes who is soon to return to France – Gertrude finally speaks. She speaks as a mother in the difficult but familiar position of mediating between her son and her new husband:

> Good Hamlet, cast thy nighted colour off,
> And let thine eye look like a friend on Denmark.
> Do not for ever with thy vailed lids
> Seek for thy noble father in the dust. (68–71)

A new note is introduced. We had thought, after the brief but potent exchange between Hamlet and Claudius, that we knew where we stood, but Gertrude's intervention has thrown doubt upon our certainties. Claudius appeared the unctuous villain, Hamlet the politically powerless yet verbally skilful victim. But now we have to take on board the possibility that Hamlet, though he may be right in many ways, is also not entirely blameless, that perhaps his mourning is indeed excessive, and he may indeed be grinding his mother and stepfather into the dust of his grief when he should be accepting that life is sometimes like that – fathers die and mothers remarry.

Gertrude drives the point home by ending her speech with a generalising remark:

> Thou know'st, 'tis common: all that lives must die,
> Passing through nature to eternity. (72–3)

But she has gone too far. It's so interesting, how effortlessly Shakespeare manipulates us with nothing but language: for four lines we had been ready to see that Gertrude had at least a point, but suddenly we are on our guard. Whether through a lack of tact or some more damning trait, that which was meant to clinch the argument leads instead to its collapse, and we are once more wholly on Hamlet's side (or not wholly; her initial words have left a particle of doubt in our minds, but more than we were a second ago) as he answers her:

> Ay, madam, it is common.

She appears not to catch his tone, or perhaps she does and chooses to disregard it. If that's the case, she says, 'Why seems it so particular with thee?' And suddenly the dam of his silence throughout the opening minutes of this scene bursts as he picks up on that apparently innocuous word, 'seems':

> Seems, madam? Nay, it is. I know not 'seems'.
> 'Tis not alone my inky cloak, good mother,
> Nor customary suits of solemn black,
> Nor windy suspiration of forc'd breath,
> No, nor the fruitful river in the eye,
> Nor the dejected haviour of the visage,
> Together with all forms, moods, shapes of grief,
> That can denote me truly. These indeed seem,
> For they are actions that a man might play;
> But I have that within which passes show,
> These but the trappings and the suits of woe. (76–86)

Stanley Cavell is, to my knowledge, the only critic to have grasped that in these lines Hamlet is doing nothing less than laying out the philosophical grounds of his melancholy:

> I understand Hamlet's 'knowing not "seems"' as expressing the presence in him of a world altogether different from theirs.

I take it as a preliminary description of his general mode of
perception – call it mourning, call it the power, or the fate, to
perceive subjectively, truly . . . Hamlet is making claim to, or
laying hold of, a power of perception that curses him, as
Cassandra's cursed her, one that makes him unable to stop at
seems, a fate to know nothing but what people are, nothing
but the truth of them.

This, if I have understood Cavell, is precisely the curse under
which, as I described it, both Kierkegaard's young man and Mann's
Adrian Leverkühn were suffering: the coldness that comes from
seeing too clearly into the nature of things.

However, that line is only the opening salvo of a speech whose
emotional thrust lies not so much in Hamlet laying bare his condition as in his persuading his mother that he and not she is right.
The rhetorical splendour of the lines, as in many of Hamlet's
longer speeches and soliloquies, conceals a cluster of questionable
assumptions. Like many a child unable to articulate his complex
feelings for his mother, Hamlet insists that he really and truly does
feel pain inside. But in pressing this point upon her he is forced to
admit that his dress and demeanour are something of a pose –
indeed, that they are most likely to be taken as such, 'the actions
that a man might play' – a formulation that will echo throughout
this play, as both *play-acting* and *action* and the relations between
them become the central issues. However, he insists, these are
mere outward show: what I feel inside can neither be said nor
shown. Yet even as he says this we realise the double-bind involved
in such formulations (a double-bind in which many thinking
Protestants will become caught in the centuries to follow), for his
insistence that he feels far more pain than either his mother or her
new husband, his uncle, has itself to be couched in what he would
deem to be 'externals', words. And Shakespeare, to drive the point
home, has his long speech end in a couplet, thus reminding us that
words are not transparent conduits to interiority but objects in the
world as well, objects which can hinder as well as help the speaker
get his message across:

> But I have that within which passes show,
> These but the trappings and the suits of woe.

Hamlet, while uttering a truth the others refuse to countenance, distorts that truth by his sharp distinction between outer and inner, false and true. As the play unfolds, Shakespeare is at pains to correct this and to bring us to a better understanding of the relation of falsehood to truth. But for the moment it is Hamlet's formulation that stands.

Claudius at this point steps in, assuring Hamlet that such assiduity in carrying out his 'mourning duties' to his father is wholly admirable, but reminding him again that everyone dies, sons have lost fathers since the beginning of time, and those sons themselves beget sons and then die. And he ends with a plea to his nephew and stepson:

> We pray you throw to earth
> This unprevailing woe, and think of us
> As of a father . . . (106–8)

For, he suggests, not only does he feel that way towards him, but he has made it known that it is Hamlet he favours as his successor. As we are to see at the very end of the play, elective monarchy in Denmark, as Shakespeare presents it, and as historians agree, went hand in hand with the elected king's recommendation of his successor – which might seem to suggest that Claudius and not Hamlet was Old Hamlet's choice, despite what Young Hamlet feels and says – but here again Shakespeare leaves things conveniently vague.

Claudius, perhaps to defuse the situation, then moves smoothly into a plea to Hamlet not to go back to university in Wittenberg but

> to remain
> Here in the cheer and comfort of our eye,
> Our chiefest courtier, cousin, and our son. (115–17)

(It is up to us to read this as he wants Hamlet to take it, as an assertion of avuncular and stepfatherly love, or as a way to keep tabs on
this dangerous pretender.) To this his mother adds her voice, and
Hamlet, for once the dutiful son, graciously acquiesces. Delighted,
Claudius insists jovially that

> No jocund health that Denmark drinks today
> But the great cannon to the clouds shall tell,
> And the King's rouse the heaven shall bruit again,
> Re-speaking earthly thunder. (125–8)

Once again Shakespeare manages to suggest to an audience a
complicated and rich web of competing claims and views. Claudius
is clearly pleased with the outcome of things and feeling benign,
and what he says is meant to express that feeling to Hamlet – and
to whoever chooses to listen. At the same time it reminds us of
something we have heard in Fold 1, that the King likes to drink
and to let off cannon, and the invocation of Heaven as merely
echoing what the King does on earth contrasts implicitly with the
other invocations of nature we've had – of the stars at night shining
in the sky and the morn in russet mantle clad walking over the
dewy hills – and leaves a bad taste in the mouth as King and court
exit, perhaps, as Q2 says, with a flourish of trumpets.

2.3 (I. 2. 129–59)

Hamlet's first speech, to Claudius, was an outburst of eleven lines.
Now, alone, his utterance comes to thirty lines. Where the first
was polished and rhetorical, this is, as scholars and critics have
long pointed out, like all Hamlet's soliloquies, groping and meditative. Gone is the sharp and false contrast between outward show,
including speech, and inner, unspeakable truth; now he is using
language to try to get at something he feels but cannot quite
express. This is less like the voice-over of modern cinema, to which
the soliloquies have been likened, than like the way Kafka or
Virginia Woolf used their diaries – full of dashes, sharp breaks,
exclamations of failure – to talk to themselves.

He begins by expressing the desire to die; more than that, to
melt away, to disappear:

> O that this too too sullied [Q solid] flesh would melt,
> Thaw and resolve itself into a dew,
> Or that the Everlasting had not fix'd
> His canon 'gainst self-slaughter. O God! O God! (129–32)

It does not really matter if we opt for flesh that is too solid or too
sullied; the important point is that, with the typical melancholic's
outlook, Hamlet finds the world 'weary, stale, flat, and unprofit-
able', and anything that flourishes there, including his own body,
not a healthy flower but a weed. All of it is corrupt, he feels, and
all should be destroyed, and the particular horror is that he is
corrupt along with it, and thus should be the first to melt and
disappear. But, unlike Kierkegaard's young man, Hamlet has a
specific reason for this state, and he moves in on it, the previous
nine lines opening up a way to confront what, until now, had just
been allowed by Shakespeare to peep through his ironic guard:

> That it should come to this!
> But two months dead – nay, not so much, not two –
> So excellent a king, that was to this
> Hyperion to a satyr . . . (137–40)

There are two separate causes of anguish adumbrated here, though
Hamlet elides them. The first is the too hasty remarriage of his
mother, and the second is Hamlet's perception of the relative
merits of her two husbands. The first is perfectly understandable,
even if the rest of the court does not seem to think so. (Shakespeare
again, with exquisite touch, leaves it unclear whether this suggests
that it is indeed normal to remarry after so short a time or whether
no one at court except Hamlet dares mention such a gross breach
of decorum.) The second, though also understandable in a
bereaved son, is nevertheless bound to seem excessive in its stark
contrast of the two husbands, a contrast which will only grow in
subsequent revisitings of this particular source of anguish.

But even this sharp contrast of Hyperion to a satyr does not remain static. The thought of his father leads Hamlet to recall the way he treated his mother, and her response:

>   . . . so loving to my mother
> That he might not beteem [permit] the winds of heaven
> Visit her face too roughly. Heaven and earth,
> Must I remember? Why, she would hang on him
> As if increase of appetite had grown
> By what it fed on; and yet within a month –
> Let me not think on't – Frailty, thy name is woman –
> A little month . . . (140–6)

One does not need to be a psychoanalytic critic to recognise that there is much here that is repressed and confused – Hamlet, after all, says so himself, 'Let me not think on't', and reaches out for some solid ground to hold on to, coming up with the kind of misogynist cliché that had been an ingrained part of the Christian culture of the Middle Ages (a woman was, after all, responsible for the greatest calamity to have befallen mankind). But that of course is no solid plank but wood as rotten as the rest, and cannot stem the flow of his memory:

> A little month, or ere those shoes were old
> With which she follow'd my poor father's body,
> Like Niobe, all tears – why, she –
> O God, a beast that wants discourse of reason
> Would have mourn'd longer – married with my uncle,
> My father's brother – but no more like my father
> Than I to Hercules . . . (147–53)

What we feel as we listen to this is that Hamlet has encountered what I would call a knot: a dense interlocking web of feelings where his father's death and his mother's remarriage to her brother-in-law unleash all sorts of emotions – sorrow, horror, and a sudden awareness of the physical nature of his mother's relations with these two men – which is too painful to cope with. Again, it hardly needs Freud or Jones to alert us to this; Shakespeare does the job perfectly. Hamlet, we feel, like any son, finds it hard to acknowledge that it is through a sexual act that he himself has been begotten. Instead of facing this he would rather melt away, cease to exist, and, if that is not possible, turn his anguish on the monstrous nature of his mother's sexual being:

> Within a month
> Ere yet the salt of most unrighteous tears
> Had left the flushing in her galled eyes,
> She married – O most wicked speed! To post
> With such dexterity to incestuous sheets! (153–7)

Language always carries you further than you thought to go – which is its glory and its horror. Here the word 'dexterity' means 'haste', but it also, as the *OED* points out, giving a date of 1548 for this meaning, implies 'address in the use of limbs and in bodily movement', so that the image of his mother and uncle frolicking in bed together comes unbidden to take its place against the earlier image of his mother 'hanging on' his father 'As if increase of appetite had grown/ By what it fed on'.

And with that Hamlet shuts the door on the knot of anguish and confusion that risks overwhelming him, whether because he feels that at the present time he can go no further or because he has heard someone coming:

> It is not, nor it cannot come to good.
> But break, my heart, for I must hold my tongue. (158–9)

2.4 (I. 2. 160–258)

Shakespeare is as skilful as Beethoven in raising questions which need to be answered and then revealing that the answer itself leads to further, bigger questions. In the first scene we have been plunged straight into the question of the Ghost, and at the start of the

much longer second scene, into the question of Hamlet, his mother
and his stepfather/uncle. Now the two come together, for the noise
that has made Hamlet bring his meditation to a sudden close is
that of the entry of Horatio, Marcellus and Barnardo with news of
what they (and of course we) have seen on the battlements.

Shakespeare does not seem to have made up his mind about
Horatio's relations with Hamlet or, indeed, about quite what
Horatio's role in the play is going to be. As so often, he is concerned
with the moment and lets the larger structure take care of itself.
What he needs is to have Hamlet be surprised enough to ask why
it is that Horatio, who was a fellow student of his at Wittenberg,
has returned to Elsinore, so as to allow the following exchange to
occur:

> *Hor.* My lord, I came to see your father's funeral.
> *Ham.* I prithee do not mock me, fellow-student.
>   I think it was to see my mother's wedding.
> *Hor.* Indeed, my lord, it follow'd hard upon.
> *Ham.* Thrift, thrift, Horatio. The funeral bak'd meats
>   Did coldly furnish forth the marriage tables. (176–81)

This is as good as his ripostes to Claudius and his mother earlier in
the scene. Its layers of irony, and the brilliant 'coldly', referring
both to the use again of roast meat as cold cut and to the human
coldness which must have led to his mother's over-hasty remarriage, at once refuse us access to Hamlet's feelings and reveal them
clearly, while also getting us firmly on his side as the one who not
only feels and suffers but has the linguistic resources to crack such
jokes. There is also, as Stephen Greenblatt has noted, a spiritual
and ethical dimension to Hamlet's quip: 'At issue', he says, 'is not
only . . . an aristocratic disdain for bourgeois prudential virtue,
but a conception of the sacred as incompatible with a restricted
economy, an economy of calculation and equivalence.' We will see
this economy at play in Polonius's advice to Ophelia and in the
downgrading of sacred rituals in such diverse episodes as the
hurried burial of Polonius and the disputed burial of Ophelia, and

even, right at the end, in Claudius's turning what should be an act of trust, the drinking of a pledge, into a means of murder. Here Hamlet's bitter remark leads him straight into his obsession:

> Would I had met my dearest foe in heaven
> Or ever I had seen that day, Horatio.
> My father – methinks I see my father – (182–4)

He has only seen him in his mind's eye, so far, but Horatio now reveals to him that *he* really has seen him. And he goes on to recount what we have just witnessed, the Ghost's appearance, armoured and solemn, and his refusal to speak to them. The telling, of course, retrospectively guides our own understanding of the encounter.

Hamlet's response is clear: 'I will watch tonight./ Perchance 'twill walk again.' Until then, he enjoins them, silence. And, when they have left, Shakespeare gives him just four lines, closing on a rhyming couplet to leave us with a sense that, for the moment, something is completed, while preparing us for what is to follow:

> My father's spirit – in arms! All is not well.
> I doubt some foul play. Would the night were come.
> Till then, sit still, my soul. Foul deeds will rise,
> Though all the earth o'erwhelm them, to men's eyes. (255–8)

FOLD THREE

3.1 (I. 3. 1–52)

Now Laertes takes centre stage with his sister Ophelia. He is concerned about Hamlet's evident interest in Ophelia, and he comes straight to the point:

> For Hamlet, and the trifling of his favour,
> Hold it a fashion and a toy in blood,
> A violet in the youth of primy nature,
> Forward, not permanent, sweet, not lasting,
> The perfume and suppliance of a minute,
> No more. (5–10)

This is the first time we see Hamlet from a point of view which is neither his own nor that of his immediate family, and we sense at once that while Laertes may, for all we know, be right, he is also driven by his own prejudices and desires. When she responds flatly: 'No more but so?', he insists: 'Think it no more', and then launches into a thirty-four-line speech which is meant to drive home his point that Hamlet is not to be trusted: he is young and impetuous, and even if he does indeed love her and is not simply keen to bed her, she must realise he is out of her reach, a king's son

who cannot simply do what he wants, 'for on his choice depends/
The sanity and health of this whole state' (20–1).

But he cannot let it rest there:

> The canker galls the infants of the spring
> Too oft before their buttons be disclos'd,
> And in the morn and liquid dew of youth
> Contagious blastments are most imminent. (38–42)

This is conventional stuff, the idea that we can see in nature how the
young plant is the one most in danger from worms and wind, but it
joins an array of examples in this play of nature turning sick when
left to its own devices. To put it in perspective: in the early comedies
Shakespeare sets up a sharp contrast between nature, which is essentially benign, and culture, which is the result of repression, with
women usually standing for the first and men, especially old men,
more especially fathers, for the second. The outcome, as in *A
Midsummer Night's Dream* and *As You Like It*, is for nature to
triumph, as the old are made to see the error of their repressive ways.
In *Hamlet*, however, as in the other plays he was writing at this time,
Troilus and Cressida and *Measure for Measure*, Shakespeare compli-
cates the issue by showing that nature, left to herself, is *not* invariably
good but is in fact liable to run to riot and excess. The question then
becomes how to let nature flourish without letting it run wild, or
how to curb it without destroying it. It is a question Shakespeare will
still be grappling with in his late plays *Pericles* and *The Winter's Tale*.

'Be wary, then,' Laertes concludes his homily, 'best safety lies
in fear' (43). And once again Ophelia shows no personality in
responding, merely compliance: 'I shall th'effect of this good
lesson keep/ As watchman to my heart.' But then she surprises
him (and us) with a bitter little speech, reminding him that if he
preaches abstinence and wariness to her, he too, now he is going to
Paris, should heed the same command. I say surprises him because
in traditional societies the spectacle of a brother warning his sister
to beware of ardent young men is commonplace, but the reverse is
rare. In a typically Shakespearean way it gives the tiniest of twists

to an otherwise predictable exchange, and allows us a glimpse of a different Ophelia. It may be that she is not blank but merely puzzled, like Hamlet, by what is going on around her, that she simply lacks, as Hamlet does, that certainty in dealing with the world which all those around them – Claudius, Young Fortinbras, Polonius and Laertes (and, as we will see, Rosencrantz and Guildenstern and Osric) – display so unselfconsciously.

3.2 (I. 3. 53–136)

At this point Polonius enters and affects surprise to see Laertes still there when he thought him already on his way to France, but then takes advantage of this to give him some last words of advice. Commentators have tended to concentrate on the triteness of the advice:

> And these few precepts in thy memory
> Look thou character. Give thy thoughts no tongue,
> Nor any unproportion'd thought his act.
> Be thou familiar, but by no means vulgar . . . (58–61)

And trite it is, to the point of being laughable. But, coming on top of Laertes's advice to his sister, it suggests a family in which the men at any rate love the sound of their own voice and like to pontificate and control. This is reinforced when, Laertes having finally gone (he had said 'farewell' in the very first line), Polonius asks Ophelia what it is he has been saying to her. When she tells him it was 'something touching the Lord Hamlet', Polonius jumps in. Rumour has it that you and he have been seeing each other recently in private, he says. If this is the case, 'I must tell you/ You do not understand yourself so clearly' (95–6). This is a new line of attack. Laertes had warned her that Hamlet was only an impetuous youth, and that, as the likely heir to the throne, he was not his own man, but her father now tells her that she must realise she does not know herself, and then presses her to tell him all: 'What is between you? Give me up the truth' (98).

That phrase, with its implication that 'the truth' is a single thing which can be either hidden or made known, 'given up' (like an object one has kept hidden in one's clothing), is one that has been pulsing through the play from the start, with Barnardo's 'Who's there?' and Horatio's repeated injunction to the Ghost to 'speak, speak. I charge thee speak.' It will throb even more loudly as the play unfolds. Here Ophelia merely answers that Hamlet has 'of late made many tenders/ Of his affection to me' (99–100). Polonius pooh-poohs this, calling her a 'green girl', ignorant of the ways of the world and prone to believe all such protestations. Once again she answers blankly: 'I do not know, my lord, what I should think.' This is just what Polonius wants to hear: 'Marry, I will teach you' (105). For him there is only one explanation: she's a pretty girl and Hamlet only wants to sleep with her. But even here he manages to turn what is after all, even if true, a perfectly natural set of impulses into something more sinister and premeditated:

> In few, Ophelia,
> Do not believe his vows; for they are brokers
> Not of that dye which their investments show,
> Being mere implorators of unholy suits,
> Breathing like sanctified and pious bawds
> The better to beguile. (126–31)

The language is dense and convoluted, difficult to take in at a first hearing, but what comes through strongly is that whatever feelings the two young people have for each other are seen by this old man entirely in terms of finance, of brokerage and investment, itself subsumed into the monetary exchange of sex. In brief, Hamlet is not to be trusted, and the best thing, therefore, is to cease to have anything to do with him.

Blank as ever, Ophelia merely answers: 'I shall obey, my lord.' And the scene is over.

FOLD FOUR

4.1 (I. 4. 1–38)

Shakespeare has kept us waiting long enough. He is ready now to lead us to the first major climax of the play, Hamlet's confrontation with the Ghost. As always, he is aware that the scene needs to be established on the Globe's stage in the broad daylight of a summer afternoon:

> *Ham.* The air bites shrewdly, it is very cold.
> *Hor.* It is a nipping and an eager air.
> *Ham.* What hour now?
> *Hor.*   I think it lacks of twelve.
> *Mar.* No, it is struck.
> *Hor.*   Indeed? I heard it not.
>   It then draws near the season
>   Wherein the spirit held his wont to walk. (1–6)

But before the Ghost appears we hear the sound of trumpets and cannon. Horatio, who seems still to be a relative stranger to Denmark, asks what it could mean, and Hamlet supplies the answer:

> The King doth wake tonight and takes his rouse,
> Keeps wassail, and the swagg'ring upspring reels;

And as he drains his draughts of Rhenish down,
The kettle-drum and trumpet thus bray out
The triumph of his pledge. (8–12)

No matter that we don't grasp exactly what he is saying, 'swaggering' and 'reels' (whether as verbs, nouns or adjectives) define Claudius as both drunken and arrogant, even if, as the next lines suggest, this is a Danish custom, and the very density of the passage conveys Hamlet's disgust at this kind of activity ('bray' is particularly good – 'sound' would have suited Shakespeare's meaning but 'bray' is powerfully negative). It is but another example of the way in which the new money economy and the corruption of the natural go hand in hand in the Court of Denmark. The Second Quarto has a further twenty-three lines in which Hamlet makes explicit his disapproval of what this does to the reputation of the Danish court, but the Folio wisely cut most of that, Shakespeare perhaps feeling that it was too moralistic and that he needed to hurry on to the climax, the entry of the Ghost, heralded by Horatio's 'Look, my lord, it comes.'

4.2 (I. 4. 38–91)

We have arrived at the moment prepared for by the first line of the play: 'Who's there?'

> *Ham.* Angels and ministers of grace defend us!
>   Be thou a spirit of health or goblin damn'd,
>   Bring with thee airs from heaven or blasts from hell,
>   Be thy intents wicked or charitable,
>   Thou com'st in such a questionable shape
>   That I will speak to thee. (39–44)

We might think that this is merely a rhetorical way of asking the Ghost who he is, but in fact every word counts. Hamlet cannot from the start decide whether this is indeed the ghost of his late father or some spirit conjured up by the Devil to lead him to disaster. As Stephen Greenblatt, who has devoted a learned book to the whole subject, reminds us, this was a common question put to ghosts in the late Middle Ages. What he fails to make clear is that while in the religious culture of the late Middle Ages there were approved and public ways, with the help of the Church, of determining the answer, by the end of the sixteenth century these had disappeared. Protestantism, concerned to wipe out what it saw as the corrupt practices of the Catholic Church in trading on people's fear of the afterlife, had done away with the whole edifice of Purgatory, with its notion that we can help souls hurry through purgatorial punishments by prayer, and in doing so had severed the ties between the living and the dead which had formed a central part of human life since time immemorial. 'First it is necessary for the heavens to turn around me here so long as they did in my life,' Belacqua had explained to Dante, 'unless prayer help me first, which must rise up from a heart that lives in grace (*se orazïone in prima no m'aita/ che surga sù di cuor che in grazia viva*).'

As most scholars now agree, the question of whether Shakespeare was a secret Catholic or a Protestant believer is the wrong one. Like most men in the late sixteenth as in the twenty-first century, he no doubt carried in his head a mass of confused and contradictory beliefs. But the point is this: Protestantism had raised questions which could not easily be put to bed. Is the Ghost that of Old Hamlet? Is it a cunning ploy by the Devil to bring Hamlet to damnation? Is it a mere projection of Hamlet's seething and confused feelings? And, above and behind all these, the giant, unspoken question: How can we know which of these it is? Dante had Virgil to guide him; Hamlet has no one.

Kierkegaard, who was so helpful on the nature of melancholy, can come to our aid again. (Indeed, though he is more interested in *Don Giovanni* than in *Hamlet*, and in his own salvation than in any work of art, his entire output can be seen as an intense, powerful and inspired exploration of the issues raised by Shakespeare's play.) For, shortly after writing *Either/Or*, he devoted an entire book to this question of the authority of visions. What happened was that a case emerged in the early 1840s in the Danish ecclesiastical courts of a pastor who claimed that Christ had appeared to him and dictated the contents of a book he produced. Challenged by the ecclesiastical authorities to withdraw such heresy, he dithered and finally confessed that he could not be *absolutely certain* that it had indeed been Christ who appeared to him, but that he was *pretty sure* that it was. Kierkegaard was incensed, and wrote *On Authority and Revelation* to demonstrate that this was precisely the one area where uncertainty could not be tolerated. In the course of the book he draws a sharp distinction between what Jesus and his disciples said and what all subsequent authorities have said. When Jesus said: 'Follow me', he meant 'follow me'. His words are not special, they are not specially powerful or poetic, but they are uttered with authority. Our world is full of poets and politicians and preachers, who may speak beautifully or persuasively, but who do not speak with authority. When they say 'Follow me', the first thing we have to do is question their motives. They are merely putting a view forward. We can admire or reject it, but we are not under any obligation to accept it, as those who heard Jesus felt they had to accept His word.

Kierkegaard is the great spokesman for and scourge of the world after the advent of Lutheranism, a world in which there is no longer any established authority. It is the world that Dürer presaged in his *Melencolia I,* the world whose political dimension Shakespeare had, in the course of the decade before *Hamlet,* so thoroughly explored. For what else are *Richard II* and the plays that followed it but the examination of what happens once God's anointed king is deposed? Richard is a wretched king, arbitrary and weak; but once Bolingbroke has deposed him by force, even though he has a great deal of right on his side, who is to decide what is right and what is wrong in the way a king rules? Anyone who wishes to seize the throne and feels he has the power to do so can find some good reason for doing so. However much the Tudors tried to cover over the questions raised by their own accession to power, those questions concerning the legitimacy of political authority would not go away – and have not gone away to this day.

Luther had of course opened a similar Pandora's box in the realm of religion. He was convinced he was right to oppose the Pope and Councils, and he was certainly right about the many corrupt practices of the late medieval Church. But he had no answer when his views were in turn challenged by more radical sects, except to reiterate that he knew he was right and they were wrong. Cervantes would soon subject individual inspiration, which had seemed to the Renaissance Platonists and others to be capable of taking the place of the Church, to a devastating critique in *Don Quixote*, which appeared in the same decade as *Hamlet*. And, as Dürer sensed in producing the pair of engravings, *Melencolia I* and *St Jerome in his Study*, behind all this lay the collapse of the medieval consensus, that set of interlocking beliefs which underlay the culture (in its anthropological sense) of the Middle Ages. This collapse drove many thinking men into the arms of Melancholy, induced in them a sense of helplessness and futility, a loss of confidence in both the world and their own abilities. In the wake of the upheavals of the Anabaptist uprisings in Germany and the violence associated with them, the embracing of melancholy as a response to the world makes perfect sense. Three and a half centuries later Yeats was to sum up the situation: 'The best lack all conviction and the worst/ Are full of passionate intensity.'

Hamlet, as we have seen, is already consumed with melancholy; can the Ghost's arrival and his words release him from this bondage?

Having raised the question of the Ghost's integrity, Hamlet nevertheless opts to address him as 'King, father, royal Dane' (45–51) and to press him on why 'the sepulchre/ Wherein we saw thee quietly inurn'd/ Hath op'd his ponderous and marble jaws/ To cast thee up again' – a passage which demonstrates the way in which Shakespeare makes language work so much harder than most playwrights – for while a possible translation of this would be: 'Tell me why you have appeared here when we all saw you safely buried', the grave's 'ponderous and marble jaws' and the verb 'cast up' convey both the security and solidity of entombment and the violent, spasmodic action seemingly required to hurl the Ghost into their presence. ('Inurned', by the way, does not mean 'put in an urn' but 'interred', which is the Quarto reading; it suggests a forcible pushing down into the earth.)

But insist as Hamlet may, the Ghost, it seems, will not speak. This time, though, it does not slip away but instead beckons Hamlet to follow him. Horatio is aghast. Don't, he warns Hamlet, all too aware of the reputation such apparitions have:

> What if it tempt you toward the flood, my lord,
> Or to the dreadful summit of the cliff
> That beetles o'er his base into the sea,
> And there assume some other horrible form . . .
> And draw you into madness? (69–74)

The future James I, in his treatise on witchcraft, had written of the way the Devil may claim his victims 'by inducing them to such perilous places at such time as he either follows or possesses them' (Jenkins, p. 212), and in *King Lear* Shakespeare was to stage a memorable scene in which Edgar pretends a 'fiend' has brought the blind Gloucester to the cliff-top (*KL*, IV. 6.), so Horatio's warning is perfectly comprehensible. Nevertheless, Hamlet chooses to ignore it, and even when the others try to restrain him by force, he fights them off with the first of a run of speeches which he is prone to utter when under particular stress, speeches whose heroic and stoic content make both the viewer in the theatre and the reader at home want to identify them as expressions of the 'true' Hamlet, but which, as we will see, is only true of him in certain moods:

> My fate cries out
> And makes each petty artire [artery] in this body
> As hardy as the Nemean lion's nerve.
> Still am I call'd. Unhand me, gentlemen.
> By heaven, I'll make a ghost of him that lets [hinders] me.
>
> (81–5)

With that he rushes into the darkness after the Ghost, leaving the others helpless and bewildered. 'He waxes desperate with imagination' is Horatio's comment, while Marcellus replies gnomically: 'Something is rotten in the state of Denmark.'

4.3 (I. 5. 1–91)

Now we have really arrived. 'Whither wilt thou lead me?' pants Hamlet. 'Speak, I'll go no further.' And then, for the first time in the play, the Ghost speaks: 'Mark me,' he says.

It is a striking feature of this play that, for all its great speeches, some as many as thirty or forty lines long, the key moments are always breathtaking in their brevity and utter simplicity: 'Mark me.' This is not a ghost that is going to scream like an oyster-wife; when it chooses to speak it will be listened to.

And it begins by describing its position:

> My hour is almost come
> When I to sulph'rous and tormenting flames
> Must render up myself. (2–4)

Does this refer to the specific hour of the night at which this meeting is taking place, or is it some eternal clock that is being invoked? We do not know and it does not matter. Hamlet, for the first time, no longer looks at himself but responds to another's pain with instinctive sympathy: 'Alas, poor ghost.' (That phrase will recur as the play approaches its climax: 'Alas, poor Yorick.') The Ghost, though, has no time for sympathy:

> Pity me not, but lend thy serious hearing
> To what I shall unfold. (5–6)

There it is again: 'Unfold'. Speak then, answers Hamlet, 'I am bound to hear,' whereat the Ghost lets fall the word we have been waiting for: 'So art thou [bound] to revenge when thou shalt hear.'

When it comes, it comes without any rhetorical flourish, a simple English verb. Suddenly, as suddenly as Beethoven in his sonatas moves from high rhetoric to utmost quietness, this has turned from an awesome and terrifying spectacle into a serious conversation between a father and his son. Hamlet asks simply: 'What?' Whereupon the Ghost steps up a gear and moves into what is going to be one of the strangest expositions in the whole of dramatic literature. First he confirms who he is, and explains that he dwells now in Purgatory:

> I am thy father's spirit,
> Doom'd for a certain term to walk the night,
> And for the day confin'd to fast in fires,
> Till the foul crimes done in my days of nature
> Are burnt and purg'd away. (9–13)

But now, by a sleight of hand that we will come to see as typical of him, he manages to move from the factual into a vague realm of the imagination which seems designed to play on the mind of his son without quite giving it anything concrete to hold on to, and thus ensnare him in his own fevered imaginings:

> *Ghost.*   But that I am forbid
> To tell the secrets of my prison-house,
> I could a tale unfold whose lightest word
> Would harrow up thy soul, freeze thy young blood,
> Make thy two eyes like stars start from their spheres,
> Thy knotted and combined locks to part,
> And each particular hair to stand an end
> Like quills upon the fretful porpentine.
> But this eternal blazon must not be
> To ears of flesh and blood. List, list, O list!
> If thou didst ever thy dear father love—
> *Ham.* O God!
> *Ghost.* Revenge his foul and most unnatural murder.
> *Ham.* Murder!

> *Ghost.* Murder most foul, as in the best it is,
>   But this most foul, strange and unnatural. (13–27)

These lines are worthy of Iago in the way they break off a flight of imagination to elicit the assertion of a bond deeper than all others, except that in *Othello* we know Iago is lying and trying to ensnare Othello for his own demonic purposes whereas here we are, at least at the moment of utterance, as overwhelmed by the Ghost's words as Hamlet is. The first part of the speech seems to be saying: 'I could tell you such terrible stories about what I suffer in Purgatory as would freeze your blood, except that I am forbidden to'; then, with 'List, list, O list', one can imagine the Ghost, if it had hands, grabbing Hamlet and drawing him close, and then asking of him the kind of question to which the only answer is: 'Of course – what is it?' And then, what it has been building towards: 'If thou didst ever thy dear father love . . . Revenge his foul and most unnatural murder.'

This is very far from 'the revenge ethic' of many ancient cultures, in which it is the automatic duty of the next of kin to avenge a murdered father, son or brother. Hamlet is not being asked as son to avenge his father's murder; he is being asked, as a son who (surely) loves his father, to avenge that father's foul and unnatural murder.

The excessive language, the language in excess of the facts, does not let up. When Hamlet raises his own rhetoric to the occasion, or rather, keeps up the heightened rhetoric he had already employed when asking his friends to 'unhand him' as he rushed to follow his fate –

> Haste me to know't, that I with wings as swift
> As meditation or the thoughts of love
> May sweep to my revenge (28–30)

– the Ghost returns, approvingly, 'I find thee apt'. And then, to bind his son even further to him, he proceeds to develop one of the more loathsome images of the play, which feeds into the general sense of horrible and unnatural growth already so strongly associated with Denmark and the court:

> And duller shouldst thou be than the fat weed
> That roots itself in ease on Lethe wharf,
> Wouldst thou not stir in this. (32–4)

And he proceeds to recount what, he says, happened to him:

> 'Tis given out that, sleeping in my orchard,
> A serpent stung me – so the whole ear of Denmark
> Is by a forged process of my death
> Rankly abused – but know, thou noble youth,
> The serpent that did sting thy father's life
> Now wears his crown. (35–40)

Here, for the first time, murder, ear and poison are conjoined, but note that 'ear' here is purely metaphorical – 'the whole mind of Denmark has been abused by a false rumour' is what the Ghost is saying. As the Ghost ends by pointing the finger firmly at Claudius without naming him Hamlet can only gasp: 'O my prophetic soul! My uncle!'

It is worth pausing here to see how far we have travelled. In Hamlet's fevered imagination his mother's too hasty marriage to his uncle and his dislike of the man had conjured up images of his uncle killing his father and seducing his mother. That had seemed the only explanation for two otherwise inexplicable events: the premature death of the father and the marriage of the mother to a man who seems both loathsome in himself and doubly so in relation to his brother, her former husband. And now the dead father has appeared to tell him that this is precisely what happened. And what he goes on to say only seems to confirm everything Hamlet had imagined:

> Ay, that incestuous, that adulterate beast,
> With witchcraft of his wit, with traitorous gifts –

> O wicked wit, and gifts that have the power
> So to seduce! – won to his shameful lust
> The will of my most seeming-virtuous queen.
> O Hamlet, what a falling off was there,
> From me, whose love was of that dignity
> That it went hand in hand even with the vow
> I made to her in marriage, and to decline
> Upon a wretch whose natural gifts were poor
> To those of mine.
> But virtue, as it never will be mov'd,
> Though lewdness court it in a shape of heaven,
> So lust, though to a radiant angel link'd,
> Will sate itself in a celestial bed
> And prey on garbage. (42–57)

Too few critics (Cavell is a noted exception) have pointed out how very strange this central passage is. The Ghost has moved apparently seamlessly from murder to something quite different, to the sexual union of his wife and his brother, in what, by the cool light of day, we can only see as the anguished howl of the betrayed husband. As with all such outbursts, it is very difficult to distinguish what is true from what only seems, to the victim, to be true. Is he right in calling Claudius 'incestuous' and 'adulterous'? How precise is he being? Does he imply, in other words, that Gertrude and Claudius had been having an affair *before* his death? As is the way with these things, he probably is not sure himself. He wants to blame the two of them for what they have done to him but at the same time he desperately wants to exonerate his wife, so, after calling the relationship incestuous and adulterous, he comes up with the common view of the cuckolded husband: it must have been witchcraft that seduced her (though 'witchcraft of his wit' might lead an unbiased listener to conclude that Claudius was a more amusing companion than was Old Hamlet). This is followed by the other frequently heard complaint in such situations: 'How could she do this? With someone like him! So inferior to me!' This merges into another anguished complaint, which could be taken in two ways. The Ghost seems to be saying that his dignified and courteous behaviour to his wife stands in sharp contrast to the mere brutal sensuality of his rival. The last lines, reflecting his confused and anguished mood, are almost impossible to make sense of, since they seem to set up a contrast between Gertrude's virtue and Claudius's lust, but seem also to imply that lust will always overcome virtue. The impartial auditor might hear the passage a little differently, and conclude that perhaps her husband was a little lacking in sensuality, which she was able to find in abundance in his replacement.

Hamlet is not, however, hearing this in the cold light of day, but in the darkness of the night after a lengthy wait and, at the time at least, we can imagine that he is as persuaded as we are by the utterance of the tormented Ghost, who only now presses on with what one might have thought was what he really had to convey to his son, information about how the murder was actually carried out. It seems that, sleeping 'within my orchard', as was his custom in the afternoon, his brother crept up to him

> With juice of cursed hebenon in a vial,
> And in the porches of my ears did pour
> The leperous distilment, whose effect
> Holds such an enmity with blood of man
> That swift as quicksilver it courses through
> The natural gates and alleys of the body,
> And with a sudden vigour it doth posset
> And curd, like eager droppings into milk,
> The thin and wholesome blood. (62–70)

The scholars tell us that Shakespeare probably heard reports of the Duke of Urbino being poisoned in similar fashion, and this seems to be borne out by Hamlet's later comment about the play he puts on at court in order to 'catch the conscience of the king' (III. 2. 233). But the real question to be asked is: why should Shakespeare choose such an unusual mode of murder? There must have been many examples in the literature of more orthodox poisonings and stabbings. Why go for something so odd and counter-intuitive?

Clearly this is part of the strange web of suggestion that Shakespeare generates in the course of this play, suggestions which seem constantly to call out for symbolic or metaphorical readings and thus prove a fruitful quarry for psychoanalysis, which is based on Freud's grasp that such metaphorical substitutions are the very language of the unconscious. It might, though, be better simply to note the play's ability to generate such readings, rather than feel we have to choose any one of them as true.

Many Elizabethans, seeing this play, would have remembered the central scene of the popular morality play, *Mankind*, written in the late fifteenth century, where the invisible devil Titivillus comes upon Mankind sleeping in the open, and, leaning over him, whispers such words into his ear that when he wakes he rejects all Church teaching and becomes a dissolute lout heading for damnation. The Devil here poisons Mankind's mind by pouring the poison of his words into his ear while he sleeps. We cannot help but think, it seems to me, that this tale of Old Hamlet being murdered by his brother by means of a vial of poison poured into his ear could itself be a vial of poison poured by a vengeful ghost into Hamlet's ear. Or so Hamlet might, with at least a part of his mind, think. In this way the folds enfold. The Ghost proceeds,

> Thus was I, sleeping, by a brother's hand,
> Of life, of crown, of queen at once dispatch'd,
> Cut off even in the blossoms of my sin,
> Unhousel'd, disappointed, unanel'd . . . (74–7)

– that is, not having received the Eucharist, not having been anointed with holy oil (i.e. not having received extreme unction), and not having made proper preparation. To add to the monstrosity, the murder left him without the last rites due to the dying Christian in the old Catholic world, thus condemning him, if one believes in it, to a period of time in the fires of Purgatory. But the triple negatives also suggest a spirit *stripped* of its rightful due, emptied out and left to float free of all its natural moorings.

The Ghost, however, does not stop there. Compulsively, it seems, he returns to his initial theme, as though the memories will not leave off tormenting him:

> If thou hast nature in thee, bear it not,
> Let not the royal bed of Denmark be
> A couch for luxury and damned incest. (81–3)

Yet once more he betrays his conflicting thoughts as he seeks both to condemn Gertrude and to exonerate her:

> But howsomever thou pursuest this act,
> Taint not thy mind nor let thy soul contrive
> Against thy mother aught. Leave her to heaven,
> And to those thorns that in her bosom lodge
> To prick and sting her. (84–8)

Stanley Cavell, one of the few critics to note the *double* burden the Ghost places on Hamlet's shoulders, makes the point forcefully:

> The Ghost asks initially for revenge for his murder, a task the son evidently accepts as his to perform . . . But after telling his story of his death, what the Ghost asks Hamlet 'not to bear' is something distinctly different – that 'the royal bed of Denmark be / A couch for luxury and damned incest.' But is this the son's business not to bear? Here the father asks the son to take the father's place, to make his life come out even for him, to set it right, so that he, the father, can rest in peace. It is the bequest of a beloved father that deprives the son of his identity, of enacting his own existence – it curses, as if spitefully, his being born of this father.

Though one might question the last sentence, the gist of the passage – that no father should embroil his child in his failure

to keep that child's mother – is surely right, and it says much
about the persuasive power of Shakespeare's rhetoric in this
strange play, a rhetoric that is here being deployed by the Ghost
and whose target is Hamlet, that the issue had never been so
clearly raised before Cavell's essay. To ask Hamlet to avenge
his murder is both understandable and, particularly if it is the
crown that is at issue, reasonable. To mix this up with how another
man usurped his place in his wife's bed, and then, as the Ghost
now does, to vanish 'with the coming of the morn', once more
urging Hamlet to 'Remember me', is unforgivable. Its effect
is, predictably, to throw Hamlet into a paroxysm of rage and
confusion.

4.4 (I. 5. 92–112)

> Hold, hold, my heart,
> And you, my sinews, grow not instant old,
> But bear me stiffly up. Remember thee? . . .
> Yea, from the table of my memory
> I'll wipe away all trivial fond records . . .
> And thy commandment all alone shall live
> Within the book and volume of my brain,
> Unmix'd with baser matter. (93–104)

But what will Hamlet remember? 'Meet it is I set it down/ That
one may smile, and smile, and be a villain', he goes on (107–8) –
but is Claudius a villain because of the murder he committed or
because he took another man's wife? Is Hamlet committing the
murder or the so-called adultery to the table or tablet of his
memory?

Curiously, the fact that the Ghost's words seem to echo what
Hamlet had felt ever since his father's death, far from confirming
the truth of what he utters, can only have the opposite effect, for
this prophetic congruence makes it more rather than less likely
that what the Ghost says to him and him alone is simply a projection of his confused feelings.

There is no time for Hamlet to sort out his whirling thoughts, for here come Horatio and Marcellus, calling out in their anxiety for his safety.

4.5 (I. 5. 113–98)

But something in Hamlet has changed. We are alerted to it almost imperceptibly, when he answers Marcellus's 'Hillo, ho, ho, my lord' not with some such phrase as 'Here I am' but with 'Hillo, ho, ho, boy. Come, bird, come', as though joining the others in a bird-hunt. They catch up with him and ask: 'How is't, my noble lord?' and 'What news, my lord?', to be greeted with Hamlet's 'O, wonderful!' When they press him to tell what has happened, he answers flippantly and seemingly beside the point:

> *Ham.* There's never a villain dwelling in all Denmark
> But he's an arrant knave.
> *Hor.* There needs no ghost, my lord, come from the grave
> To tell us this.
> *Ham.*   Why, right, you are in the right.
> And so without more circumstance at all
> I hold it fit that we shake hands and part . . .
> I will go pray.
> *Hor.* These are but wild and whirling words, my lord.
>   (129–38)

Though Hamlet seems to speak either nonsense or beside the point, we 'read' what he says perfectly well. The experience he has just been through, and which we have witnessed, has clearly been such as to put in place a wall between himself and even those he most trusts, perhaps even between himself and himself. This simple little exchange effortlessly conveys all that, and it is a great deal.

Hamlet asks only one thing of them: 'Never make known what you have seen tonight.' They say that of course they won't, but it doesn't satisfy him: 'Nay, but swear't.' When they say they have he persists, holding up his sword with its cross at the hilt:

Ham. Upon my sword.
Mar. We have sworn, my lord, already.
Ham. Indeed, upon my sword, indeed. (154–6)

Here Shakespeare introduces a further inventive twist, again reminiscent of Bach, Mozart or Beethoven, by adding a new element which in one sense is not strictly necessary but which contributes hugely to the overall 'feel' of the play: the Ghost intervenes. But he does so in a manner at once ridiculous and eerie. The line, as we have it in both the Good Quarto and the Folio, reads: 'GHOST: (*Cries under the stage*) Swear.' There follows an extraordinary scene in which Hamlet seems to taunt the Ghost: 'Ah ha, boy, say'st thou so? Art thou there, truepenny?' and the Ghost shifts its ground, calling out to them to swear now from one part of the understage and now from another, prompting more quips from Hamlet, such as: 'Well said, old mole. Canst work i'th'earth so fast?' while his terrified comrades are reduced to: 'O day and night, but this is wondrous strange.'

Jenkins (pp. 457–9), in his long note to the passage, sums up the scholarly consensus:

> We shall have accepted, along with Hamlet, (l.144), the Ghost's account of its Purgatory, and its presence down below will seem to accord with this. But 'under the stage' was the traditional theatrical location of hell, with possibilities of a kind mockingly suggested in Dekker's *News from Hell*, 'Hell, being under every one of their stages, the players . . . might with a false trap-door have slipped [the devil] down, and there kept him, as a laughing-stock to all their yawning spectators' . . . The familiarity with which Hamlet addresses it may recall the manner in which the stage Vice traditionally addressed the Devil.

There are nevertheless a number of important points he fails to make. Although he speaks of 'the impression given of something happening beyond what is or can be explained', he does not bring out sufficiently how different this scene is from that of the traditional jousting of the Vice and the Devil. For the familiarity there shown to the Devil, like the comic passages in the Harrowing of Hell sequences of the medieval miracle plays, depends on the playwright and the audience both having a secure sense of the limits to the Devil's power. When the medieval consensus disappeared that was no longer the case. Suddenly the Devil was at once nowhere and everywhere, famously, in Luther's *Table-Talk*, to be cursed and abused in the most private room in the house. Hamlet's 'Ah ha, boy' and 'Well said, old mole' signify not familiarity so much as an *attempt* at familiarity which would tame what is sensed to be untamable. It is, moreover, a strange jump from the way Hamlet addressed his beloved father in the scene we have just witnessed, to the half-taunting, half-admiring way he addresses the Ghost now he is invisible. As Jenkins says, part of the eeriness of the scene is that it is inexplicable – yet I don't think it is simply our familiarity with *Hamlet* that makes it seem both powerful and *right*, though *why* right we find it difficult to say.

The second part of Jenkins's admirable summary, which needs a little more attention than he perhaps gives it, concerns the sudden intrusion into this play, shortly after we have seen Hamlet start to play-act, of the very materiality of the Elizabethan theatre. It is not enough to point out that '"under the stage" was the traditional theatrical location of hell'. What should be stressed is that suddenly, having totally won our trust in his depiction of the Ghost, having allowed us to suspend our disbelief gracefully – and gratefully – Shakespeare is in one stroke undermining all that and reminding us that what we are witnessing is a play performed on a particular stage, the newly built Globe, with its 'cellarage' out of which things may emerge. To make drama out of something *not* emerging is striking, and it helps to keep the status of the Ghost deeply ambiguous – not just, is he the ghost of the dead king or some Devil-sent impersonation? But, is he the ghost of the dead king or a mere stage prop set up by the dramatist to frighten us or make us laugh? In this way Shakespeare forestalls those who would laugh at all ghosts in new plays as old hat and prepares the way for what is to be an emerging theme in *this* play, the relation of taking action to taking on a role both in the Danish court and in life itself.

This theme is coming to the fore even as we respond to the uncanny games of and with the underground Ghost. 'But come,' says Hamlet to his companions: swear that, however oddly I behave, 'As I perchance hereafter shall think meet/ To put an antic disposition on –' (179–80), you must give no sign that you know the reason. Jenkins glosses the phrase as 'affect madness', glossing 'antic' as grotesque, 'strange or odd', Hamlet's own description a line earlier, and he adds: 'The word is particularly used of an actor with a false head or grotesque mask' (p. 226).

But the Ghost is still there under the floorboards, and he repeats: 'Swear', which they do, with Hamlet adding: 'Rest, rest, perturbed spirit' before making it clear that it is time to go. As they do so he adds, to himself we presume, a couplet which closes off this fold and brings to an end the first movement of the play:

> The time is out of joint. O cursed spite,
> That ever I was born to set it right. (196–7)

This time the couplet seems entirely appropriate and natural. It fills out Marcellus's initial: ' 'Tis bitter cold/ And I am sick at heart' (I. 1. 7–8) and his later 'Something is rotten in the state of Denmark' (I. 4. 90), and it sets the seal on the problematic nature of the legacy the Ghost has left Hamlet.

It does more. Eliot found the play uncomfortable and was reduced to asserting that this was because Shakespeare had failed to find a plot commensurate with his feelings. Empson, another great twentieth-century poet-critic, drew the right conclusion from this, though he expressed it in his typically off-the-cuff way. Hamlet, he said, finds himself in a play he has no desire to be part of and no skill to act in. We need to listen to Empson, for he has put his finger on a key point of the play. But we need to explore rather more fully *why* this is a play Hamlet has neither the inclination nor the skill to take part in (why he curses instead of relishing the fact that it is he who has to set time right), and in this, as always, Shakespeare will be a sure guide, if only we are prepared to listen.

FOLD FIVE

(II. 1)

We need a rest, and Shakespeare knows it. On comes Polonius and with him his servant, Reynaldo. The theme of the new mercantile spirit of money and suspicion, which appears to characterise the court, is developed in what follows. 'Give him this money and these notes, Reynaldo,' instructs Polonius, and it soon becomes clear that he is talking about his son Laertes, now in Paris. Before you visit him, pursues the old councillor, I want you 'to make inquire/ Of his behaviour'. But that is not all. Reynaldo must pursue a more active path, he must put it about that Laertes is a bit of a lad, prone to 'such wanton, wild, and usual slips/ As are companions noted and most known/ To youth and liberty'. There it is again, 'youth and liberty' associated not with nature and growth but with dangerous excess. Nor is this all. He must suggest that Laertes is also addicted to 'drinking, fencing, swearing/ Quarrelling, drabbing', but – and here comes the peculiar mixture of the prudential spirit and the love of his own voice which is typical of Polonius – 'you may go so far' – but no further.

> You must not put another scandal on him,
> That he is open to incontinency –

> That's not my meaning; but breathe his faults so quaintly
> That they may seem the taints of liberty,
> The flash and outbreak of a fiery mind . . . (29–33)

Commentators have struggled to distinguish 'incontinency' from 'drabbing', but that is not the point. Polonius is a man whose moral compass is infinitely wobbly, but who seems to imagine that it is as firm and clear as a diagram; a man who is constantly quibbling over words but for whom words have long since lost their moorings in life. When Reynaldo, sensibly enough, questions what he is being asked to do, Polonius goes into a long ramble about how this is 'a fetch of warrant', a legitimate trick; or as Jenkins glosses it (p. 239), the end justifies the means, though such realpolitik is typically couched in language that feels vaguely legal and is suitably obscure. Indeed, as Polonius proceeds we witness him losing contact more and more with both language and reality. Shakespeare is giving us a kind of Dadaist rant *avant la lettre*. Inevitably, when Reynaldo breaks into his monologue with 'Very good, my lord', Polonius suddenly finds that he has lost his way: 'And then, sir, does a this – a does – what was I about to say? By the mass, I was about to say something. Where did I leave?'

This is a splendid sketch of a doddering old man losing his memory, but it is much more. It brings us to the corruption at the heart of the court, a corruption more innocent and less malicious than we find in the courts of Goneril and Regan in *King Lear*, but for that reason all the more disturbing – we cannot dismiss it as 'evil', only as the inevitable end of a culture that has lost its moral bearings. And coming so soon after Shakespeare's reminder to us of the physical conditions of the theatre in which he is working and in which this play is unfolding, it makes us aware of a simple theatrical fact: the play we are watching will come to a halt if the actors forget their lines. This is not as radical a jolt as we get in *Waiting for Godot*:

> *Vladimir:* What was I saying, we could go on from there.
> *Estragon:* What were you saying when?

Vladimir: At the very beginning.
Estragon: The very beginning of WHAT?
Vladimir: This evening . . . I was saying . . . I was saying . . .
Estragon: I'm not a historian.

In *Hamlet*, of course, someone is at hand to remind Polonius of what he was saying, but the damage has been done. A chasm has opened at our feet as we are suddenly reminded that it is not *really* an old courtier standing before us and speaking but an actor, and one who could quite easily forget his lines. Of course he has been hired precisely because he is not in the habit of forgetting his lines, and we pay for our tickets precisely in order to enter another world, the world of medieval Denmark in this instance, which is also, somehow, a contemporary world – but we do not want it to be too contemporary a world, too realistic – just realistic enough for us to inhabit it for the duration of the play. In other words, a playwright may question everything, but the one thing he must not question is the pact he has made with his audience at the start: you pay and I provide you with a spectacle to dream to. You may question every form of authority – of kings, of bishops, of geniuses – but the one authority you must not question is that of the play-wright himself. Of course there are other theatrical traditions, such as that of the medieval miracle plays, that of Brecht and his disciples, that of Japanese Noh drama, but in the dominant Western tradition, of which Shakespeare is both one of the earliest exemplars and the greatest representative, these principles hold. The playwright can play with it, prod it, but he must always make you feel that he is in control. And Shakespeare, who, especially in this play, prods it more than any other writer until the twentieth century, also knows, here as in his dealings with inflammatory theological issues, exactly how far he can go.

Here Polonius needs only to be given his cue and he is off again. Reynaldo is quick to remind him that where he left off was at 'At "closes in the consequence"', and although that is not strictly true (three more lines followed before Polonius lost his way), it is true enough, in that no one thing Polonius says makes much more

sense than any other, so that he is quite happy to pick up where his
servant tells him:

> At 'closes in the consequence', ay, marry.
> He closes thus: 'I know the gentleman,
> I saw him yesterday', or 'th'other day',
> Or then, or then, with such or such, 'and as you say,
> There was a gaming', 'there o'ertook in's rouse' . . .
> See you now,
> Your bait of falsehood takes this carp of truth;
> And thus do we of wisdom and of reach,
> With windlasses and with assays of bias,
> By indirections find direction out.
> So by my former lecture and advice
> Shall you my son. (54–68)

Line 53 in the Folio has Reynaldo give a cue of two lines rather
than one, and Jenkins notes that this has 'the air of an actor's
elaboration' (p. 232), which is not surprising, since the whole
exchange could clearly be lengthened or curtailed, depending on
how much elaboration was felt to be needed. Margreta de Grazia
has observed, very acutely, how many speeches in this play consist
of lists, and how often the three texts differ in length at those
points, suggesting that, of all Shakespeare's plays, this is the most
flexible as well as being the longest (in Q2 and F). And this is not
surprising, for it is the most Beckettian of his plays, in the sense
that a good deal of it consists of words that have little meaning but
for that very reason powerfully convey the vacancy or horror that
has given rise to them. All too often we want to scream at the
speaker to shut up, to stop a little and think – but the play, of
course, goes on.

As it goes on here, once Reynaldo has left, with the entry of
Polonius's other child, Ophelia. Here the paradox of language
being inadequate to convey what is felt and yet, through its very
inadequacy, powerfully conveying all that is needed is given a new
twist, for the terrified Ophelia is coming to report Hamlet's

seemingly incomprehensible behaviour as he broke into her closet and confronted her,

> with his doublet all unbrac'd
> No hat upon his head, his stockings foul'd,
> Ungarter'd and down-gyved to his ankle,
> Pale as his shirt, his knees knocking each other,
> And with a look so piteous in purport
> As if he had been loosed out of hell
> To speak of horrors . . . (78–84)

This is the first glimpse we have of the new Hamlet, 'playing' the madman, though his attitude towards Horatio and the others in the previous scene had hinted at it, and he has indeed told them he will do so. Yet it is also a powerful evocation of a Hamlet deeply disturbed by his recent experiences: the 'play' and the 'reality', though Hamlet himself may not realise it, merge all too easily.

Polonius is convinced that this is simply a sign of love-madness, and he presses Ophelia for further details. She obliges:

> He took me by the wrist and held me hard.
> Then goes he to the length of all his arm,
>> ['He backs till he holds her at arm's length' – Jenkins,
>>   p. 234.]
> And with his other hand thus o'er his brow
> He falls to such perusal of my face
> As a would draw it. Long stay'd he so.
> At last, a little shaking of mine arm,
> And thrice his head thus waving up and down,
> He rais'd a sigh so piteous and profound
> As did seem to shatter all his bulk
> And end his being. (87–96)

Effortlessly, Shakespeare presents us with the opposite of the scene we have just witnessed. Where Polonius spoke at length and said almost nothing, Hamlet, even though we have his actions filtered through the double prism of Ophelia's report and his feigned madness, says nothing yet conveys much. Conveys his anguished perusal of Ophelia's face for clues as to her true being and to an understanding of women in general and his own mother in particular. Conveys his plea to her to be what he would have her be.

Polonius, of course, only sees in this what he would like to see: 'This is the very ecstasy of love', an ecstasy which, he fears, 'leads the will to desperate undertakings'. Did she encourage him in any way? he asks. No, she replies, I did what you told me, 'I did repel his letters and denied/ His access to me' (109–10). Castigating himself for his lack of judgement in suggesting that Hamlet was merely trifling with her affections, but only because he fears the consequences, Polonius decides that the best thing is for her to tell the King all she has told him. 'Come,' he ends, suddenly decisive, and they go.

FOLD SIX

6.1 (II. 2. 1–39)

Rosencrantz and Guildenstern. As Stoppard understood so well, they are not to be separated, any more than Laurel and Hardy or Vladimir and Estragon or K's two assistants in *The Castle*. Which suggests that they are both a music-hall act and the stuff of nightmare. (In this play in which Hamlet seeks to understand in what way he is himself and not another, pairs proliferate as if to mock his quest.)

'Welcome, dear Rosencrantz and Guildenstern,' begins the King. 'Good gentlemen, he hath much talked of you,' proceeds Gertrude, when Claudius has reminded them of their long friend-ship with Hamlet and told them of Hamlet's strange behaviour and his need to know more. In other words, just as Polonius set his spies on Laertes, so Claudius and Gertrude would set them on Hamlet. 'And sure I am,' Gertrude goes on, 'two men there is not living/ To whom he more adheres'. Though her words are couched in what would appear to be the language of the court, formal and gracious, it is striking that she too seems naturally to formulate her desires in terms of expenditure, profit and loss:

> If it will please you
> To show us so much gentry and good will
> As to expend your time with us awhile
> For the supply and profit of our hope . . . (II. 2. 21–4)

The old-fashioned virtues of 'gentry' (i.e. courtesy) and 'good will' seem to sit comfortably for her with the new virtues of expenditure, supply and profit. One wonders how this mixture of old and new sounded to the ears of an Elizabethan audience.

When they respond, Shakespeare makes sure it is quite symmetrically, each starting and ending with a half-line and having two and a half lines in between. Whereupon, almost comically, the King comes in with: 'Thanks, Rosencrantz and gentle Guildenstern', and Gertrude with: 'Thanks, Guildenstern and gentle Rosencrantz.'

Upon which, after Guildenstern has uttered the pious wish that Heaven should help them to help Hamlet, and Gertrude added an 'Amen', they are ushered away to be led by an attendant to Hamlet, and Polonius enters.

6.2 (II. 2. 40–84)

He has come to announce the arrival of yet another pair. They are the ambassadors Claudius had sent to the King of Norway. At the same time Polonius tells Claudius that he thinks he has 'found/ The very cause of Hamlet's lunacy' (48–9). When Claudius relays this to Gertrude, however, she is sceptical: 'I doubt it is no other but the main,/ His father's death and our o'er-hasty marriage' (56–7). Has she, we wonder, always felt their marriage was over-hasty, or has she only been forced into recognising this by Hamlet's words and attitude to her? There is no time to ponder the issue, for something else is upon us, something new but also something old. For the ambassadors, Voltemand and Cornelius, have come to tell the King of Denmark that Young Fortinbras had mustered forces purportedly to attack the Poles but in actual fact to invade Denmark. The old sick King of Norway, on discovering this, reprimanded his son, and the young man has now sworn to uphold the treaty with Denmark and the King has given the permission to sally forth against the Poles. For this purpose, Fortinbras needs to pass through Denmark (Shakespeare does not scruple to tinker with geography when it suits him); the ambassadors come to ask Claudius's permission for this. Claudius is handed the King of Norway's letter, the first of many pieces of writing to litter this play, which, he says, he will read at leisure and, in the meanwhile, offers them hospitality which they accept.

They too go, and Polonius is ready to resume his account of what he believes to be the cause of Hamlet's strange behaviour.

6.3 (II. 2. 85–167)

By now we are getting used to him, but here he surpasses himself, as Shakespeare discovers how to make comedy and tragedy work with rather than against each other (as they do in, say, *Measure for Measure*):

> My liege and madam, to expostulate
> What majesty should be, what duty is,
> Why day is day, night night, and time is time,
> Were nothing but to waste night, day, and time.
> Therefore, since brevity is the soul of wit,
> And tediousness the limbs and outward flourishes,
> I will be brief. Your noble son is mad.
> Mad call I it, for to define true madness,
> What is't but to be nothing else but mad?
> But let that go. (86–95)

Polonius's inability to advance is comic; it is also an instance of what is endemic to this play, the way time seems to be suspended ('the time is out of joint'), in the first instance for Hamlet but increasingly, as the play unfolds, for the other characters and for the audience as well. There is something else. Hamlet, we have seen, feels that there is a kind of envelope between himself and the world and in particular between himself and language: other people appear to use it unselfconsciously to say what they want but he is always only too aware of the physicality of words coming between himself and what he wants to say. At other moments, though, the fact that most people imagine language to be transparent becomes a sign of their blindness to their own motives, and their language betrays them to reveal to us what they are hiding from themselves. Thus one of Hamlet's central tactics consists of derailing the speeches of others and setting them on tracks that were not envisaged. Polonius, however, hardly needs Hamlet to trip him up; he is perfectly able to do it by himself. So lacking in self-awareness is he that words and half-remembered turns of phrase have become the motors of his speeches, leading him further and further away from what he was trying to say in the first place. This speech in particular is a wonderful example of this, as 'day' leads to 'day' and then to 'night', and 'mad' leads to 'mad' and 'true madness' and 'mad' again. The only way to escape is to give up – 'but let that go'.

However, everyone in this play is a critic, and Gertrude cuts Polonius short with: 'More matter with less art.' In other words: 'Get to the point.' But what *is* the point? As in *Tristram Shandy*, what seems like digression often turns out to be the main theme, or rather the clear distinction between theme and digression is progressively blurred. Polonius defends himself: 'Madam, I swear I use no art at all', and he is right, and right to rebuke her for conflating art and outward flourish. Poor Polonius, however, cannot seem to get out of the mire he appears to inhabit, where the sounds of words automatically trigger other words and any sense he was groping for seems to be perpetually deferred:

> And now remains
> That we find out the cause of this effect,
> Or rather say the cause of this defect,
> For this effect defective comes by cause. (100–3)

Eventually, however, he produces a letter (yes, another) which he claims Ophelia has given him. It is clearly from Hamlet, and we now get our second glimpse of him in his new state, prior to his actually appearing before us, but this time the clash between *what* we hear and *how* we hear it is even more pronounced than when Ophelia herself had reported Hamlet's actions, since what we have here is a very private missive, a love letter, no less, read out in public by an old buffoon: '*To the celestial and my soul's idol, the most beautified Ophelia –*' At this point he breaks off to subject Hamlet's words to his own criticism: '"... *beautified Ophelia*— That's an ill phrase, a vile phrase, "beautified" is a vile phrase' (109–11).

Gertrude cannot hide her impatience: 'Came this from Hamlet to her?' But Polonius is where he delights to be, centre stage, listening to his own voice, even if it is uttering another man's words – but then, as we will see, one of the questions raised by the play is: what are one's own words?

Polonius proceeds:

Good madam, stay awhile, I will be faithful.

> *Doubt thou the stars are fire,*
> *Doubt that the sun doth move,*
> *Doubt truth to be a liar,*
> *But never doubt I love.*
> *O dear Ophelia, I am ill at these numbers. I have not art to reckon my groans. But that I love thee best, O most best, believe it. Adieu.*
>
>> *Thine evermore, most dear lady, whilst this*
>> *machine is to him,   Hamlet.*
>
> (115–23)

What is so extraordinary is that Hamlet comes through the double barrier of his own clumsiness at writing and Polonius's delivery. Comes through, one is inclined to say, precisely *because* of those things. In *Love's Labour's Lost* four young men are shown to be caught up only in their own idea of what love is when the sonnets they thought they were delivering in private are overheard by others. Here the opposite happens. The very ordinariness of the little quatrain, and the clichéd nature of Hamlet's admission that he is no good at writing poetry and protestation of love, is suddenly given enormous pathos by his strange way of signing off, the genuineness of 'thine evermore, most dear lady' followed by 'whilst this machine is to him'. Jenkins glosses the last phrase as 'whilst this bodily frame belongs to him', and tries to persuade us that 'the word machine, without the prosaic associations it has acquired in a later age, refers admiringly to a complicated structure composed of many parts' (p. 243). But why 'admiringly'? I suspect that Heiner Müller was a better reader of Shakespeare than the learned editor when he entitled his schizoid *Hamlet Hamletmachine*. Hamlet confesses (despairingly, I would say) to Ophelia that he feels himself to be the sum of mechanical parts rather than a living whole, and he expresses this feeling here to the one person, apart from Horatio, to whom we ever find him confiding, the one person he trusts to be a human being and not a machine.

Having finished reading, Polonius explains: 'This in obedience hath my daughter shown me' – for him Ophelia is just an appendage, a cog in his 'machine' (as Hermia is to Egeus in *A Midsummer Night's Dream*) and in the larger machine of the state of which he himself is just a cog. For, he goes on, what would you and the Queen have thought of me if I had kept quiet or 'look'd upon this love with idle sight'? No, he says, 'I went round to work', and, he tells them, explained to her that Hamlet was 'out of thy star', and she should lock herself away from him and return all his gifts. As a result of which, he ends, Hamlet

> Fell into a sadness, then into a fast,
> Thence to a watch, thence into a weakness,
> Thence to a lightness, and, by this declension,
> Into the madness wherein now he raves
> And we all mourn for. (147–51)

It is typical of Polonius that he should break down what is one thing into what he sees as its constituent parts. But it is more than that. It is an aspect of the court culture of accounting, of profit and loss, and it is also, strangely, something that Hamlet, with his sense of humans as machines and of the time being out of joint, is also prone to, though for him it is a sign of the horror in which he feels himself embedded.

Polonius is on a roll and cannot be stopped. Leave it to me, he says, when the King and Queen show some hesitancy in going along with his diagnosis:

> I will find
> Where truth is hid, though it were hid indeed
> Within the centre. (157–9)

His way of doing so is the same as he used with his own son. In words at once ludicrous and chilling he explains his plan:

> I'll loose my daughter to him.
> Be you and I behind an arras then,
> Mark the encounter. (162–4)

He will turn her loose to him, as one does to ensure two animals of one's choice will mate, and he and the King will hide and see what happens. That fateful word 'arras', denoting tapestry made in the town of Arras, and thus any wall hanging or even curtain, has become one of the best-known words in the play, but for a first-time theatregoer the speech only reinforces the web of associations linked with Polonius and the court: the attempt to find where truth is hidden and pluck it out; and the instinct to hide where, unseen, you may see and know. One of the things the play will demonstrate is the utterly mistaken view of human nature embodied in such terms. And it will start to do so at this very moment, for who should now appear but Hamlet himself, 'reading on a book', as the Folio has it.

6.4 (II. 2. 168–218)

This is our first sight of Hamlet since his encounter with the ghost of his father, although, as with the Ghost himself, Shakespeare has already prepared the way, first with Ophelia's account of him and then with the public reading of his letter to her, so that we feel we have already seen him in his new state. Our sense that we know this play before we have actually seen it may depend less on its world-wide fame than on the way it is constructed, in that what we see and hear is all too often something, or a version of something, we have already seen and heard.

Yet Hamlet's ensuing exchanges with Polonius only develop the kind of cutting wit we have already witnessed him employing in his opening exchanges with Claudius and his mother, reinforcing our sense that the actual appearance of the Ghost, with his account of his murder, is less decisive in creating the character we are presented with than the trauma of his mother's (over-hasty?) marriage to his despised uncle.

Polonius urges the King and Queen to leave. 'I'll board him presently,' he says. Glossed as 'I'll accost/address him at once' by the Arden editors, this shows how dangerous it is to take the meaning of Shakespeare's words but forget the words themselves. They are, after all, the building blocks from which the play is made. Here Polonius has changed from being a spy to being a soldier, ready to jump into an enemy ship as soon as his own comes alongside it, so as to seize control of it (an image that will become reality later in the play as Hamlet escapes the fate Claudius has planned for him in England because the ship in which he is sailing is boarded by pirates). Hamlet, however, has other ideas. His first move is to pretend he does not recognise Polonius:

Pol.   How does my good Lord Hamlet?
Ham. Well, God-a-mercy.
Pol.   Do you know me, my lord?
Ham. Excellent well. You are a fishmonger.
Pol.   Not I, my lord.

Ham. Then I would you were so honest a man.

Pol. Honest, my lord?

Ham. Ay sir. To be honest, as this world goes, is to be one man picked out of ten thousand.

Pol. That's very true, my lord. (171–80)

We feel that much more is going on in this exchange, as we do in Hamlet's earlier exchange with his uncle and mother, than it is possible to bring to the surface. Wit, certainly, such as we find in Shakespeare's fools as they continually wrong-foot their interlocutors; but also – since Hamlet is not a licensed fool like Lear's Fool, nor a clown like those we find in the early comedies – a kind of despair, as though his wit were his way of keeping afloat. That feeling will grow in the course of the scene. Here Hamlet wrong-foots Polonius from the start by pretending he does not know him, then by imputing an insultingly low profession to him (the editors remind us that fishmongers were connected with sexual trade and so are anything but 'honest') and then, when he looks likely to take offence, turning the tables by saying something general about the corruption of the entire world.

Suddenly he swerves away again as Polonius, on the defensive, tries to be conciliatory while coming through as condescending, with his 'very true, my lord':

Ham. For if the sun breed maggots in a dead dog, being a good kissing carrion – Have you a daughter? (181–2)

Shakespeare will develop this in Lear's great rants in *King Lear* with their sudden descent into a dense maelstrom of sexual imagery – but here it has already been prepared for not only in the connotations of 'fishmonger' but in Laertes's earlier words to Ophelia and the imagery of corruption associated with Denmark by Hamlet and the soldiers on the battlements. Most of all it picks up on Hamlet's 'Not so, my lord, I am too much in the sun' to Claudius. The image is of the sun bringing forth maggots from the carcass of an animal, but 'breed' and 'kissing' allow the unpleasant image of the sun as both corrupter and lover to hover over the scene – all the more powerful because of the usual positive associations of the sun with love. Hamlet gives Polonius no chance to take all this in before letting fly with: 'Have you a daughter?', which could be an innocent question, but, coming on top of what we have just had, associates her with sex, procreation and corruption. Polonius can only respond with: 'I have, my lord', whereupon Hamlet has him where he wants him: 'Let her not walk i'th'sun. Conception is a blessing, but as your daughter may conceive – friend, look to't' (184–6). At one level, let her not, carrion that she is, expose herself to the sun, lest she breed maggots; at another, let her not frequent the royal family; at a third, it reminds us of Hamlet's desire to melt away, not exist, and his unspoken feelings about procreation. As Jenkins says (p. 247): 'After Polonius's plan to "loose" her (162) the audience may appreciate the irony of this.' I doubt if 'appreciate' is the right word, though. It suggests leisure to take in the nuances, whereas the exchanges go so fast that the audience can only cling on and hope to grasp the general sense of what is at play here. But that, Shakespeare knows, is enough, for, he knows, the echoes will reverberate even as we are propelled forward.

'How say you by that?' Polonius exclaims. Then, to himself: 'Still harping on my daughter.' He tries another tack: 'What do you read, my lord?'

> *Ham.* Words, words, words.
> *Pol.* What is the matter, my lord?
> *Ham.* Between who?
> *Pol.* I mean the matter that you read, my lord. (191–5)

It is as if everyone in the play is intent on dragging Hamlet back to a clear linear set of meanings which he either cannot or will not recognise; for as with a sixteenth-century Kaspar Hauser or Rimbaud, the materiality of language keeps intruding on the meaning, making it impossible for him to engage in a normal conversation. We have already seen this intrusion of the materiality of language in Polonius's speeches, but while Polonius was unaware of this, letting the sounds of words dictate the direction in which he moves, Hamlet is driven towards silence by his very awareness of it. Words are not transparent for him as they are for most of us most of the time, unnoticed as they convey meaning. They remain, stubbornly, just words. On another level, of course, the actor is being utterly honest – these things he is mouthing are just words to him, words he has to learn and memorise and repeat at the appropriate moment.

We can begin to see now how much more central we need to make Empson's insight that Hamlet is reluctant to take part in a play others are performing: they *act* while he merely he feels himself to be *an actor*. What Empson says is: 'He walks out to the audience and says: "You think this is an absurd old play, and so it is, but I'm in it, and what can I do?"' Though Empson is primarily talking about how Shakespeare deals with the fact that the old *Hamlet* ghost was a source of mirth when he set out to write *his* version, I don't think we should limit it to that. For seeing the play this way helps us to see it not as primarily about Hamlet's reluctance to act, or the problem of the succession, or Hamlet's sexuality. Rather, it suggests how alienated Hamlet feels from the court, how unwilling he is to enter the play he sees the King, the Queen and the courtiers performing, the play about a happy marriage and a secure King and Queen on the throne of a prosperous country. At the same time we have already had hints, in the latter part of his encounter with the Ghost and in his concluding soliloquy there, that he may also be reluctant to take part in the play the Ghost is offering him, the play of filial revenge. But it cuts deeper than that. If Hamlet does not seem able to be part of either of the plays that are on offer, this does not mean that he belongs in another, more satisfying, play. For these two are the only plays in town, and if he cannot take part in either he cannot live at all. This is, as we will see, what he spends the rest of the play trying in vain to do something about.

After more banter, and Polonius's grudging admission that there seems to be method in Hamlet's madness, he decides he has seen and heard enough:

Pol.   My lord, I will take my leave of you.

Ham. You cannot, sir, take from me anything that I will not
        more willingly part withal – except my life, except my
        life, except my life. (213–17)

This is one of the places where editors, and Jenkins among them,
tend to opt for a text that is neither that of the Quartos nor of
the Folio, but a combination of both. The Second Quarto has:
'You cannot take from me anything that I will not more willingly
part withal – except my life, except my life, except my life.' The
Folio has: 'You cannot, sir, take anything from me that I would
more willingly part withal – except my life, except my life.' Which
version is preferable, the Quarto, the Folio, or the amalgamation
of the two? There are more words in *Hamlet* than in any other
Shakespeare play – more than any performance could accommodate, say the scholars, and as one examines them and tries to decide
which are most likely to reflect Shakespeare's final decision, they
start to blur, as they do for Hamlet himself and to become nothing
but words, words, words. We will have to live with the uncertainty,
while recognising the important thing, that if Hamlet's (feigned?)
'madness' does not exactly have method in it, it certainly allows
him to say what he feels, and, occasionally, to say it loud and clear,
but in such a way as to obscure its meaning. Hamlet's courteous
and courtly phrases here are so powerful because, like the conclusion of his letter to Ophelia, they seem to allow us – amazingly –
direct access, via his wit, to his profoundest feelings: he tells
Polonius, in the most polite language, that he is mightily glad he
is leaving, but that what would make him gladder still is for him,
Hamlet, to be able to leave this life, with its seemingly impossible
demands upon him.

So much, at least, is clear.

6.5 (II. 2. 219–313)

Since this is a play in which events tumble over themselves at
dizzying speed and yet nothing much happens, Polonius's exit is

the cue for the entrance of the pair, Rosencrantz and Guildenstern.
And the banter continues, though these two are, as we would
expect from young men who have grown up with Hamlet, less
tedious than the old councillor, and capable, up to a point, of
keeping up with him, matching him for suggestive double
entendres:

> *Ham.* My excellent good friends. How dost thou,
> Guildenstern? Ah, Rosencrantz. Good lads, how do
> you both?
> *Ros.* As the indifferent children of the earth.
> *Guild.* Happy in that we are not over-happy: on Fortune's cap
> we are not the very button.
> *Ham.* Nor the soles of her shoe?
> *Ros.* Neither, my lord.
> *Ham.* Then you live about her waist, or in the middle of her
> favours?
> *Guild.* Faith, her privates we. (224–34)

Guildenstern suggests that they are merely nature's foot soldiers,
but hints too that they are nothing less than nature's private parts.
Hamlet then, as is his wont, abruptly changes the subject and
suggests that to live here in Denmark is to live in a prison. (The
next thirty lines are in the Folio but not the Quarto, suggesting
that Shakespeare, in his revision – if that is indeed what F is – felt
the need to develop the dialogue.) 'We think not so, my lord,'
returns Rosencrantz. This leads Hamlet into one of those strange
moments when he is seen to be 'kidding on the level', speaking
what he feels while giving the impression that he is only playing a
part, just as he did in his closing words to Polonius:

> *Ham.* Why, then, 'tis none to you; for there is nothing either
> good or bad but thinking makes it so. To me it is a
> prison.
> *Ros.* Why, then your ambition makes it one: 'tis too narrow
> for your mind.

> *Ham.* O God, I could be bounded in a nutshell and count
> myself a king of infinite space – were it not that I have
> bad dreams. (249–56)

In one breath Hamlet seems to take up an idealist position, while
in the next he appears to reject it. It is perfectly possible, Hamlet
says, merely to imagine a possibility for it to be the case. But one
can substitute imagination for reality *only for so long* – sooner or
later reality reasserts itself, if only in one's unconscious. The
modern viewer or reader will recall William Golding's terrifying
novel given over to precisely this state of affairs, *Pincher Martin.* Its
eponymous hero, wrecked on a bare rock in the middle of the
ocean, manages to survive for a while, but the hideous truth dawns
on him gradually and then in a final terrifying rush that the rock,
in all its solidity, in all its complex topography, is nothing but the
projection outwards of his own tooth as he passes his tongue over
it. In response to the question of how long it takes Pincher Martin
to die, Golding replied: 'Eternity.' But Golding is only the last in
a long line of artists who have explored this state of affairs. We,
who have the benefit of so much nineteenth-century literature
exploring just this paradox, the opium-induced dreams of a de
Quincey or a Baudelaire, the erotic fantasies of an Emma Bovary
or an Anna Karenina, the crazed fantasies of a Raskolnikov, the
refusal of Ivan Ilyitch to accept that he is dying, can see that
Hamlet has been there first.

All the while he is exchanging witticisms with his old comrades
Hamlet is trying to discover why they are there. Finally he comes
out with it straight: 'What make you at Elsinore?' (270) (the point
at which the Folio and Quarto once more converge). 'To visit you,
my lord, no other occasion,' insists Rosencrantz. 'Were you not
sent for?' Hamlet insists, but again they stonewall, and Hamlet has
to press them: 'I know the good King and Queen have sent for
you.' But they still will not confess: 'To what end, my lord?' asks
Rosencrantz, and it is worth noting how the very formality with
which Hamlet is always addressed as 'my lord' comes to seem
almost insulting when combined with the desire of everyone in the

King's employment to wrench his secret out of him, to treat him, in other words, in anything but a lordly way.

After further probing they finally admit: 'My lord, we were sent for.' 'I will tell you why,' Hamlet promptly answers them, and proceeds with another of those strange confessions that are not quite confessions and which he seems to need:

> I have of late, but wherefore I know not, lost all my mirth, forgone all custom of exercises; and indeed it goes so heavily with my disposition that this goodly frame the earth seems to me a sterile promontory, this most excellent canopy the air, look you, this brave o'erhanging firmament, this majestical roof fretted with golden fire, why, it appeareth nothing to me but a foul and pestilent congregation of vapours. What piece [What a piece, F] of work is a man, how noble in reason, how infinite in faculties, in form and moving how express and admirable, in action how like an angel, in apprehension how like a god: the beauty of the world, the paragon of animals – and yet, to me, what is this quintessence of dust? Man delights not me – nor woman neither . . . (295–309)

It has often been remarked that Hamlet, the Renaissance courtier, is here quoting almost verbatim the great essay *On the Dignity of Man*, by the Florentine Neoplatonist, Pico della Mirandola (1463–94), a summary of that movement's view of man which, in contrast to the medieval Christian view, argued that man could, if he directed his faculties in the right way, become something akin to a god. Panofsky, in the book on Dürer from which I quoted earlier, seeks to link the artist's *Melencolia 1* to this tradition via the notion of the genius who operates under the influence of Saturn, but, I suggested, his passion for the Florentines made him misread Dürer. What we have in the engraving is a figure who has been deprived of the medieval tradition where man knew his place within a biblical scheme in which salvation would come through Jesus Christ, but who has found that the Florentine optimism in the powers of man to achieve a kind of divinity by his own efforts is turning into a cruel deception. Here Hamlet here shows the same attitude; could, indeed, be Dürer's Melancolia speaking. The very wonder of the universe, the very sense of his own potential ('in apprehension how like a god'), has suddenly turned everything to ashes and all he is left with is the sense of man as 'the quintessence of dust', the alchemical term ironically inverted, since alchemy was designed to turn base matter into gold. And all for no reason, he says, but whether he says this because he believes it or because he wishes to hide the real reason from those he rightly perceives as the King's spies, we cannot tell. Melancholy, as Kierkegaard saw, is all-encompassing, and when we are in its grip all questions about its provenance fall away.

But just when we seem to be embarked on a journey in one direction we suddenly, with the introduction of a new topic, find we have changed tack – except that the 'new direction' all too often leads back to the very issues we thought we had left behind.

6.6 (II. 2. 314–417)

The new direction is introduced almost as an afterthought and proceeds to take centre stage for what turns out to be a sizeable portion of the play. Hamlet has just said that man, 'this quintessence of dust . . . delights not me'. Rosencrantz responds:

> To think, my lord, if you delight not in man, what Lenten entertainment the players shall receive from you [there was, of course, no entertainment in the season of Lent]. We coted [outstripped] them on the way, and hither are they coming to offer you service. (314–17)

Hamlet starts to respond to this news with the kind of barbed double entendre that characterises his relations with the court, but suddenly changes direction: 'He that plays the king shall be welcome – his Majesty shall have tribute on me'. It is as though the thought of the players allows him to rediscover his instinctive self, unseen until now, since it has been pushed down by his adversarial relation to the court and by the shock of his encounter with the Ghost. For the first time since the play started, Hamlet begins to forget his father's death and his mother's remarriage. But such forgetting is not easy, and for a while the two things – his delight at the advent of the players and his burdensome thoughts – fight for dominance within him.

'He that plays the king shall be welcome – his Majesty shall have tribute on me.' He who only *plays* the king, Hamlet seems to be saying, is someone I can love and whose vassal I am happy to be – unlike the *false* king who is at present demanding my allegiance – the one who has usurped the role rightly held by another and will not acknowledge his lack of entitlement. Underneath this, and certainly unseen by Hamlet, but surely picked up by the audience, there lies a possible critique of the old King, his father, Old Hamlet, coming back into his life as a ghost, another player who will not acknowledge his lack of substance.

But the thought of the king who is only an actor carries him into a new realm. Or not quite new – nothing, it seems, is ever quite new in this play – for we have seen how in the previous speech about man's greatness and smallness the very description of the universe and of man seems suddenly to leave its moorings and soar, until brought crashing down to earth by the conclusion. Here, though, the thought of the players seems to sustain him for a very long time indeed:

> – his Majesty shall have tribute on me, the adventurous knight shall use his foil and target, the lover shall not sigh gratis, the humorous man shall end his part in peace, the clown shall make those laugh whose lungs are tickle a th'sear ['who are of such sensible and nimble lungs that they always use to laugh at nothing' – Jenkins, p. 254), and the lady shall say her mind freely – or the blank verse shall halt for't. What players are they? (318–25)

For the first time we see Hamlet neither acting a part nor being acted upon, and we find him relishing his own imagination and rhetoric as he enters the world of the players. Jenkins, in his dry note, puts it well:

> The humorous man [the man of humours, not the clown, who comes next in the list], like the knight with his weapon, and the lady with her tongue, is to have full rein to enact his stock role. Hence he will play out in peace (unmolested) his unpeaceful part, and play it to its peaceful end, when his rages are all spent. (p. 254)

For the theatre is the one place where you can give free rein to feelings within a clearly circumscribed role in full recognition that you will not be called to account for them and can, when your part is done, find another in order to give free rein to quite other feelings. And this helps us see that Hamlet has in one sense been using the court as his theatre, playing on that stage first the Melancholic and then the Madman. Unfortunately, as he recognises, it is not a stage but – on the Globe stage at least – the reality.

After giving free rein to his newly found high spirits, Hamlet returns to the present: 'What players are they?' There follows a long passage that theatre historians have had a field day with and critics have scratched their heads over. For, Rosencrantz explains, they are actors who have left the city, where they worked, driven out by the newfangled children's companies, which are now all the rage. How so? asks Hamlet, and he wonders at their not realising that the children in turn will grow up and become the adults whose places they are in the process of usurping. Then he identifies this with his own problems, musing that those who once laughed at Claudius, now that he is King pay good money to buy his portrait. But he is interrupted by the sound of trumpets and Guildenstern announces: 'There are the players.'

It seems that all this refers to a theatrical dispute in London just at the time *Hamlet* was being written, when a children's company began to act in the Blackfriars Theatre, performing, among other things, Ben Jonson's *Cynthia's Revels* and *Poetaster*, where a character says: 'This winter has made us all poorer than so

many starved snakes; nobody comes at us, not a gentleman, nor a
–' (III. 4. 328–30). But Shakespeare, unlike Jonson, does not
usually go in for topical references, and the problem is compounded
by the fact that the Second Quarto omits all reference to the child
actors, the 'little eyases' who are 'now the fashion' and 'berattle the
common stages' in Rosencrantz's account. Did Shakespeare add
the passage later? If so, why? One can see a vague connection
between the usurping children and the generational conflict that
seethes beneath the surface in *Hamlet*, whether it be between
Hamlet and his father and uncle, Laertes and Polonius, or Old and
Young Fortinbras. And one can see – Hamlet points it out – a
connection between the inconstancy of the public, always keen to
show its admiration for the new man in power or the new theatrical phenomenon, and the present situation. But then *Hamlet*
seems to be written in such a way that we will always find connec-
tions between something in it and something else that hovers close
to its edges, waiting to come to life. What has perhaps not been
commented on so often is that the very oddity of introducing a
specific highly topical London reference into the utterly different
context which the playwright has been at pains to create for us, the
dark and dangerous Court of Elsinore, only adds to the nightmarish quality of the play, the feeling it generates that anything
can suddenly come into its orbit and linger there to trouble us by
its apparent lack of specific relation to the central theme.

Whatever the reason, the episode is engulfed by the trumpet
flourish, which heralds the arrival of the Players and is Hamlet's
excuse to get rid of his two old comrades, though he does so with
a flourish of his own, a further example of his kidding on the level.
Are we – are they – to take what he says as the truth, or as more
play-acting, or as a true sign of madness?

> *Ham.* You are welcome. But my uncle-father and aunt-mother
> are deceived.
> *Guild.* In what, my dear lord?
> *Ham.* I am but mad north-north-west. When the wind is
> southerly, I know a hawk from a handsaw. (371–5)

At this point Polonius enters. 'That great baby you see there is not yet out of his swaddling-clouts,' remarks Hamlet. You will see, he says to the others, he comes to announce the arrival of the Players.

Hamlet is now surprisingly rude to Polonius – 'buzz buzz', he says as the latter starts to speak, but the old councillor is too taken up with his exciting news to cotton on to the fact that Hamlet seems to know it already. 'The best actors in the world', he announces,

> either for tragedy, comedy, history, pastoral, pastoral-comical, historical-pastoral, tragical-historical, tragical-comical-historical-pastoral, scene individable, or poem unlimited. Seneca cannot be too heavy, nor Plautus too light. For the law of writ and the liberty, these are the only men. (392–8)

While scholars on the whole agree that Polonius, as usual, is more interested in hearing himself speak than in saying anything, they are nevertheless convinced that what he says here, and what Hamlet says a little later, can be mined for information not only about Elizabethan theatre practice but also about Shakespeare's view of the theatre. There is a simple reason for this: we have so little information on all this and are so infatuated with Shakespeare that any scrap of evidence is scrutinised as if it were Holy Writ. When that piece of evidence comes from Shakespeare himself, and from his most famous play as well, the temptation is irresistible.

Yet Hamlet ignores the old man's words and, in a move typical of both him and the play, switches to a seemingly totally unrelated subject, though even Polonius quickly sees its relevance:

> *Ham.* O Jephthah, judge of Israel, what a treasure hadst thou!
> *Pol.* What a treasure had he, my lord?
> *Ham.* Why
>
> > One fair daughter and no more,
> > The which he loved passing well.
>
> *Pol.* [*aside*] Still on my daughter.
> *Ham.* Am I not i'th' right, old Jephthah? (399–406)

Jephthah, in the biblical Book of Judges, swore to sacrifice the first thing he saw on returning home and was horrified to find it was none other than his daughter. Accepting her fate, she went into the wilderness with her maids and bewailed her virginity. *Jepthah, Judge of Israel* was the title of a well-known ballad, from which Hamlet proceeds to quote. Saying that, however, does not do justice to this extraordinary passage. We need to look at the rest of it:

> *Ham.* Am I not i'th'right, old Jepthah?
> *Pol.* If you call me Jepthah, my lord, I have a daughter that I love passing well.
> *Ham.* Nay, that follows not.
> *Pol.* What follows then, my lord?
> *Ham.* Why,
>   As by lot God wot
>   and then, you know,
>   It came to pass, as most like it was.
>   The first row of the pious chanson will show you more,
>   for look where my abridgement comes. (406–16)

The ballad's first stanza runs:

> I read that many years agoe
>   when *Jepha*, Judge of *Israel*,
> Had one fair Daughter and no more,
>   Whom he loved so passing well.
> And as by lot God wot
> It came to passe most like it was,
> Great warrs there should be,
>   And who should be the chiefe, but he, but he.

An undistinguished piece by any standards, stumbling along in almost Polonius-like fashion. But see how Shakespeare uses it. Hamlet quotes the crucial third and fourth lines, either to draw from Polonius the inference he does indeed draw, or because he really is obsessed by Ophelia, or both. Then, when Polonius bites and responds that he too has a daughter whom he loves, Hamlet questions this. It doesn't follow, he says: both of you may have daughters, but that doesn't mean that you both love them greatly. When Polonius asks him what does follow, Hamlet, in his usual fashion, chooses to take the words in a way other than they are meant, and proceeds to quote from what follows in the ballad. But this time he chooses one nonsensical line-filler: 'As by lot God wot', and then a clumsy but enigmatic line: 'It came to pass, as most like it was.' It is as if, under the pressure of the writing, Shakespeare discovers how to convey Hamlet's madness/wildness through his use of bits and pieces of the common repertory of the time, but in the process making the words lose their meaning, if they ever had any, and become something more like cries, groans, shrieks and grunts, pure bodily expressions of wildness and frustration. For a moment it becomes irrelevant *who* is speaking. At one level it is the playwright who is filling the theatre with his voice and body; or, if you prefer, the play. Not Hamlet and not Shakespeare. This, I suspect, is what drew Heiner Müller to *Hamlet*. And Shakespeare must have been pleased with what he had discovered, for he developed it to even greater effect in the snatches of old ballads sung by the Fool and Poor Tom on the heath in *King Lear*.

6.7 (II. 2. 417–542)

Then, as quickly as he had introduced Jephthah's daughter, Hamlet discards her, as the players finally enter. And as, earlier, the mere thought of the players seemed to have filled him with pleasure and excitement, an excitement, for once, untinged with any thought of self-protection or self-projection, so he now greets them in a tone which we have not heard before. We have come to love his quick wit, but it has always been barbed with bitterness; here there is only warmth.

You are welcome, masters. Welcome, all. – I am glad to see thee well. – Welcome, good friends. – O, old friend, why, thy

face is valanced [draped – i.e. bearded] since I saw thee last.
Com'st thou to beard me in Denmark? – What, my young lady
and mistress! By'r lady, your ladyship is nearer to heaven than
when I saw you last, by the altitude of a chopine [a high-soled
shoe]. Pray God your voice, like a piece of uncurrent gold, be
not cracked within the ring. – Masters, you are all welcome
. . . We'll have a speech straight. Come, give us a taste of your
quality. Come, a passionate speech. (417–28)

Hamlet is the only person in this play who seems capable of
speaking like this – truly, a nobleman and courtier, and a generous
and witty one to boot, in a court where both are in short supply.
Only he would have been able both to be spontaneous – he is
amazed at the actor's new beard and at how the youth who plays
the female role has grown – and to find surprising and delightful
images to convey his feelings. And then there is the further
element, which will always enter these plays when, as in the comedies, women disguise themselves as men – or, as here, when attention is drawn to the feminine – that women were played by boys,
so that the theme that has been with us since Shakespeare drew
attention to the Ghost's descending into the understage area of the
Elizabethan playhouse, of this being 'only' a play, surfaces again
momentarily here. Shakespeare, it seems, is unwilling to let us
forget it, just as he is unwilling to make it overwhelm the 'reality'
of the Court of Denmark he has been creating from the first line
of the play.

This extended section, which, it is worth reminding ourselves,
need not exist at all, in the economy of the plot, now takes a new
turn, as the man who is obviously the lead actor is asked by Hamlet
to recite a speech he says he once heard, a speech from a play
which, Hamlet says, did not please the multitude, but rather the
discerning few, 'an excellent play, well digested in the scenes, set
down with as much modesty as cunning'. 'I remember,' he goes on,

one said there were no sallets [tasty morsels] in the lines to
make the matter savoury, nor no matter in the phrase that

might indict the author of affection, but called it an honest
method, as wholesome as sweet, and by very much more hand-
some than fine. (437–41)

The speech he requests is Aeneas's recounting to Dido the sack of
Troy by the Greeks and the death of Priam. Can the Player recall it?

>   If it live in your memory,
>   begin at this line – let me see, let me see –
>   *The rugged Pyrrhus, like th'Hyrcanian beast –*
>   'Tis not so. It begins with Pyrrhus –
>   *The rugged Pyrrhus, he whose sable arms,*
>   *Black as his purpose, did the night resemble,*
>   *When he lay couched in the ominous horse . . .*
>   *And thus o'ersized* [covered] *with coagulate gore,*
>   *With eyes like carbuncles, the hellish Pyrrhus*
>   *Old grandsire Priam seeks.*
>   So proceed you. (444–60)

Polonius is full of praise: ' 'Fore God, my lord, well spoken, with
good accent and good discretion.' The Player picks it up:

>   *Anon he finds him,*
>   *Striking too short at Greeks. His antique sword,*
>   *Rebellious to his arm, lies where it falls,*
>   *Repugnant to command. . .* [20 lines]
>   ....
>   *Out, out, thou strumpet Fortune! All you gods*
>   *In general synod take away her power,*
>   *Break all the spokes and fellies from her wheel,*
>   *And bowl the round nave down the hill of heaven*
>   *As low as to the fiends.* (464–93)

But Polonius has had enough: 'This is too long,' he says, for once
surprisingly succinct himself. Hamlet, in high spirits, responds: 'It
shall to the barber's with your beard.' 'Prithee, say on,' he instructs

the Player, and then, pointing to Polonius: 'He's for a jig or a tale of bawdry, or he sleeps.'

Shakespeare had found a rich vein of humour before in having those watching or listening to some entertainment comment on it, and had also found it a valuable way to point up contrasts of character and expectation, and thus to drive the plot forward while seeming to be introducing a diversion – notably when the 'mechanicals' put on their play at the end of *A Midsummer Night's Dream* and the performance is intercut with the court's comments upon it. A variant of this has already been introduced into *Hamlet*, with Polonius reading out loud to the King and Queen Hamlet's letter to his daughter, and commenting on it as he does so. Here though, for the first time, a comment by a spectator is itself commented upon, as Hamlet light-heartedly, but in keeping with his new-found rudeness to the old courtier, dismisses Polonius's criticism by, rather surprisingly, bracketing him with the groundlings who only want a rowdy dance and a dirty story or they will go to sleep.

'Say on,' he instructs the Player, 'come to Hecuba.' Always ready to oblige, the Player skips some lines and plunges in at Hecuba: '*But who – ah, woe!* [F: *ah who*] *– had seen the mobbled queen.*' This arcane word, meaning 'muffled', one of a whole string of such recherché terms in the speech, provokes a thoughtful or perhaps delighted response in Hamlet, who repeats it to himself: 'The mobbled queen', and, from Polonius, a quiet, 'That's good', though whether because he genuinely feels this or has decided to fit in with Hamlet's obvious admiration for the speech it is impossible to determine. The Player, oblivious to all this, presses on for a further fourteen lines, till Polonius calls a halt with: 'Look whe'er he has not turned his colour and has tears in's eyes. Prithee no more.' Hamlet assents: ' 'Tis well. I'll have thee speak out the rest of this soon.'

There are many questions to be asked about this passage. First of all, who is right – Hamlet or Polonius? Is the speech 'set down with as much modesty as cunning', with 'no sallets [tasty morsels, possibly ribaldries] in the lines . . . nor no matter in the phrase that might indict the author of affection', or is it overwrought and too long? Critics and scholars have been divided on this, though most agree that it belongs to a style that had once been in fashion on the Elizabethan stage, what Bottom the Weaver calls 'Ercles' [Hercules'] vein, a tyrant's vein' (*MND,* I. 2. 33–4). Shakespeare had not been above using it himself in his early plays, such as *Titus Andronicus,* and had parodied it in *A Midsummer Night's Dream,* but it clearly isn't exactly a parody here. But if not, then what is it?

As many critics have noted, there are certain parallels between what we have been learning about Old Hamlet, Gertrude and Claudius, and the events referred to in the speech: Pyrrhus, a Greek, having hidden, along with his comrades, in the Trojan Horse, emerges under cover of night and goes in search of Priam, the aged King of Troy, the father of the man who has wronged the Greeks by running away with the wife of one of their leaders. Pyrrhus finds him and kills him, leaving his wife, Hecuba, distraught. Does Hamlet see himself in Pyrrhus and Claudius in Priam? Or does he see in Hecuba the loving wife whose response to the death of her husband is strikingly at odds with his own mother's? As is the way with this play, the parallels leap at you yet remain tantalisingly just out of reach.

But Hamlet has after all requested precisely this speech, and it is one whose outlines would have been familiar to most Elizabethans. It is, as Hamlet says, the account of Priam's slaughter as it was told in 'Aeneas' tale to Dido'. In the second book of the *Aeneid* Virgil chooses to fill in the background to Aeneas's wander-ings by recounting with extraordinary vividness the fall of Troy, the murder of its king, and Aeneas's escape amidst the fighting and the flames. It was one of the most celebrated episodes in the poem and had been translated by the Earl of Surrey when he first experi-mented with English blank verse in the first half of the sixteenth century, then turned into drama by Marlowe and Nashe in their early tragedy, *Dido, Queen of Carthage* (*c.* 1587). What Shakespeare seems to do here is to take the story from Virgil, to add a generous sprinkling of Ovid, his favourite Latin poet, and then present the whole in the kind of Senecan style that was so popular in the theatre of the Elizabethans, but whose high-flown rhetoric had begun, by the time *Hamlet* was written, to be severely criticised.

Eliot, famously, both recognised the central importance of the Senecan style and ethos to the drama of the period and registered his unease with it. He was uneasy because he recognised Shakespeare's greatness and how significant a figure Seneca was for Shakespeare, yet could not but feel disdain for Seneca's 'philosophy'. 'Seneca', he suggests, 'is the *literary* representative of Roman stoicism.' And 'Stoicism is the refuge for the individual in an indifferent or hostile world too big for him; it is the permanent substratum of a number of versions of cheering oneself up . . . The stoical attitude is the reverse of Christian humility.'

Eliot, like Dr Johnson, gives us plenty of food for thought. And, like Johnson, this is because he is both right and wrong at the same time. He has a nose for a problem but deals with it in a predictable manner. By that I mean that Johnson tends to fall back automatically on to a set of firmly held neoclassical principles and Eliot on to a set of Christian principles, which are what led them to see the problem in the first place but at the same time obscured for them the real point at issue. Here Eliot may well be right about Christian humility, but by using this argument to criticise Senecan stoicism he turns the debate into one about the pros and cons of different visions of life. The real problem with Senecan theatre is that it takes the trappings of ancient Greek tragic theatre without the substance. And for very good reason. The theatre of Aeschylus, Sophocles and Euripides was rooted in a particular culture, a culture which, as Kierkegaard, Dodds, John Jones and others have been at pains to point out, is rooted not in the individual but in the house, the *oikos*, and the city, the *polis*. It is a communal theatre, one still close to religion and the gods, where what is at stake is the tragic sacrifice of the hero in order to cleanse the community, whether that be the house, as in the *Oresteia*, or the city, as in *Oedipus Tyrannus*. And with the cleansing, with the lament for the tragic hero/victim, comes a sense of pity, but also a sense of release, an upsurge of gratitude, spoken by the chorus, who here, as always, speak for the community of spectators. By the time Seneca was writing there was no communal theatre because there was no community. There was a stifling Empire and, at its centre, a court which did the bidding of a tyrannical emperor. We do not even know if Seneca's plays were ever performed or simply read to friends. They take over the superficialities of Aeschylean language and graft it on to plots which are merely melodramatic. There are profound reasons in Sophocles why Jocasta hangs herself and Oedipus puts out his eyes, reasons which have to do, in the first instance, with a failure to respect the gods; in Seneca there is plenty of gore, and plenty of mention of gods, but what we see are individuals taking revenge on each other by committing acts even more atrocious than those they seek to avenge; and there is never any sense that this will lead to a cleansing of the society or a restoration of the community – because there *is* no community.

Elizabethan playwrights, relishing the new freedom the professional theatre gave them and relishing the possibilities of the theatrical language that had developed in the course of the sixteenth century, with its potent combination of Humanist rhetoric and popular speech, found Seneca a godsend when he began to be translated into English. (One of the set pieces of a popular manual of rhetoric, Richard Rainolde's *The Foundacion of Rhetoricke* of 1563, is entitled 'What lamentable Oracion Hecuba Quene of Troie mighte make, Troie being destroied'.) Seneca gave them the licence, as it were, to indulge in their newly acquired skills and to terrify their audiences. As Eliot sensed, 'senecanism' 'may not have been Shakespeare's "philosophy"; . . . it may only have been Shakespeare's instinctive recognition of something of theatrical utility.' But what kind of utility? By the time he came to write *Hamlet*, as I have said, the Senecan style, which Marlowe and Kyd had made so popular, was beginning to seem old-fashioned, even to be the subject of satire. So why exactly does Shakespeare choose to introduce it into *Hamlet*? In other words, the question is not what the passage *says* but what it *does*.

It is what anyone familiar with classical tragedy will immediately recognise as 'the Messenger's Speech' – the speech a messenger utters on returning from witnessing the death of the hero. Though modern productions of the classics seem fearful of these extended passages of narration in the theatre, and producers tend to ask the actors charged with delivering them to act them out as they speak, they should be spoken quietly and simply, letting the words do all the work, so that through them we may glimpse what the Greek stage could not and would not show: an actual death occurring. A producer of *Hamlet* has no such problems with this speech:

> *The rugged Pyrrhus, he whose sable arms,*
> *Black as his purpose, did the night resemble*
> *Where he lay couched in the ominous horse,*
> *Hath now this dread and black complexion smear'd*
> *With heraldry more dismal. Head to foot*
> *Now is he total gules, horridly trick'd*
> *With blood of fathers, mothers, daughters, sons,*
> *Bak'd and impasted with the parching streets,*
> *That lend a tyrannous and a damned light*
> *To their lord's murder.* (448–57)

Pyrrhus, after lying in wait in the wooden horse with all the other Greeks in his black armour, is now rushing through Troy covered all over with blood from the indiscriminate murder of its citizens to which dirt and dust from the streets of the burning city has attached itself. The central conceit Shakespeare chooses to convey this is that of heraldry, where black and gules (red) are key colours. The effect is to turn the whole scene into a gory and awesome *spectacle* while draining it of any taint of *feeling* – we have no sense of the suffering of mothers and children, nor of the bloodlust of the conquerors. The effect is compounded by giving every noun its adjective – the horse is *ominous*, the light is *tyrannous* and *damned*, Pyrrhus is *hellish*, Ilium is *senseless*. So it continues:

> *For lo, his sword,*
> *Which was declining in the milky head*
> *Of reverend Priam, seem'd i'th'air to stick;*
> *So, as a painted tyrant, Pyrrhus stood,*
> *And like a neutral to his will and matter,*
> *Did nothing.*

> *But as we often see against some storm*
> *A silence in the heavens, the rack stand still,*
> *The bold winds speechless, and the orb below*
> *As hush as death, anon the dreadful thunder*
> *Doth rend the region; so after Pyrrhus' pause*
> *Aroused vengeance sets him new awork,*
> *And never did the Cyclops' hammers fall*
> *With less remorse than Pyrrhus' bleeding sword*
> *Now falls on Priam.* (473–88)

The killing of Priam appears to take place in slow motion and amidst an eerie silence, which lends the whole a nightmarish quality, the sense that it is not really happening, a feeling that is the polar opposite of, say, the Messenger's account of the death of Oedipus in *Oedipus at Colonus*.

There is a protracted passage in Shakespeare's early poem, *The Rape of Lucrece,* in which the heroine, having been raped by the tyrant Tarquin, gazes at a tapestry or wall painting in the hall of her house, and the poet describes in meticulous detail what she sees. At times, indeed, the images she sees seem more alive than the 'real life' events we have been reading about. This was a commonplace of classical and Renaissance writing, known as *ecphrasis*, whereby poets would be able to narrate stories connected only tangentially with the main story by having their protagonists come upon a painting and then describing it in vivid detail. Indeed, an early and famous example is to be found precisely in Book Two of the *Aeneid*, the classic account of the fall of Troy. *Ecphrasis* feels forced to us, but it was a standard rhetorical device and Shakespeare uses it to perfection in his poem. We could say that here he turns *ecphrasis* on its head: instead of giving life to a painting he drains life from the world by turning it into a painting.

At times the whole thing tips over into the plainly ridiculous. Dryden noted the absurdity: 'Would not a man have thought that the poet had been bound prentice to a wheelwright?' But that is to attribute the speech to Shakespeare and not to the exigencies of his play. Pyrrhus finds Priam, aims a blow at him, which misses, but

Priam, an old man, nevertheless falls. In a kind of sympathy with him, the poet goes on, the great towers of Troy come crashing down:

> *Then senseless Ilium,*
> *Seeming to feel this blow, with flaming top*
> *Stoops to his base, and with a hideous crash*
> *Takes prisoner Pyrrhus' ear.* (470–3)

At first the absurd image of a wall falling down and pinning Pyrrhus down by the ear comes into one's head, and it is only gradually that one realises this is metaphorical, that what the poet means is that Pyrrhus becomes *distracted* by the noise of the crashing building, and pauses in his slaughter of Priam. But such blatant absurdity, which is the staple of the spectacle of Pyramus and Thisbe put on by the 'mechanicals' in *A Midsummer Night's Dream*, is on the whole avoided here, even if only just. We are not meant to laugh, though exactly how we are meant to react is very difficult to put into words.

I think the passage functions for the audience, subliminally, as a sign that says: 'This is theatre.' It reminds us of the fact that what we have before us is not a real messenger but a player, an actor, delivering a set speech. The passage thus joins all the other moments in this play in which the illusion of Elsinore is momentarily breached and the physicality of theatre, of words, of letters, is highlighted. The Player, Hamlet himself, and we the audience, as well as Polonius, are returned to babyhood, to the time when we uttered not words but sounds which gave us pleasure and expressed our needs. That is why, at one level, *Hamlet* is simply so enjoyable.

In contrast to the mess and confusion of his own life (and ours), in which nothing is certain, nothing is clear, here is a story that, if terrible, is also riveting, and where people are wholly bad (Pyrrhus) and wholly good (Priam and Hecuba). Shakespeare knows instinctively why people flocked to the plays of Marlowe and Kyd; he admires the ability of those playwrights to turn it on,

crank it up. But he knows too why audiences have moved on from
there, why, if the theatre is to touch them, it will have to question
as well as to declaim – and that what it will have to question above
all is the nature of declamation. In this Marlowe and Kyd are
like Verdi and Puccini, Shakespeare like Mozart. Indeed, only
Shakespeare and Mozart seem to have been able both to produce
heart-stopping rhetoric and music, and to use rhetoric and music
as a means of exploring different levels of reality, of asking questions about the power of language, the power of music. Though
the early *Titus Andronicus* is rather different from the work of
Marlowe and Kyd in both plot and style it is nevertheless clearly
working within their orbit. In *Troilus and Cressida*, written at
around the same time as *Hamlet*, scholars think, Shakespeare went
all out to debunk the myth of the greatness of the ancient Greeks
and Trojans, who are shown to be as nasty, devious and mean as
are the Elizabethans in any of the city comedies by Shakespeare's
contemporaries. Both *Titus* and *Troilus* are uneasy plays, difficult
to watch and difficult to like. In *Hamlet*, however, Shakespeare
manages to have his cake and eat it: the play incorporates with
surprising ease both 'Ercles' vein' and the utter directness of 'Who's
there?', both the speech of the Player and 'How weary, stale, flat,
and unprofitable/ Seem to me all the uses of this world!' He can do
this because he has grasped the link between acting as an imperative in life and acting as play-acting. Instead of the blandness of
'All the world's a stage', which says nothing because it says everything, *Hamlet* asks us to consider just what the relation is between
a role in life and a role on the stage. Here, instead of the easy nod
of assent that greets Jaques's fine speech, we can only react with an
uneasy shifting in our seats and a sense that *this* play is really, if
obscurely, speaking to *us*, to our unease, but also to our sheer
pleasure in theatre.

Whether, as some critics think, it's hearing the Player recite that
gives Hamlet the idea, or whether, as seems more likely, he already
has it in mind when he asks the Player to recite, we cannot know.
But when the recitation has ended, and after asking Polonius to see
to the comfort of the company, Hamlet draws the Player aside and

puts his proposition to him: would the company be prepared to act that well-known play, *The Murder of Gonzago* (invented of course by Shakespeare for the purpose)? And, if so, would he be prepared to slip into it an extra sixteen or so lines Hamlet will write specially for the occasion? The Player says that would be no problem, and, with that, first Polonius and the players and then Rosencrantz and Guildenstern exit, leaving Hamlet alone on stage.

6.8 (II. 2. 542–601)

What follows is the longest of Hamlet's soliloquies. Harry Levin has made the intriguing suggestion that it runs precisely parallel to the Player's speech, being roughly the same length and similarly divided into three movements. Whether an audience would pick this up in the theatre is a moot point, but in its weight and depth it certainly closes off this fold impressively and locks all that has gone before into place.

Hamlet is not only left alone after this enormous and hugely varied scene, he marks it with: 'Now I am alone.' In his first soliloquy, which closed the first encounter between him and the court, he had given vent to his desire to melt away and be no more rather than live in his present melancholy state, shattered as he is by his mother's marrying his despised uncle so quickly after his beloved father's death. Here too he turns on himself in self-reproach:

> O what a rogue and peasant slave am I!
> Is it not monstrous that this player here,
> But in a fiction, in a dream of passion,
> Could force his soul so to his own conceit
> That from her working all his visage wann'd,
> Tears in his eyes, distraction in his aspect,
> A broken voice, and his whole function suiting
> With forms to his conceit? And all for nothing!
> For Hecuba!
> What's Hecuba to him, or he to her [F: Hecuba],
> That he should weep for her? What would he do

> Had he the motive and the cue for passion
> That I have? He would drown the stage with tears . . .
>
> (544–56)

Hamlet takes the Player's tears at the end of his performance as an indictment of himself. If the Player could be moved when merely reciting a speech about people who lived long ago and for whom it is impossible for him to care, how much more would he be moved if he were to experience the pain that I am experiencing? he says. But this is the wrong inference to draw. The idea that if one sheds a few tears for something one does not feel strongly about one will shed a lot of tears for something one does is just bad psychology, typical, perhaps, of a highly educated and sensitive young man, but one that simply will not bear examination.

But Shakespeare has started to explore a rather different, though related, and far more important issue: that of the relation between emotion and its external manifestation. Proust will explore this in all its hideous comedy in his great novel, from Legrandin, the snob, insisting a little too forcefully on his disdain for high society and his love of the quiet countryside, to Mme Verdurin's dislocating her jaw in her attempt to demonstrate the passion she feels on listening to Wagner; but through Hamlet's misunderstanding of his condition Shakespeare had already examined the nature of that condition. The Player could cry for someone as remote as Hecuba, he goes on,

> Yet I,
> A dull and muddy-mettled rascal, peak [mope]
> Like John-a-dreams, unpregnant of my cause,
> And can say nothing – no, not for a king,
> Upon whose property and most dear life
> A damn'd defeat was made. Am I a coward? (561–6)

How do we respond to events that are meaningful to us when ritual has been drained from our lives – ritual which would shape, publicly, our response to grief and guide our actions? It was a

question Kierkegaard was much concerned with, and it lies at the
heart of this soliloquy. Am I a coward? leads to: how do I respond
when someone plucks my beard, tweaks my nose, accuses me of
being a liar? And the answer is: I take it lying down. Why? Because
'I am pigeon-liver'd and lack gall/ To make oppression bitter'
(573–4). That Hamlet is thinking of one thing only, how Claudius
has treated him, is brought out into the open by the next few lines:

> Bloody, bawdy villain!
> Remorseless, treacherous, lecherous, kindless villain!
> Why, what an ass am I! This is most brave,
> That I, the son of a dear father murder'd,
> Prompted to my revenge by heaven and hell,
> Must like a whore unpack my heart with words
> And fall a-cursing like a very drab,
> A scullion! Fie upon't! Foh! (576–83)

'Kindless' recalls his first response to Claudius's overtures: 'A little
more than kin and less than kind' (i.e. not one of the community
of men – mankind); while the 'lecherous' shows us that Hamlet,
like his father, cannot disentangle the murder from the adultery;
and 'by heaven and hell' that he still cannot decide which it is that
has brought the Ghost forth to lay his heavy command upon him.
The final exclamations (in both Quarto and Folio) testify to his
continuing inability to make sense of it all and his desperate need
to do so, as language disintegrates and sound, the animal cries of
the body, take over.

   But what Hamlet, in his rush to pass judgement on himself,
has failed to grasp is that in the new world in which he finds
himself, where Luther's Reformation has made all ritual suspect
and where the simple code of vengeance which animated the
Norse sagas has long since disappeared, 'revenge' is no longer a
simple or even a meaningful option. Hamlet is not only unsure of
what has been done to his father, he is unsure whether the Ghost
has come to set him on the right path or to lead him to perdition.
In other words, he cannot, naturally, take part in the old play, and

he cannot, naturally, take part in the new play of court intrigue and subservience to the reigning monarch. No wonder he ends with an anguished cry, which reveals his pain both at what he is suffering and at the fact that there are no words for it.

So Margreta de Grazia's at first startling claim that all talk of Hamlet's 'inwardness' is based on a flawed grasp of the history of inwardness, a Romantic condition that simply has no place in the Renaissance, is right to the extent that Hamlet's continuous setting up of inwardness against outwardness is the result of his misunderstanding of his own condition; but it is wrong and our intuitions have always been right in that this is a play one of whose central *themes* is the nature of the contrast between inner and outer. Hamlet misunderstands himself and his situation, but that misunderstanding, as one would expect from a Wittenberg-trained student, depends on an appeal to the contrast between inner and outer that was a key part of Luther's message. Whether or not the play offers an alternative view of human feeling and action is something that will emerge in the course of its unfolding. For the moment we register the unease and the ready recourse (already seen in his first words, 'I have that within which passes show') to a stark contrast of feeling/lack of feeling, outer/inner, which sounds convincing but fails to satisfy him (or us) for very long.

Hamlet's sense of horror at what Claudius has done to him and his family leads into the third part of his meditation. He has heard that the guilty are sometimes so struck by seeing their crimes and sins portrayed on stage that they instinctively reveal their guilt, and so has decided to put a play on before Claudius that will bring him face to face with his putative crime, and so perhaps force out of him some act that will reveal clearly and without any shadow of doubt whether the Ghost was or was not a devil, who 'abuses me to damn me'. Triumphantly he ends: 'The play's the thing/ Wherein I'll catch the conscience of the King' (600–1).

But the comforting snap of the couplet locking into place reveals less a step well taken and more the false comfort of wishful thinking. For, after all, what could be less likely to furnish clear proof of guilt than facing a culprit with a mirror of his crime? King

David, in the Book of Samuel, has slept with the beautiful wife of his soldier Uriah, and has sent Uriah to his death to cover up his misdemeanour. Nathan the prophet comes to him and recounts to him the story of how a wealthy and powerful man robbed a poor man of his few possessions, but David merely remarks that the rich man should clearly be punished. Nathan has to say to him, 'Thou art the man' before David can recognise the parallels. Nothing tells Hamlet that Claudius will grasp that the play is meant to apply to him, and, even if he does, why should his consequent actions reveal his guilt or innocence beyond any shadow of doubt? Mightn't an angry response merely show his anger at anyone daring to suggest that he was responsible for his brother's death? But so powerful is the persuasive quality of theatre that we, as audience, quell our doubts and prepare to see if what happens next will bring about a resolution.

FOLD SEVEN

7.1 (III. 1. 1–55)

We switch once more to Claudius, interrogating Rosencrantz and Guildenstern about Hamlet. Can't you find out from what he says why he's acting so wildly? he asks. Well, says Rosencrantz, he admits he feels 'distracted', but he won't give the reason why. And Guildenstern adds:

> Nor do we find him forward to be sounded,
> But with a crafty madness keeps aloof
> When we would bring him on to some confession
> Of his true state. (III. 1. 7–10)

Jenkins does not deem line 7 worthy of a footnote, but it is not too much to say that without a proper understanding of it we cannot understand the entire play. 'Sound' could be translated as 'probe', which is what the editors of Arden 3 give here and at II. 1. 41, but that is a poor substitute for an understanding of the verb's literal meaning. It comes from the Old French *sonder*, which, as the *OED* explains, means 'to employ the line and lead, or other means, in order to ascertain the depth of the sea, a channel, etc., or the nature of the bottom'. In figurative contexts it means 'to measure,

or ascertain, as by sounding'. Hamlet, says Guildenstern, is reluctant (not 'forward') to be 'sounded' in this way. Moreover, with a
'crafty madness' (cunningly pretending to be mad) he deflects our
questions 'when we would bring him on to confession/ Of his true
state'. The implication, which has been there in the court circle all
along, is that there is something 'at the bottom' of Hamlet's actions,
which can, by means of spying on him and interrogating him with
enough guile and perseverance, be 'sounded', whose nature (or
'true state') can thus be 'ascertained', and which may be 'confessed'.

But what if this image of human character is misleading?
What if human beings are not like the ocean, whose depth can be
ascertained by the use of certain instruments? The assumption
that it can be is one with Claudius's and the court's assumption
that everything can be understood in terms of measurement and
cost. But what if they are wrong? Hamlet, for one, though he tends
sometimes to fall in with this language, instinctively resists it,
notably when in his little parable of the pipe he rebukes Rosencrantz
and Guildenstern (at III. 2. 341ff.) for trying to 'pluck the heart
out of my mystery'. Shakespeare has shown us, in Hamlet's
soliloquies, that the self is not a machine but rather a seething and
confused mass of contradictory impulses, which can only be
imperfectly understood, and then only by talking or acting, not
by mechanical investigation. That a human being is even more
than that will only emerge as a central theme as the play draws to
its end.

The two courtiers, when pressed further by Claudius and
Gertrude, go on to tell of the arrival of the players. 'Of these we
told him,/ And there did seem in him a kind of joy/ To hear of it'
(17–19). We have sensed the joy in Hamlet's speech and actions in
the previous scene, but this external confirmation is particularly
interesting in that, without their realising it, the spies vouchsafe a
piece of information which, if they or their master could only
understand it, would force them to rethink the model of the self
with which they operate. This 'kind of joy' aroused in Hamlet by
the mention of the players we will meet again just once, but at a
crucial moment, when Hamlet recalls another 'player', the old

court jester Yorick. But that is some way ahead. At the moment the remark goes without comment, and Rosencrantz and Guildenstern take their leave.

Claudius now asks Gertrude to leave as well, explaining that he and Polonius are going to spy on an encounter between Hamlet and Ophelia which they have set up:

> For we have closely [privately] sent for Hamlet hither
> That he, as 'twere by accident, may here
> Affront Ophelia. (29–31)

That offhand phrase, 'as 'twere by accident', is a key one too. They are shaping the action, but in such a way as to make it seem natural. This is the way Shakespeare's villains always work, from Richard III to Iago, usurping the powers of God, so to speak, yet also, of course, duplicating the activity of the playwright, but in such a way as to hide their own part in the matter. (They seem not to be concerned that Ophelia is there with them; in their eyes she is merely a pawn in a bigger game.)

Claudius goes on:

> Her father and myself, lawful espials,
> We'll so bestow ourselves that, seeing unseen,
> We may of their encounter frankly judge . . . (32–4)

It's fascinating how close *Hamlet* runs, all the way through, to Shakespeare's comedies. The sight of two old men, the Uncle and the Father, hiding in order to spy on young lovers, is pure comedy. But not here, of course. 'Lawful espials', 'like 'his true state', conveys all the more powerfully for not being so understood by those who say these words, that it is possible, with enough ingenuity, to see what the 'true state' of someone is, and, for authority, such ingenuity, including spying on those one considers a danger to oneself, is always lawful.

At this point Shakespeare chooses to distinguish for the first time between Gertrude, the mother, and Claudius, the uncle.

First, her basic desire for a happy outcome and her warmth towards both Hamlet and Ophelia is stressed:

> And for your part, Ophelia, I do wish
> That your good beauties be the happy cause
> Of Hamlet's wildness; so shall I hope your virtues
> Will bring him to his wonted way again,
> To both your honours. (38–42)

Then, after Polonius has given Ophelia her stage directions and dropped the rather surprising hint that he is not altogether at ease with his role –

> We are oft to blame in this,
> 'Tis too much proved, that with devotion's visage
> And pious action we do sugar o'er
> The devil himself (46–9)

– Claudius gives us the first indication of his guilt. Until then we have had the Ghost's word for it, but now we – though not Hamlet – are given conclusive proof:

> O 'tis too true.
> How smart a lash that speech doth give my conscience.
> The harlot's cheek, beautied with plast'ring art,
> Is not more ugly to the thing that helps it
> Than is my deed to my most painted word.
> O heavy burden! (49–54)

My feeling is that Shakespeare would rather not have committed himself, and has been putting off for as long as possible the decision as to how much of Claudius's guilt to show; that he senses that once he has made it clear that Claudius is the villain the play will turn into the melodrama he has been trying to avoid, since he rightly feels that this will detract from the secret sources of its power. But he is too good a craftsman or too much a man of his time not to recognise that sooner or later he will need to make a decision on this score if the play is to work at all. I am aware that this may be a very modern way of seeing the play, one imbued with the values of Mallarmé and Eliot, Borges and Beckett, and that many if not most readers and viewers of the play will be thankful that it is as it is, and feel that it would have been a weaker thing had Shakespeare found a way to keep the issue open till the end. I raise the question here because it seems to me to be of more than historical interest.

But no sooner have we had to take in one thing than another is upon us. For Hamlet is heard approaching and the two conspirators quickly hide.

7.2 (III. 1. 56–88)

Just as Hamlet's first soliloquy – 'O that this too too solid/sullied flesh would melt,/ Thaw and resolve itself into a dew . . .' (I. 2. 129–30) – had been an anguished cry for the dissolution of the self so that he would not have to be faced with the hideous thoughts and decisions that were overwhelming him, so now we find him mired in unbearable confusion, still longing to bring things to an end. This soliloquy, though, is more formal, more rhetorical and balanced than the two previous ones, which perhaps accounts for its subsequent fame: 'To be or not to be,' caesura, 'that is the question.' Followed by 'Whether . . .' (two lines), and 'Or . . .' (two lines). The choice, though, now seems to be between two heroic alternatives: to suffer or endure 'the slings and arrows of outrageous fortune', that is, the buffetings of an outrageous fate, or to go into battle against them and die a noble death. The alternatives do not seem to include triumph over fortune, and taking arms against a sea of troubles suggests that the speaker knows that the two opponents are absurdly mismatched and that he will inevitably be overwhelmed and go down. But Shakespeare does something astonishing with lines 5 and 6. He transforms, in six short and common words, this heroic vision into an image of peace and repose: '. . . And by opposing end

them. To die – to sleep,/ No more.' Again we feel we are witnessing
thought in action, so that 'to die' follows naturally from the image
of the hero striding into the waves to do battle with them, but
then, after the pause signalled by the dash, 'to die' is discovered
also to be 'to sleep', and then comes the very different, less abrupt,
more meditative pause signalled by the comma and the enjamb-
ment, 'no more', a phrase both completely general and utterly
specific. Four more lines develop the thought of that sleep and
that 'no more', exploring the bliss of an end to 'the heart-ache
and the thousand natural shocks/ That flesh is heir to', and then
the very cadences of his speech lead him back to that 'to die,
to sleep'. This time a comma rather than the dash of five lines
earlier brings the two concepts together, but at once the notion of
sleep leads on to a new thought: 'To sleep, perchance to dream –
ay, there's the rub.' Can the perturbed soul be sure of finding
peace in death? Is it not just as likely that, like the ghost of
his father, he will find that even the grave will not hold him?
That even here he will have bad dreams? And now his very
command of rhetoric leads Hamlet into a long passage in which
he does nothing but elaborate on this in perfectly balanced
phrases – 'Th'opressor's wrong, the proud man's contumely,/ The
pangs of dispriz'd [unvalued] love, the law's delay' – which bring
him exactly nowhere. He tries to recapitulate: who would 'grunt
and sweat under a weary life' if he was sure that death would
effectively end it all? But no one knows if it does, since no one has
ever returned from 'The undiscover'd country' – and so it is
perhaps better to stick with the devil we know than take on the
one we don't. But, just as he had used the manifest sorrow of the
Player over the death of an ancient queen to lash himself for his
lack of feeling, so here he concludes by returning to his sense of
himself as a coward for not immediately fulfilling his father's
commandment:

> Thus conscience does make cowards of us all,
> And thus the native hue of resolution
> Is sicklied o'er with the pale cast of thought,

And enterprises of great pitch and moment
With this regard their currents turn awry
And lose the name of action. (83–8)

Hamlet's rhetoric is so powerful that we too are swept along with it. It takes an effort to recall his doubts about the Ghost's provenance and the fact that this was what triggered his unease with its commands. To call these commands an 'enterprise of great pitch and moment' is like dramatising the dark and confused nature of our decision-making as taking arms against a sea of troubles – a beautiful and heart-lifting image, but very far from the problematic tangle in which we actually live our lives.

Larkin, who knew a thing or two about such feelings, wrote a poem about them, 'Poetry of Departures'. It begins:

Sometimes you hear, fifth-hand,
As epitaph:
He chucked up everything
And just cleared off,
And always the voice will sound
Certain you approve
This audacious, purifying,
Elemental move.

And they are right, I think.
We all hate home
And having to be there:
I detest my room,
Its specially-chosen junk,
The good books, the good bed,
And my life, in perfect order:
So to hear it said

He walked out on the whole crowd
Leaves me flushed and stirred,
Like, *Then she undid her dress*

Or *take that you bastard*;
Surely I can if he did?

7.3 (III. 1. 88–163)

Hamlet's troubled musings are brought to an end by the appearance of Ophelia:

> Soft you now,
> The fair Ophelia! Nymph, in thy orisons
> Be all my sins remember'd. (88–90)

Both his immediate response to her presence and his more formal
address to her are, we feel, very Hamlet-like in their openness and
generosity. 'Soft you now,/ The fair Ophelia', like the ending of his
letter to her, 'But that I love thee best, O most best, believe it', feels
utterly authentic, wrenched from the heart, while the latter, his
address to her, has the graciousness of the accomplished courtier
– which does not mean that it is in any way hypocritical.

What follows is a marvellous exchange, where we feel both are,
at the outset, constrained, partly, where Ophelia is concerned, by
her awareness that they are being spied upon, but partly too by
their youthful embarrassment. We feel their love through the
prism of their formal language in a very Jane Austen-like manner.
She starts by trying to return his letter:

> Take these again; for to the noble mind
> Rich gifts wax poor when givers prove unkind. (100–1)

The inadvertent couplet puts the stress on 'unkind', that word
which runs through the play, always oscillating, as we saw in
Hamlet's first response to Claudius, between its modern meaning
of 'doing (or not doing) a kindness to', and 'forming (or not
forming) a part of the family of mankind'. Hamlet, however,
rebuffs her, first insisting that he gave her nothing, then,

abandoning verse for workaday prose, questioning her honesty and finally accusing her of being no better than a common whore. She defends herself, but he persists:

> *Oph.* Could beauty, my lord, have better commerce than with
>   honesty?
> *Ham.* Ay, truly, for the power of beauty will sooner transform
>   honesty from what it is to a bawd than the force of
>   honesty can translate beauty into his likeness.
>   (109–14)

But then, with one of those abrupt switches of direction which are so typical of him, he suddenly comes out with: 'I did love you once.' 'Indeed, my lord,' she responds, 'you made me believe so.' 'You should not have believed me,' he responds, quick to cover up the vulnerability he has briefly allowed to surface.

And this is why we warm to him. Because he is always one step ahead of us – we cannot contain him, nor can parts in any of the plays that are offered him in the course of this one: Claudius and Gertrude's play, Old Hamlet's play, the players' plays. Having shifted the gears, he does not stop:

> Get thee to a nunnery. Why, wouldst thou be a breeder of
> sinners? I am myself indifferent honest, but yet I could accuse
> me of such things that it were better my mother had not borne
> me . . . What should such fellows as I do crawling between
> earth and heaven? We are arrant knaves all, believe none of us.
> Go thy ways to a nunnery. Where's your father? (121–31)

It becomes clear in the course of this Dostoevskian rant that what is really troubling him, and has been troubling him all along, is not his father's death but his mother's remarriage, not, even though he now knows it, the murder of his father, but the 'adultery' of his mother. This is the knot he finds it impossible to untie, a knot which we all instinctively understand but which it is difficult to express. It can be done, though, and not, I believe, in overtly psychoanalytic language, since it is something all human beings have had to deal with. He cannot bear the thought of his mother's sexuality, a thought normally buried in the respect that is naturally given to parents but now brought out into the open by the mother's remarriage, and exacerbated in this instance by the father's unseemly dragging of the son into his own deep and unresolved problems of jealousy and sexuality.

But we should not stop at the mother's sexuality as though it were the answer to everything. Behind *that*, it seems to me, lies another issue: bringing the parents' sexuality into the open, as a remarriage inevitably does, brings with it the painful recognition that the child was not necessary but contingent, that we are all the products of chance couplings. This is difficult, indeed almost impossible, to take in and it leads, in Hamlet's case, to a desire never to have been: 'It were better my mother had never borne me.'

Where have we heard such words before? In the bleak early chapters of the Book of Job, in which Job, rendered almost mad by the repeated blows fate has dealt him, systematically and almost ritualistically set about *uncreating* what God, in the opening chapters of Genesis, had created:

After this opened Job his mouth, and cursed his day. And Job spake and said, Let the day perish wherein I was born, and the night in which it was said, There is a man child conceived. Let that day be darkness; let not God regard it from above, neither let the light shine upon it. Let darkness and the shadow of death stain it; let a cloud dwell upon it; let the blackness of the day terrify it. As for that night, let darkness seize upon it; let it not be joined unto the days of the year, let it not come into the number of the months. Lo, let that night be solitary, let no joyful voice come therein. Let them curse it that curse the day, who are ready to raise up their mourning. Let the stars of the twilight thereof be dark; let it look for light, but have none; neither let it see the dawning of the day: Because it shut not up the doors of my mother's womb, nor hid sorrow from mine

eyes. Why died I not from the womb? Why did I not give up
the ghost when I came out of the belly? Why did the knees
prevent me? or why the breasts that I should suck? For now
should I have lain still and been quiet, I should have slept:
then had I been at rest. (Job 3.1–13)

Hamlet does not have Job's eloquence, and is far less single-
minded, but nevertheless the parallels are striking: both feel that
what they have to endure is intolerable, both feel that the bottom
has dropped out of their lives and beliefs, and their response is to
wish they had never been born, because *existing* is what is troubling them.

Hamlet, of course, is only partly talking to himself. Here he
is also talking to one of the two women in his life. And his
rant about procreation leads from *his* mother to *her* father:
'Where's your father?' 'At home, my lord.' 'Let the doors be shut
upon him, that he may play the fool nowhere but in's own house.
Farewell' (132–4). He must turn to go at this moment, for she
says, out of his hearing: 'O help him, you sweet heavens', showing
once more *her* generosity of spirit and perhaps her love for him.
But he is ferocious, turning to her with one more withering curse:
'If thou wilt needs marry, marry a fool; for wise men know well
enough what monsters you make of them. To a nunnery, go – and
quickly too. Farewell.' To which, again, she responds with the
prayer, 'Heavenly powers, restore him.' But this only leads him to
a further rant on women's deceit and their use of cosmetics: 'God
hath given you one face and you make yourselves another.' His
wish not to be brings with it a puritan desire to strip things of
their false coverings and so reveal the truth beneath – a notion
Hamlet himself has already poured scorn on in his sparring
with Rosencrantz and Guildenstern and their desire to plumb his
depths.

This time he does indeed depart, leaving Ophelia for once
alone on stage, though even here she is of course being spied on
by the King and her father. Her great lament, 'O what a noble
mind is here o'erthrown! The courtier's, soldier's, scholar's,

eye, tongue, sword,' etc. (152–63), has often been used to describe Hamlet, but all it shows is how one member of the court, a young woman in love with him, sees him, as a Sidney-like paragon of courtliness. It does not correspond to how Hamlet sees himself, of course, which is not to say that it is not closer to the mark than his own self-assessment – but we the spectators know that it is not and cannot be the whole truth. Nevertheless, like his earlier soliloquy, it leaves us with a noble music ringing in our ears:

> And I, of ladies most deject and wretched,
> That suck'd the honey of his music vows,
> Now see that noble and most sovereign reason
> Like sweet bells jangled out of tune and harsh,
> That unmatch'd form and feature of blown youth
> Blasted with ecstasy [madness]. O woe is me
> T'have seen what I have seen, see what I see. (157–63)

7.4 (III. 1. 164–90)

Ophelia's music is in striking contrast to what follows. Claudius and Polonius come out of their hiding place to discuss what they have just seen. Claudius is convinced that it is not love that has unhinged Hamlet, and fears the worst. Hamlet is brooding on something else, he feels, and whatever it is, it bodes him, Claudius, no good. He decides that the best thing is to dispatch Hamlet to England as his ambassador, to remind the English of the tribute they owe him. Perhaps a nice sea voyage will clear Hamlet's brain, he says to Polonius, who is, however, unwilling to abandon his theory that love for his daughter lies at the root of it all. But Polonius relishes his role as spy and, while going along with the King's plan, asks that he be given one more chance to find out what is really causing Hamlet's strange behaviour: let his mother summon him to her bedchamber, he says, and ask him privately to explain himself to her, 'And I'll be plac'd, so please you, in the ear/ Of all their conference', a grotesque and wonderful image (we

recall 'Take prisoner Pyrrhus' ear') which will take on ironic over-
tones as a result of subsequent events. 'It shall be so,' says Claudius,
in another of those couplets that often ironically close a scene
whose consequences cannot be so easily boxed in, 'Madness in
great ones must not unwatch'd go' (189–90).

FOLD EIGHT

8.1 (III. 2. 1–45)

At once we are back with Hamlet and three of the players, and into another of those speeches that all playgoers will feel sure they have heard before even if they have never seen the play, in which the very fame of the passage can easily stop us responding to it as, within the context of the play, it needs to be responded to.

Hamlet is giving the players instruction on how to perform, and theatre historians have had a field day with it, for it is one of the few places in the whole of Elizabethan literature in which such instruction is given. I have a DVD of John Barton taking a group of world-famous RSC actors in a Shakespeare workshop designed to shed light on Shakespeare as primarily a man of the theatre rather than a poet, and Barton begins by taking the actors through this speech as though it were Shakespeare's very own word on the subject:

> Speak the speech, I pray you, as I pronounced it to you, trip-
> pingly on the tongue; but if you mouth it as many of your
> players do, I had as lief the town-crier spoke my lines. Nor do
> not saw the air too much with your hand, thus, but use all
> gently; for in the very torrent, tempest, and, as I may say,

whirlwind of your passion, you must acquire and beget a temperance that may give it smoothness. O, it offends me to the soul to hear a robustious periwig-pated fellow tear a passion to tatters, to very rags, to split the ears of the groundlings, who for the most part are capable of nothing but inexplicable dumb-shows and noise. I would have such a fellow whipped for o'erdoing Termagant. It out-Herods Herod. Pray you avoid it. (1–14)

What Hamlet says he wants here, is 'temperance', the middle way, and 'smoothness', both so beloved of the Italian Humanists. What he cannot stand is actors hamming it up for the sake of the ground-lings, whom he clearly despises as wanting 'inexplicable dumb-shows and noise' (we recall his assertion that Polonius, like the groundlings, only cares 'for a jig or a tale of bawdry, or [before] he sleeps': II. 2. 496).

Are these Shakespeare's views, and, more importantly, whatever Shakespeare's views, is this what the play before us has actually been giving us? The answer has to be, no. The play we are watching has so far given us a terrifying ghost who is also mocked and tries to impress by creeping about under the stage and banging on its floor; a hero who is anything but balanced and who moves suddenly and violently rather than slowly and gracefully, and veers from silence to sharp and acid repartee, from protestations of love to gross insults aimed at an innocent young woman; an old man who keeps forgetting his lines; and an actor who appears out of nowhere to make an interminable speech written in a bombastic rhetoric which at times spills over into the ridiculous. We are nearer to Ionesco's *The Bald Prima Donna* than to Castiglione's *The Courtier*, and the groundlings will have had a field day (it is probably one of the main reasons why the play has been and goes on being so hugely successful). But there has also been much for the Humanists in the audience to appreciate: Hamlet's quoting of Pico della Mirandola on the dignity of man; his long medita-tions on the meaning of life; Ophelia's tribute to him as having once been the epitome of a Renaissance prince. What we have not had is temperance and smoothness. That much at least is unequivocal.

To take Hamlet's prescription here as Shakespeare's last word is like taking Gargantua's letter to his son Pantagruel, a model of Humanist rhetoric and instruction, as the blueprint for Rabelais's great work. This, of course is what critics of Rabelais, trained in Renaissance Humanism, used to do until, during the second half of the last century, a more accurate view of Rabelais' work began to gain ground. 'Most dear sonne,' begins Gargantua,

> amongst the gifts, graces and prerogatives, with which the sovereign *Plasmater* God Almighty, hath endowed and adorned humane Nature at the beginning, that seems to me most singular and excellent, by which we may in a mortal estate attain to a kind of immortality, and in the course of this transitory life perpetuate our name and seed, which is done by progeny issued from us in the lawful bonds of Matrimony: whereby that in some measure is restored unto us, which was taken from us by the sin of our first Parents, to whom it was said . . .

This is splendid if rather boring stuff, but it is not what we love and remember Rabelais for. Yet it is not exactly parody either. What it is – and we can see this in Swift's admiration for his dull but admirable patron, Sir William Temple – is the expression of admiration for an ideal, but one which unfortunately is betrayed as soon as it is put into words, when it emerges as mere platitude. Writers as different as Rabelais, Shakespeare, Swift and Sterne seem to have sensed that the only true way to express this ideal, with much of which they agreed, was by indirection, and that to try and express it directly was immediately to betray it. By expressing in their writing everything that is anathema to the Humanist, yet forcing us to question the authority of what is being said, they feel that they can most accurately express the fate of the Humanist ideals in a world in which more has changed than the Humanists are willing to recognise. They feel too that the

Humanists simply leave out too much, and too much that is vital, for the expression of their ideals ever to be wholly persuasive. Thus *A Midsummer Night's Dream* may not be ironic at the expense of Duke Theseus and his court but it certainly does not endorse their judgement of the spectacle the 'rude mechanicals' put on for them. Not, of course, that Shakespeare's play shies away from laughing at the antics of Bottom and the other mechanicals. But a full response to it has to recognise that there is more to the world than is ever dreamt of in Theseus's philosophy, and that Bottom, recognising that the dream he has dreamed is bottomless, may be closer to the truth than the highly educated courtiers who laugh at him.

What Hamlet goes on to say to the players is, if anything, even more revered by theatre historians and directors (at least in didactic mode) than what has gone before:

> Suit the action to the word, the word to the action, with this special observance, that you o'erstep not the modesty of nature. For anything so o'erdone is from the purpose of playing, whose end, both at the first and now, was and is to hold as 'twere the mirror up to nature; to show virtue her feature, scorn her own image, and the very age and body of the time his form and pressure . . . And let those that play your clowns speak no more than is set down for them – for there be of them that will themselves laugh, to set on some quantity of barren spectators to laugh too . . . That's villainous, and shows a most pitiful ambition in the fool that uses it. (17–45)

However, a number of scholars, such as Robert Weimann, Patricia Parker, Margreta de Grazia, David Wiles and Bart van Es, have begun to explore what is going on here in a more historically nuanced way than the neo-Humanists of the RSC. They recognise that what Hamlet (but not *Hamlet*) is advocating was, in the year 1600, a new form of theatre, what we might in shorthand call realist theatre; theatre, that is, where the events on the stage are entirely self-contained and where the actors are seemingly unaware of the audience. The defence of such plays is that they hold the mirror up to nature, and it is still the defence made of all modes of realism, both in drama and in fiction. It has become so much the standard view of theatre that we have difficulty in remembering that it is a fairly recent development, despite the questioning of this kind of theatre by Brecht, Beckett, Ionesco and almost every major playwright of the last hundred years. But this was not the way theatre worked in ancient Greece or in medieval England, and, as Weimann and others have shown, it was not a notion entrenched in the spectators' consciousness until well into the seventeenth century. Before that, the audience never consisted of passive spectators who, having paid for their entry, waited to have a mirror held up to them. Rather, audience and performers were in dialogue, though that dialogue took many forms, from the quasi-religious theatre of ancient Athens through the Corpus Christi plays of the English Middle Ages to the comic interludes and other popular forms of the fifteenth and early sixteenth centuries. The figure of the Vice and then of the Clown in the theatre that preceded Shakespeare's performed the role of mediating between play and spectators by commenting on the action, often comically, from a position midway between 'the play' and the audience. As Weimann has shown, this was clearly expressed by the stage position the Vice or Clown took up, on the floor with the spectators rather than on the stage with the other actors. Shakespeare's clowns, in plays like *The Two Gentlemen of Verona* and *The Merchant of Venice*, go on performing this role in changing circumstances, being to some extent integrated into the plot but never completely, always retaining something of their 'in between' role.

Here the theatre historians begin to differ among themselves. For obviously there is no clown (apart, as we will see, from a crucial intervention towards the end of the play) in *Hamlet*, and after that the role changes: what we get in *Twelfth Night* and, supremely, in *King Lear* is the introduction of the Fool, the licensed or court jester who both takes over the role of the Vice and the Clown and becomes a crucial part of the plot.

All theatre historians are agreed, however, that an important part of what happened was that the resident clown of Shakespeare's company, the Lord Chamberlain's Men, Will Kemp, who was famous for his ad-libbing and his physical prowess, left the company and was replaced by Robert Armin, a very different sort of actor whose way of operating had to be catered for. But did Kemp leave of his own free will or was he pushed? Did he go because the kind of play Shakespeare wanted to write would no longer accommodate him, or did Shakespeare change his way of writing to suit the change in personnel? And was this really crucial?

For James Shapiro it clearly was. He entitles the first chapter of his deservedly popular book about one year in Shakespeare's life, *1599*, 'A Battle of Wills', and he writes:

> The parting of ways between [Will] Shakespeare and [Will] Kemp – ironically, if unintentionally mirrored in Hal's icy repudiation of Falstaff – was a rejection not only of a certain kind of comedy but also of a declaration that from here on in it was going to be a playwright's and not an actor's theatre, no matter how popular the actor.

Shapiro's book is full of such absolute breaks, and while this may account for the book's success with the public at large it achieves it at a cost. And the main loser is *Hamlet*.

Other scholars, such as Weimann and Wiles, have come closer to the mark, it seems to me, in recognising that what we have in *Hamlet* is the strange but extraordinarily powerful effect Shakespeare creates by having the tragic hero and the clown figure merge, but their emphasis on theatre history still seems to me to lead to blindness as to what is actually at stake here. They are content to point up Hamlet's link with the tradition of the Vice and the Clown and to leave it at that. Yet if I am right in feeling that Hamlet's suffering and behaviour stem from the fact that he cannot find a play to be part of, that he cannot find it in himself to enter wholeheartedly into the play either of the Ghost or of Claudius and the court, then his inhabiting an intermediary position, outside the play we are witnessing and in touch with the audience, becomes not merely a fact of theatrical history but one way in which Shakespeare dramatises the new kind of metaphysical anguish he is exploring here.

What holds Hamlet back? A suspicion about the validity of *either* of the plays on offer, a sense that if he were to enter either he would be play-acting, not fully himself. And the way he expresses this is through the kind of banter, the kind of wordplay, that raises questions about the language of others, and this, of course, is precisely the role traditionally occupied by the Vice and the Clown. It is a supreme irony of this play, then, that Hamlet, who comes alive through his quips and ad-libbing, should seek here to ban this from the repertoire of the players: 'Let your clowns speak no more than is set down for them,' he says, and keep them from making the spectators laugh, for it will detract from the seriousness of the play they are watching, and 'That's villainous, and shows a most plentiful ambition in the fool that uses it.'

Ironic, yes, but then of Hamlet too it might be said, as it is said of Lear, that he does 'but slenderly know himself'. Why should that surprise us?

8.2 (III. 2. 46–90)

In *Love's Labour's Lost* and *A Midsummer Night's Dream* the play-within-the-play came at the end and was the burlesque climax to a comedy of love. Here it has a much more precise function than the release of tension and the generation of laughter. In fact, if 'the play's the thing wherein [to] catch the conscience of the King', then it has a crucial position within the unfolding plot, and, not surprisingly, comes at the very centre of Shakespeare's play.

There is the bustle of preparation, but soon Hamlet and Horatio find themselves briefly alone. Their closeness is at once evident from the way they address each other. 'Here, sweet [not simply 'my' – though it's true that the foppish Osric addresses him in similar style towards the end] lord, at your service,' says Horatio, and Hamlet responds: 'Horatio, thou art e'en as just a man/ As e'er my conversation cop'd withal' (you are as true and as well-balanced a man is I ever encountered) (53–5). When Horatio protests, Hamlet goes on to develop what he means by 'just': you are no flatterer, one of those who 'are not a pipe for Fortune's finger/ To sound what stop she please'. In *Othello* Shakespeare will make the play hinge on Othello's false impression of Iago as just such a man, but here we know Horatio is indeed the one solid rock in a totally unstable world.

Hamlet has just time to instruct Horatio to watch Claudius like a hawk and see how he reacts to the play, before trumpets are heard, heralding the arrival of the royal party. 'They are coming to the play. I must be idle,' mutters Hamlet, and that last word is nicely ironic: he must look unoccupied, he says – but all the way through it is his *idleness* he has not been able to bear, the sense that in this new world left by his father's death and his mother's remarriage there is nothing for him to *do* – until now, when, as we will see, far from being idle, or being still and watching a play, he will be almost pathologically active.

8.3 (III. 2. 91–132)

He begins right away. To Claudius's bland: 'How fares our cousin Hamlet?' he responds with a mixture of aggression and fantasy. Taking, as is his habit, the words uttered in a sense other than they are meant, he pretends to understand 'fares' not as a present tense of a verb meaning 'do, be', but of a verb derived from 'fare: to eat', and so answers: 'Excellent, i'faith, of the chameleon's dish. I eat the air, promise-crammed. You cannot feed capons so.' The chameleon was thought to feed on air, while capons were stuffed, and the sentence as a whole clearly implies that Hamlet feels that his uncle's accession to the throne has robbed him of his rights. As we have seen, there is nothing in the constitution of Denmark as presented in the play which suggests that the son should inherit the throne from the father; on the contrary, it is an elected monarchy, though the reigning monarch can clearly, as Claudius has said he has done, voice a preference for who will succeed him, and this will no doubt be taken into account. But this is an element of the play that Shakespeare has deliberately left vague, so that Hamlet's gripe, if it is that, that he has been passed over, is felt as both justified and unjustified, depending on the moment.

At the same time, like Hamlet's 'Words, words, words', this reminds us that an actor must always 'eat the air, promise-crammed', for the food he feeds on is always fake food, never the real thing. Thus Shakespeare plays with us, revealing and then concealing the negative aspect of what it means to act on a stage and using that to develop our sense of Hamlet the person and his sense of himself.

Claudius certainly takes his answer as a rebuke and responds stiffly: 'I have nothing with this answer, Hamlet.' But Hamlet is off at a tangent again, suddenly addressing Polonius:

Ham. My lord, you played once i'th' university, you say?
Pol. That did I, my lord, and was accounted a good actor.
Ham. What did you enact?
Pol. I did enact Julius Caesar. I was killed i'th' Capitol. Brutus killed me.
Ham. It was a brute part of him to kill so capital a calf there. (97–105)

This is where theatre historians can really contribute to drawing out the meaning of individual moments in Shakespeare. They now think it was highly likely that the roles of Caesar and Brutus in Shakespeare's own *Julius Caesar*, which had only recently been performed in the new Globe theatre where *Hamlet* was being staged, were taken by the same actors as were now playing Polonius and Hamlet, so that, as Jenkins succinctly puts it, ' "Hamlet" would already have killed "Polonius" in a previous play, and, ironi-cally, is to perform the same "brute part" in this' (p. 294). Jenkins is not a critic one would associate with the name of Borges, which lends all the more credence to this dizzying scenario, made even more poignant if the conjecture of some theatre historians is accepted that Shakespeare – who it seems was not particularly distinguished as an actor, specialised in playing old men and may have played both the Ghost and Polonius – is here conversing with the star of the company, Burbage, for whom, in all probability, the role of Hamlet was created.

There is more. Brutus was not just the hero of all republicans; his ancestor, an earlier Brutus, was one too, and figures as such in Shakespeare's early foray into Roman history, his long poem, *The Rape of Lucrece*, where this Brutus brings the cruel tyrant and rapist Tarquin to justice and starts Rome on its republican path. Nor is it incidental that a Brutus or Brut was taken to be the legendary founder of Britain. A calf, later in the line, is a term for a fool, but again theatre historians point out that 'to kill a calf', whatever that means, appears to have been part of traditional mumming entertainment.

What this shows, if true, is that *all* Shakespeare's audience – nobility, intellectuals and groundlings – would have had no difficulty taking in the dizzying play of mirrors opened up by this brief exchange, with its metatheatrical high jinks, only possible when playwright, company *and* audience are familiar with each another.

The play again swerves in a new direction. Gertrude asks Hamlet to sit by her and he responds: 'No, good mother, here's metal more attractive' (punning on the magnetic power of iron), and turns to Ophelia. There follows a brief exchange in which Hamlet's sexual aggression is again evident but Ophelia's passivity seems, for once, to be a form less of acquiescence than of inner firmness, thus revealing her, if not as feisty a lady as the heroines of Shakespeare's mature comedies, Rosalind and Viola, then certainly as a match for Hamlet:

> *Ham.* Lady, shall I lie in your lap?
> *Oph.* No, my lord.
> *Ham.* I mean, my head upon your lap.
> *Oph.* Ay, my lord.
> *Ham.* Do you think I meant country matters?
> *Oph.* I think nothing, my lord.
> *Ham.* That's a fair thought to lie between maids' legs.

Oph. What is, my lord?

Ham. Nothing.

Oph. You are merry, my lord.

Ham. Who, I?

Oph. Ay, my lord.

Ham. O God, your only jig-maker. What should a man do but be merry? For look you how cheerfully my mother looks and my father died within's two hours.

Oph. Nay, 'tis twice two months, my lord.

Ham. So long? Nay then, let the devil wear black, for I'll have a suit of sables. O heavens, die two months ago and not forgotten yet! Then there's hope a great man's memory may outlive his life half a year. But by'r lady a must build churches then, or else shall a suffer not thinking on, with the hobby-horse, whose epitaph is, 'For O, for O, the hobby-horse is forgot'. (110–32)

So much is going on here one grows dizzy with the effort of processing it. First, the obscenity. Hamlet does not hold back. In 'country matters', meaning physical love-making, it would be easy to stress the first syllable; while 'nothing' would play on a man's 'thing' and on the figure nought, suggesting a woman's sexual organ. But it would be wrong to leave it at that. One reason why Ophelia can keep up the banter is that Hamlet has, from the start, adopted the role of the clown. As David Wiles points out:

When Hamlet describes himself as Ophelia's only jig-maker he is excusing his gross sexual obscenities . . . [But he] is signalling also that he has adopted the clown's role, jesting and singing to introduce the play that is about to happen. He positions himself informally, lying at Ophelia's feet, and studying Claudius's face. Placed both verbally and visually half-way between play and audience, he is 'as good as a chorus'. Mingled with puns and parody, his jests betray Tarlton's penchant for jibes and Kemp's for extempore alliteration.

What neither Wiles nor Jenkins comments on is the pain behind the exchange, evinced by Hamlet's compulsive return to his mother's over-hasty marriage. A.D. Nuttall pointed out in a famous lecture that Hamlet does not even construe Ophelia's ' 'Tis twice two months my lord' correctly: 'Oh, heavens, die two months ago and not forgotten yet,' he responds, whether because the quip is the important thing or because in his anguish at his father's death and his mother's subsequent remarriage four and two months both feel like yesterday. Nor do they say enough about the closing lines. Here Hamlet refers to the old, Catholic practice, now outlawed, of building chantry chapels for the rich departed, where priests would keep their memory alive by singing psalms and offering prayers for the dead in perpetuity (such, as we have seen, as Dante's Belacqua hoped would be said for him to speed his way through Purgatory). Without such visible means of keeping memory alive, Hamlet is suggesting, it is all too easy for it to be quickly lost. And he ends by comparing this to the disappearance in his day of the mummers' play, another, but this time pagan, relic of a medieval culture of communal festivity and remembrance.

Most fascinating of all, though, is the paradox embedded in the catchphrase with which he concludes. It appears to be the refrain of a popular song, and we find Shakespeare alluding to it in *Love's Labour's Lost* (III. 1. 25–6). Jenkins states that 'we seem to have an instance of a catch-phrase continuing in popularity after the original point of it had been lost. What is certain', he goes on, 'is that the hobby-horse, while very much remembered, became a by-word for being forgotten and as such the occasion for numerous jokes in Elizabethan plays' (p. 501). But this, as so often with Jenkins, while laying out the evidence with scrupulous clarity, fails to get to the heart of the matter. For here we have a perfect example of what is known as the paradox of the Cretan liar, after the ancient conundrum of the Cretan who said all Cretans were liars. Since he is a Cretan he must be a liar, but then what he has said is true and so not all Cretans are liars; on the other hand, since all Cretans are liars he cannot be telling the truth, so all Cretans are not liars, etc. In the passage before us we must imagine Hamlet growing into the part of the jig-maker or clown and perhaps even singing and dancing (obscenely?) as he utters the well-known refrain. The refrain asserts that the hobby-horse has been forgotten, but in saying and singing and jigging it we are more than reminded of the hobby-horse and all that went with it: we experience it in the theatre, our bodies respond. As we will see when we arrive at Hamlet's memories of the old court jester, Yorick, such doubleness is not only amusing, it is the way Shakespeare approaches the paradoxes that lie at the heart of his play.

8.4 (III. 2. 133–4)

And so we come to the play-within-the-play. Or at least to the dumb-show that precedes the play, and which is given in stage directions which are virtually identical in the Quarto and Folio. We see a King and Queen in an arbour, embracing. 'He takes her up, and declines his head upon her neck.' Then he lies down on a 'bank of flowers' and, seeing him asleep, she leaves him. Another man enters, takes the crown from off the sleeping King's head, kisses it, pours poison in his ear, leaves. The Queen returns, finds the King dead, 'makes passionate action'. The other man returns with three or four companions, seems to condole with her, and the dead body is carried away. 'The Poisoner woos the Queen with gifts. She seems harsh awhile, but in the end accepts his love.'

Perhaps the most famous problem of the many problems associated with *Hamlet* attaches to this episode. It concerns Claudius's reaction, or rather, lack of reaction. Why does he seem unmoved by the dumb-show? Is it that he does not see it, because he is too busy settling into his place and talking to those around him? Or that he does not recognise himself and his actions? Or does he see it and recognise his actions in it but maintain a mask of ignorance? All three views have had passionate advocates, but there are objections to all of them. First of all it is unlikely that Shakespeare would take the trouble to set all this up and then have Claudius ignore it. Then, since Claudius has more or less admitted his guilt in his asides, how could he not recognise himself? And, finally, why, if he manages to conceal his feelings here, does he give vent to them in the middle of the play proper which follows?

In answer to the objection to the third theory it has been argued that he manages to hold back for one dramatisation of the murder but not for two. Yet might it not be that it is not so much a question of his resistance being worn down as of his anger at what Hamlet has presented him with – with its blatant suggestion that he has murdered his brother – finally boiling over and his feeling that he can stand such insults no more, whether he is guilty or not?

The second theory is the most intriguing. It was first put forward by W. W. Greg as long ago as 1917, and has recently been revived by Stanley Cavell. Greg argues that Claudius does not react because Hamlet hallucinated the entire murder. Cavell feels that critics have been too quick to dismiss this as nonsense, and that their counter-arguments do not hold up in the face of the facts. He himself, however, wishes to argue that Claudius is clearly guilty, but does not recognise the murder enacted before him *because it does not correspond to how he actually did it*. He argues thus because he wants to propound a psychoanalytic explanation whereby the dumb-show – and the Ghost's account on which it is based – gives form to Hamlet's deep feelings about his father and mother, with Hamlet taking the place of the unnamed poisoner, who inseminates the Queen (psychoanalytically inclined critics seem quite happy to substitute Gertrude for Claudius here, for no good reason that I can see) 'through the ear'.

I think Cavell is on the right track but he is far too Freudian for me. The first thing that should be said is that the Mime, which comes bang in the centre of the play, looks both backwards and forwards, both back to some primal scene which has taken place before the play began but has, in effect, provided the impetus for it to begin, and forward to the scene of carnage with which it ends. But it is a very imprecise mirror of both. Unlike the murder, what we have here is not the King's brother but the King's nephew murdering the sleeping King, as Hamlet would like to murder his uncle Claudius; and unlike the concluding bloodbath this is a murder carried out secretly in a peaceful orchard.

Yet the fact that it is a mime, that it is silent, makes it much more akin to dream than to theatre, which is where the psycho-analysts come in. Unlike them, though, I want to start from the contrast between the life embodied in Hamlet's last singing of the little ditty, 'For O, for O, the hobby-horse is forgot', and the silence of the mime that follows. I think Shakespeare deliberately leaves it vague at this point whether Claudius does not see, masks his response, or is left bemused by what he sees, because what Shakespeare is interested in is Hamlet, not Claudius. Silence and vision stand over against the hearing of verse and the physicality of dance as psychosis stands over against health. And to add to this sense that we are inside a kind of traumatic dream re-enactment or imagined re-enactment of something forever out of reach is the unnatural way the crime is committed, by means of poison poured in the ear, not the mouth.

Scholars will complain that this was simply the way a well-known murder, to which Hamlet is soon to refer, took place a few decades earlier in Italy – but Shakespeare still chose to use *this* murder and not the many more obvious ones as his point of reference, so again the question is: why?

There is of course no definite answer. My sense is that the *effect on us* first of the Ghost's account and now of Hamlet's reconstruction of it is to elide a wide range of things. Let us first think of it from Hamlet's point of view. A nightmare vision is presented of murder and adultery, of a father's murder and a mother's implication in it, and, grotesquely, the murder is committed by poison entering through the ear. Does this not at some level represent Hamlet's sense of what his father's ghost *is doing to him* – poisoning his life by pouring poison into his ear? Even more eerie is the showing of this in a scene without sound. This is the stuff of nightmare, and it stands as one pole in this play, the opposite pole to Ophelia's tribute to Hamlet as the paragon of courtly virtues.

From Shakespeare's perspective, this is also one pole in a play which has, almost from the start, been exploring the limits of the audience's powers of imagination, moving in and out of the world of Elsinore and the world of the Globe in at times dizzying fashion.

At this moment, though, everything stops and even sound is cut off. It is the equivalent of Dante's circle of ice, the very lowest circle of hell, in which even the tears are frozen on the cheeks of the damned.

8.5 (III. 2. 134–49)

'What means this, my lord?' asks Ophelia, breaking the silence. And Hamlet, taking the role of Clown or Chorus, explains – to her and of course to us, but with his usual ironical ellipsis: 'Marry, this is miching malicho. It means mischief.' No one has been able fully to explain the phrase 'miching malicho', but it is clear it means something bad and something sneaky; 'stealthy iniquity' is how Jenkins takes it (p. 296), but we need not worry, for Hamlet himself clarifies: 'It means mischief'.

The Prologue to the spoken play now appears and Hamlet has fun at his expense and at that of the theatre in general: 'We shall know by this fellow. The players cannot keep counsel: they'll tell all.' But what else are plays, we ask, if not the spectacle of actors 'telling all'? The larger question is what does this 'all' consist of? Does it not smell of the 'soundings' Rosencrantz and Guildenstern would take, of the belief Claudius and Polonius have that Hamlet has a 'secret' that can be brought into the open? The players will mouth the lines written for them and thus reveal the plot as the play advances – but is that really all life is? Do they 'tell all' about the larger questions of what it means to be alive and the child of parents, what we are to do with our lives, what happens to us after death? It may be that the very ease with which they tell all that the playwright has given them to tell actually helps occlude the real questions – which is certainly the view of Samuel Beckett. And it is, it seems, Shakespeare's as well.

After a further exchange full of sexual innuendo on Hamlet's part and a quiet put-down by Ophelia, the Prologue begins to speak. Hamlet is scathing about this too: 'Is this a prologue, or the posy of a ring?' (Some pretty conceit such as those commonly engraved on the inside of rings.) ' 'Tis brief, my lord,' responds the enigmatic Ophelia. 'As woman's love,' Hamlet shoots back, but there is no time for her to respond as the Player King and Queen have entered and the King launches into his first speech.

8.6 (III. 2. 150–264)

As Jenkins notes, 'The play within the play is at once marked off from the surrounding dialogue by the rhyming couplets and by an artificial elaboration of style characteristic of an older period' (p. 506). As with the Player's speech earlier, the problem remains: is this parody, and if so, why? And if not, what is it exactly?

The whole set-up is strikingly reminiscent of the play put on by the 'mechanicals' at the end of *A Midsummer Night's Dream*: poor performers perform a poor play and are ridiculed by those watching – except that the place and function of the play in *Hamlet* – in the middle, not at the end, and, in Hamlet's eyes at least, in the verification of the Ghost's words and the flushing out of the murderer – give the whole thing a fraught and nightmarish quality which is the opposite of the laughter generated by the equivalent scene in *A Midsummer Night's Dream*. Indeed, the worse the writing and the acting, the less we know how to deal with it:

P. King.   *Full thirty times hath Phoebus' cart gone round*
         Neptune's salt wash and Tellus' orbed ground,
         And thirty dozen moons with borrow'd sheen
         About the world have times twelve thirties been
         Since love our hearts and Hymen did our hands
         Unite commutual in most sacred bands.

P. Queen. *So many journeys may the sun and moon*
         Make us again count o'er ere love be done.
         But woe is me, you are so sick of late,
         So far from cheer and from your former state,
         That I distrust [feel anxiety for] you. Yet though I
           distrust,
         Discomfort you, my lord, it nothing must;
         For women's fear and love hold quantity,

> *In neither aught, or in extremity.*
> *Now what my love is, proof hath made you know,*
> *And as my love is siz'd, my fear is so . . .* (150–65)

What the King says, simply, is that thirty years have passed since they got married, and the Queen responds with the hope that their marriage will last as long again. However, she says, you have recently seemed unwell and this makes me afraid, though my anxiety should in no way upset you, for that is the way of women. Is the style in which this is said merely archaic? Or does the Player Queen in particular remind us uncomfortably of Polonius as she struggles to articulate her anxiety in leaden couplets and the more she struggles the less she seems able to do so? To my ear, it is, though the effect is less of bumbling pretentiousness (it is more natural to speak at length in a play than in 'real life'), than of a rather touching earnestness mingled with naivety, precisely what one finds when reading the poetry of the first half of the sixteenth century, and what Pound, for one, found deeply moving in Arthur Golding's 1567 translation of Ovid's *Metamorphoses*.

The play now takes on a darker tone as the King announces that he is soon to die and hopes that after his death the Queen will find a husband worthy of her. But she interrupts this with a vehement protestation:

> In second husband let me be accurst;
> None wed the second but who kill'd the first. (174–5)

It is in response to this that Hamlet makes his first choric interruption: 'That's wormwood,' he says. Wormwood, a late Middle English word for the plant that produces absinthe (cf. vermouth), was proverbial for its bitterness. Does he take her to be saying that only a wife who kills a first husband ever marries a second? Surely not. She is merely protesting that only one who was so monstrous as to kill a first would wed a second husband – i.e. that no wife would ever marry again. And she repeats this in a different form:

> A second time I kill my husband dead,
> When second husband kisses me in bed. (179–80)

Yet it has to be said that her choice of words does at least allow the possibility to float over the scene that she will kill her first husband and, in a sense, kill him again and again each time she embraces the second. That is how *Hamlet* works – at almost every stage a set of alternative possibilities hovers over it, lending it its peculiar quality of nightmare and impenetrability.

The King, in the play, unlike Hamlet, does not seem to notice these alternatives. He responds with a long and rambling speech, Polonius-like again ('. . . But orderly to end where I begun . . .'), whose gist is that no one knows what will happen and it is folly to say now that we will never do something later: 'Our thoughts are ours, their ends none of our own.' The Queen, however, is adamant:

> *Both here and hence pursue me lasting strife,*
> *If, once a widow, ever I be a wife.* (217–18)

Hamlet interrupts once more: 'If she should break it now.' But the King in the play merely says: ' 'Tis deeply sworn.' Leave me, he goes on, I am weary and need to sleep. 'Sleep rock thy brain,' she responds, 'And never come mischance between us twain.' So she goes, says the stage direction, and he sleeps.

The scenario is a common one in ballads and poems of the late Middle Ages, usually given the generic title 'The Sleeper Betrayed': while the man sleeps his lover steals away to rejoin another. Skelton, in the early sixteenth century, wrote a beautiful version, which has the refrain: 'With "Lullay! Lullay!" like a childe/ Thou slepest too long, thou art begilde.' The first two stanzas run:

> 'My darling dere, my daisy floure,
> Let me,' quod he, 'ly in your lap.'
> 'Ly still,' quod she, 'my paramoure,
> Ly still, hardely, and take a nap.'

His hed was hevy, such was his hap [luck]!
All drowsy, dreming, drownd in slepe,
That of his love he toke no kepe.

With 'Ba! Ba! Ba!' and 'Bas! Bas! Bas!'
She cherished him both cheke and chin,
That he wist never where he was,
He had forgotten all deadly sin.
He wanted wit her love to win!
He trusted her payment and lost all his pray,
She left him sleping and stale away.

Clearly this corresponds to a male anxiety that the wife will not, like the mother, always be there to sing him lullabies, and that perpetual vigilance is both necessary and impossible to maintain.

Hamlet now turns to his mother:

Ham. Madam, how like you this play?
Queen. The lady doth protest too much, methinks.
Ham. O, but she'll keep her word.
King. Have you heard the argument? Is there no offence in't?
Ham. No, no, they do but jest – poison in jest. (224–30)

Unlike Polonius, who took exception to the Player's speech on stylistic grounds, here Gertrude is concerned, like many modern playgoers, with the psychology of the characters. She raises a question about the Queen's sincerity, though the phrase, another of the myriad 'quotes' to be found in this play, is usually quoted without the qualifying 'methinks'. This is brilliant on Shakespeare's part, because it tells us nothing about Gertrude except that she is wholly taken up by the play – the remark could be a sign either of her actual or of her pretended innocence, we cannot tell. And Claudius's ensuing remark is likewise neutral – is he concerned with the fact that the play might contain scenes unfit for women's eyes and ears, or that it might somehow be casting a slur upon him? Until it unfolds, of course, and we learn that the King will be poisoned by his nephew, there is nothing obviously subversive about it.

Hamlet, however, in answer to Claudius's enquiry, explains that the play is called *The Mousetrap*, and 'is the image of a murder done in Vienna', that it is 'a knavish piece of work', but that guiltless spirits should think nothing of it – 'we that have free souls, it touches us not'. And he ends with a typically compacted and riddling phrase, though it seems to have been proverbial, 'Let the galled jade wince, our withers are unwrung', meaning let the horse flinch which is rubbed sore, by a saddle or spurs perhaps, but for those without any such sore spots it should cause no trouble.

The scholars tell us that there was a play in circulation called *The Murder of Gonzago*, about a murder committed in Urbino, not Vienna (though some think the latter might be simply a misreading of the former), in the very manner in which the play (and Shakespeare's play) presents it, but, as I suggested earlier, that does not in itself explain why Shakespeare should have chosen this precise form of murder for his play. But we are not there yet (this time round). For what we have now is the entry of a new character, who is explained by Hamlet to be 'one Lucianus, nephew to the King'.

This character, who 'plays the part' of Claudius in the murder reported to Hamlet by the Ghost, could surely have been given as the King's brother. By choosing to make him the nephew Shakespeare carries out one of those subversions which help to trap and confuse us. For the play-within-the-play, as it is enacted here in the very centre of the play proper, in effect echoes both the primal scene of the play proper and its closing scene, while not being precisely like either. Like the primal scene, it entails the murder of a king by poisoning in an orchard by the lover of his wife; like the final scene, it entails the murder of a king by poisoning by his nephew. Thus a manifestly 'playlike' play in the middle of the play proper half-mirrors the extraordinary story that is said to form the backdrop to the play proper and the equally extraordinary story that will unfold before our eyes at the end. *Hamlet* truly is a remarkable construction, quite as full of echoes and mirrorings as Velázquez's *Las Meninas*, with its central conceit of the ostensible subjects of the work only dimly present in a mirror at the back of the enormous room, a mirror which hangs on the wall next to an open door in which a figure is seen in silhouette entering the room. But if that is the case they must be standing next to us, outside the actual canvas, while the painter, so visible to us, is presumably absent from the picture on which he is at work.

Ophelia, at this point, names the role Hamlet has been adopting throughout this performance: 'You are as good as a chorus, my lord.' Hamlet, as we know, never merely responds, he always uses the remarks of another as a springboard for his own invention, so here he comes back: 'I could interpret between you and your love if I could see the puppets dallying.' In other words, I would certainly be able to supply the dialogue if I were to see you and your lover performing, as in a puppet-play. The man who 'interprets' at a puppet-play supplies a running commentary on the action, and is often the puppeteer himself. It is suggestive, coming after his reference to himself as a machine in his letter to her, that Hamlet should now think of Ophelia and her lover (whether himself or another) as having no more freedom than puppets, whose every movement is manipulated by another. But she chooses to pick up not on this but on the 'dallying': 'You are keen, my lord, you are keen.' You are (too) sharp-tongued, she says, but he chooses to understand 'keen' as sharp, and applying it to both the edge of a blade and to sexual desire he replies, obscenely, 'It would cost you a groaning to take off my edge.' But, as in earlier scenes, she is ever a match for him: 'Still better, and worse' – that is, you are always able to cap a remark with a better one, but it is always in worse taste. And, of course, he cannot resist capping *that*: 'So you mis-take your husbands' – so you 'take' your husbands in marriage ('for better for worse,' runs the marriage service); or, so you take them for a ride (mis-take); or, so you fail to see what I am trying to say to you beneath my sarcastic words (mistake).

But he has had enough, and seems now not so much to pre-empt the speech Lucianus is about to deliver (do we imagine him, all this time, poised to speak his lines as the rugged Pyrrhus was poised for too long to strike down the aged Priam?) as to coax it into being, rather as Electra and the Chorus coax Orestes into the killing of their mother in Aeschylus's *Choephoroe*. 'Begin, murderer,' he says. 'Leave thy damnable faces [horrid grimaces] and begin.' Returning to the Senecan rhetoric of the Player's speech he prompts: 'Come, the croaking raven doth bellow for revenge.'

But before we look at that it is worth recapitulating what we have seen and heard so far: a husband so tired he only wants to sleep and talk of his impending death; a wife who protests that she will never remarry; and sexual banter between Hamlet and Ophelia. It is striking that in all this there has been no talk of murder, except metaphorically as second marriage, and a harping on the sexual appetites of women, with Ophelia and the Queen eliding and separating in a dream-like way. This has been at the centre of Hamlet's thoughts and feelings from the time we first see him to the present moment. It is almost as if the murder is an afterthought, and, here, something that must be come to, eventually, and almost reluctantly. Hamlet, we feel, has to gear himself up, drag the rhetoric of ravens and revenge out of himself, before it can come into being before us.

The stage murderer does not need much prompting: 'Thoughts black, hands apt, drugs fit, and time agreeing,' he begins, and proceeds to pour poison into the sleeper's ear. Hamlet explains: 'A poisons him i'th' garden for his estate. [No mention of lust here, the murder is purely for gain.] His name's Gonzago. The story is extant, and written in very choice Italian ['choice' is good, as Polonius might say, another deflection from content and into form]. You shall see anon how the murderer gets the love of Gonzago's wife' (255–8).

But Claudius has had enough. He gets up. 'What,' quips Hamlet, 'frighted with false fire?' Just as a gun may make a noise but if it is a blank that is discharged nothing will happen, so a play, he suggests, is only make-believe. 'How fares my lord?' asks Gertrude, alarmed, while Polonius cries out for the play to stop. But all Claudius says is 'Give me some light. Away.' 'Lights, lights,

lights,' all cry (though the Quarto gives the line to Polonius alone). This reminds us that we have been watching a play supposed to be performed indoors, unlike the performance of *Hamlet* taking place under the skies in the Globe, but also that the King feels the need to see more clearly in the murk and confusion of his guilty thoughts.

There is a rush for the exit, and soon only Hamlet and Horatio are left on stage.

8.7 (III. 2. 265–88)

We would expect a quick consultation as to the success or otherwise of their plan. Instead, Hamlet bursts into song:

> Why, let the stricken deer go weep,
> > The hart ungalled play;
> For some must watch while some must sleep,
> > Thus runs the world away. (265–8)

Again, a darting glance at what has happened swept up into popular ballad. The first couplet is easy enough: Claudius has been struck by the arrow of the performance, Hamlet suggests; had he not he would have been happy to 'play'. The second couplet is harder: Why 'must'? And why 'runs the world away' rather than 'so goes the world'? Wiles suggests that the phrase refers to the Globe playhouse, like Kemp's jest in his book about his dancing from London to Norwich that 'I have . . . danced myself out of the world', signalling his parting of the ways with the Globe and its company in 1599. But that seems to be straining things and still does not explain 'away'. It is better perhaps to let it float as a hint of Doomsday, all the more eerie for being couched in so light a tone. But it is a further example of the almost Picassoesque way Shakespeare uses collage in this play to make his points and create the mood he wants.

Wiles is on more solid ground when he points out that the feathers and shoes Hamlet goes on to describe are the attributes of morris men and fools, and that his 'this' in 'Would not this, sir . . . get me a fellowship in a cry of players' refers not only to the play he has just written (and directed), but to the little song and dance he has just performed – would this not be my passport to the profession of actor? he asks. Horatio, like Ophelia, is prepared to play the game: half a share, he quips, but Hamlet is adamant: 'A whole one, I.'

But by now we too as audience are prepared to play these word games. Hamlet may have earned himself a place in a professional company, but he is living, speaking, sighing, singing, dancing proof that no human being is 'whole', and that 'I' is a small word that covers a big lie.

But he is off into another little ditty:

> For thou dost know, O Damon dear,
>   This realm dismantled was
> Of Jove himself, and now reigns here
>   A very, very – pajock. (275–8)

Jenkins's note on 'Damon' could not be bettered: 'A traditional shepherd name from pastoral poetry, appropriately addressed to one who has the ancient virtues of the golden age before the realm was "dismantled" ' (p. 305). Hamlet is clearly referring to Claudius, who, in his eyes, has 'dismantled' the realm of Jove, his father, and now rules as a patched or motley fool, a more threatening and ambiguous figure than the 'ass' the rhyme requires. (Jenkins glosses 'pajock' as: 'probably a form of "patchcock", a base contemptible fellow, a savage'.)

Wiles is surely right too when he points out that serious plays had been in the habit of being rounded off with a jig, a merry song and dance, usually bawdy, in which the Clown performed, and that the Elizabethan audience, faced with this little episode after the melodramatic play, would have instinctively seen Hamlet at this moment as the Clown and jig-maker.

Horatio, a little slower, comes back with: 'You might have rhymed.' But Hamlet has moved on again: 'O good Horatio, I'll take the ghost's word for a thousand pounds. Did'st perceive?' (280–1) 'Very well, my lord,' responds Horatio. But the fact is that we are no wiser now than we were at the start about Claudius's guilt, and were of course always unlikely to be, given the nature of the test. As I have already argued, Claudius's abrupt exit could just as well be due to his anger at Hamlet's continual imputation of his guilt as a sign of the guilt itself. Hamlet's remark that he would be prepared to bet a thousand pounds now that the Ghost was telling the truth may strike us as rash.

'Come,' Hamlet says, reprising his role as jig-maker, 'some music; come, the recorders.' But at this moment who should re-enter but Rosencrantz and Guildenstern? The jig is over and the reality that is the play of the court takes over.

8.8 (III. 2. 289–378)

The King, says Guildenstern, 'is in his retirement marvellous distempered'. That is, the King, having withdrawn, is furious. But Hamlet, in his usual fool's way, chooses to take the word in its alternative meaning of unwell. 'With drink?' he asks disingenuously. 'No, my lord,' responds Guildenstern, 'with choler', that is, with anger. But again Hamlet chooses to take it in its alternative sense of sickness, an excess of bile, and innocently suggests it might be better to consult the doctor than himself. Guildenstern reprimands him: 'Good my lord, put your discourse into some frame, and start not so wildly from my affair' (300–1). But the question is – and remains throughout this play – what frame should we put things in? And is it even possible to put frames round discourse? For as a result of the melancholy into which he has fallen Hamlet has become aware of the fact that there is no single frame that governs all discourse but that each group brings a different 'frame' to its view of the world, his father providing one, Claudius another, the players a third. This Nietzschean insight, as Cavell rightly calls Hamlet's initial 'I know not seems', is what holds him back from wholehearted participation in any action, whether his pursuit of Ophelia or his taking of revenge.

There are two further points to be made about this brief exchange, which are pertinent to our response to the play as a whole. First, something we touched on in our discussion of Hamlet's first appearance in I.2. By always choosing to understand the discourse of his interlocutors in ways other than they mean it he not only helps us see that everything, including language, is 'framed'; he also puts a spanner in the smooth-running machine that is conversation within a frame tacitly accepted by all. At every moment the forward thrust of the dialogue, which in most plays is transparent, yielding information that will drive the plot, is stopped in its tracks, or briefly re-routed on to a different track. (Shakespeare's language, of course, is never simply transparent, but the point here is that Hamlet keeps shoving our noses into the materiality of 'words, words, words'.) This functions, whenever Hamlet is in conversation with a member of the court, rather like Brecht's notion of interruption, about which Benjamin has written so well. By breaking up the stream of continuity, Benjamin explains, Brechtian theatre allows us to see that events could be other than they are. Benjamin himself, when he comes to write his aphorisms on the philosophy of history, points out that 'Universal history has no theoretical armature. Its method is additive; it musters a mass of data to fill the homogenous, empty time. Materialistic historiography, on the other hand, is based on a constructive principle. Thinking involves not only the flow of thoughts, but their arrest as well.' One of the reasons we warm to Hamlet, as to the Marx Brothers, is that by constantly arresting the normal flow of thoughts they set us both laughing and thinking.

The second point is less obvious but equally important. Because of Hamlet's position as the King's nephew and the Queen's son he is always addressed as 'my lord', and this both establishes a rhythm and adds a further disturbing element. For if Hamlet spoke as he is expected to, that 'my lord' would simply merge into the discourse. If it was the court fool who spoke Hamlet's lines, as happens with such lines in *Lear*, Hamlet would not be addressed as 'my lord'. But Hamlet is both lord and fool, and that is the problem both for him and for his interlocutors.

That repeated 'my lord' on the part of those who address him also balances Hamlet's own fondness for phrases such as 'soft now', which punctuate his speeches, even to himself. We feel the different registers pulling us in different directions.

The two courtiers have now come to summon Hamlet to his mother's chamber, where she wishes to speak to him. Fine, Hamlet says, and is there anything else? Rosencrantz tries to seize the initiative: 'My lord, you once did love me.' 'And do still,' Hamlet answers, 'by these pickers and stealers.' He is at it again: Jenkins points out that by 'pickers and stealers' Hamlet simply means 'hands' (p. 308) – but this is deeply twisted and ironic, because the meaning derives from the phrase in the Catechism, 'to keep these hands from picking and stealing'. Ironic, then, but also reinforcing the idea of the body as a machine which can easily get out of control, as the hands, in those who do not make a conscious effort to hold them back, will reach out and pick and steal.

Rosencrantz presses on: 'Good my lord, what is your cause of distemper? You do surely bar the door upon your own liberty if you deny your griefs to your friend.' And Hamlet, in one of those sudden bursts of apparent clarity which are so disconcerting, says: 'Sir, I lack advancement.' How can that be, responds the other, 'when you have the voice of the King himself for your succession in Denmark?' 'Ay sir,' returns the prince, 'but while the grass grows – the proverb is something musty' (326–35).

The proverb runs: 'While the grass grows the horse starves.' This, then, appears to be a clear indication that what is troubling Hamlet is nothing other than the issue of the succession. Denmark, as Rosencrantz's remark makes clear, was not a hereditary monarchy, the incumbent only having the power to give his 'voice' to one candidate or another. Yet Shakespeare, as we have repeatedly seen, leaves us in deliberate confusion as to whether this is in fact the case. Hamlet certainly does not seem to think so. He feels his rightful 'advancement' has been taken from him and that to have the 'voice' of a middle-aged and healthy king is no comfort at all. This is the line taken by those, like Margreta de Grazia, who are keen to free Hamlet of the taint of indecision through excessive soul-searching foisted upon him by Romantic critics. But while the motive is surely laudable the case they make is not entirely convincing. For, compared to Hamlet's outbursts against his uncle's lechery and his mother's compliance, these remarks seem a little too pat. Is Hamlet merely saying this to divert attention from the real cause of his 'distemper' (the very word used earlier of Claudius)? We can never know, but in the theatre the effect on the audience is not that of a long-awaited revelation bursting forth but of yet more verbal sparring, with neither side letting down their guard.

Hamlet, before the two courtiers entered, had called for recorders, and now they arrive, just in time for Hamlet, who, we have seen in his dealings with the players, likes to hold forth quite as much as Polonius, though to better effect, to use them not to play on but to give Rosencrantz and Guildenstern a little lesson on the nature of man. Why, he asks them, using a hunting image, 'do you go about to recover the wind of me, as if you would drive me into a toil [a net]?' 'O my lord,' responds Guildenstern, forgive me if I have seemed intrusive, it's only my love for you that makes me seem rude. Hamlet affects puzzlement:

Ham. I do not well understand that. Will you play upon this pipe?

Guild. My lord, I cannot.

Ham. I pray you.

Guild. Believe me, I cannot.

Ham. I do beseech you.

Guild. I know no touch of it, my lord.

Ham. It is as easy as lying. Govern these ventages with your fingers and thumb, give it breath with your mouth, and it will discourse most eloquent music. Look you, these are the stops.

Guild. But these cannot I command to any utterance of harmony. I have not the skill.

Ham. Why, look you now, how unworthy a thing you make
of me. You would play upon me, you would seem to
know my stops, you would pluck out the heart of my
mystery, you would sound me from my lowest note to
the top of my compass: and there is much music, excellent voice, in this little organ, yet cannot you make it
speak. 'Sblood, do you think I am easier to be played
on than a pipe? Call me what instrument you will,
though you fret me, you cannot play upon me.

(341–63)

Earlier we saw Rosencrantz and Guildenstern reporting to the
King that Hamlet was difficult to 'sound', and saw how such
metaphors fit in with the ethos of the King and court, which holds
that people are hollow vessels into which we can, with ingenuity
and cunning, reach in and pluck out their 'mystery'. Now Hamlet
is outlining a different view of man: man is not a machine but
more like a musical instrument, which cannot be played upon by
those who are alien to it and ignorant of how it works. Like a
recorder, says Hamlet, but of course much more complex. Even
Hamlet himself, we have sensed, does not really know how to play
his own instrument; how much less likely that another would be
able to do so.

The conclusion to this splendid Humanist disquisition returns
us to Hamlet the deployer of barbed wit. Switching from the
image of man as a wind instrument to man as a stringed instrument, he says: though you equip me with frets (the ridges on some
stringed instruments which mark the placement of the fingers)
you cannot play me; but also, though you irritate me (make me
fret) you still will not be able to play me. There is no time for the
other to respond, for at this moment, and prolonging this enormous scene even further, Polonius enters to say that the Queen
needs to speak to Hamlet at once. But the prince is in full flight
and will not be brought down to earth so easily. He now proceeds
to give Polonius and the rest (including ourselves) a practical
lesson in Nietzschean framing:

Ham. Do you see yonder cloud that's almost in shape of a
     camel?
Pol. By th' mass and 'tis – like a camel indeed.
Ham. Methinks it is like a weasel.
Pol. It is backed like a weasel.
Ham. Or like a whale.
Pol. Very like a whale.
Ham. Then I will come to my mother by and by. (367–74)

Of course Polonius is, in a sense, humouring him as a respectful
courtier would humour a prince. Hamlet recognises this when, in
an aside, he mutters that 'They will fool me to the top of my bent'.
But the exchange also demonstrates, as the disquisition on human
beings and musical instruments just has, that we read the world
through the glasses we have on. If you tell me this cloud looks like
a camel I am likely to pick out its camel-like features and really see
a camel; if you tell me it looks like a whale I will pick out its whale-
like features and really see a whale. Wittgenstein famously explored
this issue by means of the silhouette that can equally well be seen as
a duck and as a rabbit, but never as both at once. Most practitioners
of narrative choose not to raise the issue, so that a novelist will write,
'Her hands were small and delicate' and feel he has sufficiently
described one aspect of one of his characters and given us a sense of
the kind of person she is (though that need not stop the lady in
question turning out to be the murderer, say, or a vindictive bitch),
but a few, like Kafka, will want to make us see how subjective these
types of description are by writing: 'Her hands were certainly small
and delicate, but they could quite as well have been called weak and
characterless.' Shakespeare is in *Hamlet* at the Kafka/Wittgenstein
end of the literary spectrum. Discourse has to be put in some frame
– but, asks this play, who decides which is the right frame?

8.9 (III. 2. 379–90)

Once again, at the end of a fold, all exit, leaving Hamlet on his
own to turn things over in his mind. And how we see him at this

point is, to begin with, as the Avenger. This, it seems, is the frame
he has now chosen, and it comes with the appropriate Senecan
language:

> 'Tis now the very witching time of night,
> When churchyards yawn and hell itself breathes out
> Contagion to this world. Now could I drink hot blood,
> And do such bitter business as the day
> Would quake to look on.

But he cannot keep it up.

> Soft, now to my mother.
> O heart, lose not thy nature . . .
> Let me be cruel, not unnatural.
> I will speak daggers to her, but use none. (379–87)

'Soft now', the Hamlet signature tune, heralds a coming down to
earth, as he prepares for the fateful meeting. It is followed by an
expression of his need to stick to his new determination to act the
part of the Avenger, but the very fact that he needs to say this
suggests that he is less than comfortable in the role.

    And so he goes in to her. It is the first meeting between mother
and son alone that we will have been witness to. Except, of course,
that they are not alone. Polonius, hidden, watches.

FOLD NINE

9.1 (III. 3. 1–35)

But before we can finally get to that scene Shakespeare switches to Claudius. It is our first sight of him since he rose from the play in distress or anger. 'I like him not,' he muses,

> nor stands it safe with us
> To let his madness range. (1–2)

For that reason, he says to Rosencrantz and Guildenstern, I want you to go with him to England – the plan that he has had in mind for some time.

They leave to get ready and in comes Polonius with news that Hamlet is on his way to his mother's closet. He himself, he says, will hide 'behind the arras . . . to hear the process' (what is said). The reason he gives brings out well the atmosphere of spying and suspicion that pervades the court:

> 'Tis meet that some more audience than a mother,
> Since nature makes them partial, should o'erhear
> The speech of vantage. (31–3)

9.2 (III. 3. 36–98)

He goes and, for the first time in the play, Claudius is alone; he starts to speak. This is our chance at last to see things from his point of view, and Shakespeare equivocates no longer:

> O my offence is rank, it smells to heaven;
> It hath the primal eldest curse upon't –
> A brother's murder. (36–8)

Yet the emphasis is not on his guilt but on the fact, as he sees it, in tortured theological debate with himself reminiscent of Marlowe's Dr Faustus, that he cannot ever find peace or pardon from God, since, though Christ is merciful, he could only receive that mercy were he to give up all the things for which he has committed the crime: 'My crown, mine own ambition, and my queen.' In this world, he goes on, it is possible to 'buy out the law', but not so with God:

> There is no shuffling, there the action lies
> In his true nature [the deed is exposed], and we ourselves
>   compell'd
> Even to the teeth and forehead of our faults
> To give in evidence. (61–4)

And so, like Hamlet in *his* soliloquies, he finds that all his feverish argument has simply brought him back to the impasse from which he started:

> O wretched state! O bosom black as death!
> O limed soul, that struggling to be free
> Art more engag'd! (67–9)

And yet, like many a Christian sinner before and after, he cannot let it go at that. (After all, even Titivillus, the invisible devil of *Mankind,* admits that 'A short prayer thirleth [pierces] heaven' – l.558.)

> Help, angels! Make assay.
> Bow, stubborn knees; and heart with strings of steel,
> Be soft as sinews of the new-born babe.
> All may be well. (69–72)

It's a wonderful touch on Shakespeare's part that the predominant tone of the second half of the play, which is now starting to unfold, should be established not by the hero but by the villain: the hope, sensed to be vain even as it is uttered, that 'all may be well'.

It is wonderful too how Shakespeare so orders things that the source and origin of all the spying in the play should now himself turn out to be the one being spied upon. For as Claudius finishes his speech, and, presumably, kneels in attempted prayer (so Q1), Hamlet appears. 'Now might I do it pat,' he muses, 'now a is a-praying./ And now I'll do it.'

But we need to see it as Shakespeare presented it – most probably to Burbage, playing Hamlet:

> Now might I do it pat, now a is a-praying.
> And now I'll do't. (73–4)

The pentameter fills line 73, and the full stop at the end of the line, plus the transition to the start of line 74, leaves a massive pause between his comment on what he sees and his injunction to himself (of course it is up to the actor to determine whether line 74 is said as an imperative, an optative or a simple future, but the latter reading feels unconvincing). And then an even bigger pause ensues, as Shakespeare leaves the rest of the line empty, as well, most unusually, as the start of the following line. Directors usually have Hamlet draw his sword at this point. But what follows is, of course, not action but a thought:

> And so a goes to heaven;
> And so am I reveng'd. (74–5)

Note that Hamlet, sword in hand, suddenly held in suspense, is very like the rugged Pyrrhus of the Player's speech, his sword hanging for an eternity over the cowering Priam as his mind is momentarily taken by the crash of a building falling in the burning city. And note too how, most unusually, Hamlet has started to talk to himself in the ironic tone he has hitherto used in talking to members of the court. For, as the musings that follow make clear, what he recognises suddenly is that to kill Claudius in prayer would be anything but revenge, since it would ensure that he went straight to heaven, unlike his brother, who, we remember, was very clear that he was 'Cut off even in the blossoms of my sin,/ Unhousel'd, disappointed, unanel'd' (I. 5. 76–7).

This scene has called forth such torrents of commentary that its basic outline is in danger of getting lost. Readers from Dr Johnson on have been at pains either to seek to understand 'the inner workings' of Hamlet's mind, or to condemn him for going well beyond the revenge ethic in wishing not merely to kill his father's murderer but to ensure his eternal damnation. I don't think we should be too concerned about either. As we have seen with the sketching in of the notion of Purgatory in the play, Shakespeare is far from being a dogmatic Catholic or Protestant but is ready to use whatever is at hand as grist to his mill. The play inhabits a universe where God exists, but in no very clear way, and where the late medieval world picture of Heaven, Hell, Purgatory and an afterlife is still present, but how literally it is taken is always moot.

What all this amounts to is that spectators will take Hamlet's anguished debate with himself about whether or not to kill Claudius now he has the opportunity, like Claudius's own anguished debate as to whether he can or cannot be saved, in a wide range of ways, from full belief to blatant scepticism and the thought that he is merely making excuses for not acting. It seems to me again, though, that what we have is a Hamlet who would dearly like to be part of a revenge drama, but who, for whatever reason, is unable to embrace that wholly. Note how, as he comes to the peroration of his speech and faces the fact that now is not the time for the doing of the deed, the Senecan tone starts once more to make itself heard, as though he would compensate for his lack of action by an excess of words. And in the Senecan tradition words always are, in a sense, deeds:

> And am I then reveng'd,
> To take him in the purging of his soul,
> When he is fit and season'd for his passage?
> No.
> Up, sword, and know thou a more horrid hent:
> When he is drunk asleep [Q2 drunke, asleep], or in his
> rage,
> Or in th'incestuous pleasure of his bed,
> At game a-swearing, or about some act
> That has no relish of salvation in't,
> Then trip him, that his heels may kick at heaven
> And that his soul may be as damn'd and black
> As hell, whereto it goes. (84–95)

He exits, leaving Claudius to mouth the by now almost obligatory couplet which closes but does not close, though this time the speaker is fully aware of this fact:

> My words fly up, my thoughts remain below.
> Words without thoughts never to heaven go. (97–8)

FOLD TEN

10.1 (III. 4. 1–6)

Polonius and Gertrude. It seems that even with royalty, provided it is female, Polonius cannot rein in his propensity to instruct. Hamlet is on his way, he tells her, 'Look you lay home to him.' Tell him his jokes are getting out of hand, he goes on, and that you have had to do everything in your power to protect him from getting what he, frankly, deserves. I'll hide here.

Actually what he says, wonderfully ironically for this most talkative of men, is: 'I'll silence me even here' – words we will soon have occasion to recall.

10.2 (III. 4. 7–218)

And so the stage is set for another momentous confrontation, this time not between Hamlet and the ghost of his father, but between Hamlet and his very living mother.

They begin warily. 'Now, mother, what's the matter?' he asks. 'Hamlet, thou hast thy father much offended.' 'Mother,' he responds, going on the attack, 'you have my father much offended.' But she will have none of this insolence, as she sees it: 'Come, come, you answer with an idle tongue.' And, when he persists, she tries a different tack: 'Have you forgot me?' In other words, have

you forgotten that I bore you and raised you up, have you forgotten
what we are to one another? But he will not yield:

> No, by the rood, not so.
> You are the Queen, your husband's brother's wife,
> And, would it were not so, you are my mother. (13–15)

Like all family quarrels, this one changes register at an alarming
rate. Having offered him memories of how close they once
were and been rebuffed, she changes tack again: if that's your
attitude I will set others on to you who will be able to speak to
you. She probably turns away, signifying that the interview is over,
for he is suddenly insistent, even perhaps manhandling her:
'Come, come, and sit you down, you shall not budge.' I won't
let you go, he tells her, until I show you your true self in the mirror
of my words.

But she, terrified by his abruptness, cries out: 'What wilt thou
do? Thou wilt not murder me? Help, ho! [F: Helpe, helpe.]'

At her words Polonius suddenly pipes up behind the arras:
'What ho! Help! [F: helpe, helpe, helpe]'

Hamlet turns: 'How now? A rat! Dead for a ducat, dead.' And
he stabs through the fabric of the arras.

Pol.   O, I am slain.

Queen. O me, what hast thou done?

Ham.   Nay, I know not.
Is it the King? [*Lifts up the arras and discovers Polonius, dead.*]

Queen. O what a rash and bloody deed is this!

Ham.   A bloody deed. Almost as bad, good mother,
As kill a king and marry with his brother.

Queen. As kill a king?

Ham.   Ay, lady, it was my word –
Thou wretched, rash, intruding fool, farewell.
I took thee for thy better. (24–32)

It is worth looking at the passage in detail, because much has been made of it. A great many critics have seen in this moment the point at which Hamlet takes his destiny in hand and leaves all procrastination behind him. This testifies to a desire on their part to find a turning point, a moment of decision, perhaps even of salvation or redemption, a desire of course shared by Hamlet himself. But this interpretation has to be seen for what it is: a reading of life and what we should expect from it which is very Augustinian and very Protestant. I want to suggest that it is resisted by the play, in favour of a wiser, more realistic vision of what life is really like. And this moment in the play provides a good example. Hamlet, who has just come from failing to carry out his father's injunction when he had Claudius at his mercy, is startled by a shout from behind the arras and stabs wildly, in what is a perfect example of Sartrean bad faith – for if it is Claudius, as he suspects/ hopes it is, he will have killed him without, in a sense, wanting or meaning to ('What hast thou done? 'Nay, I know not.'). His 'How now? A rat!' is wonderfully ambiguous, for although Hamlet thinks of Claudius as a rat, he can also take refuge in the thought that he did indeed imagine it was a literal rat. Jenkins refers us to a 1552 text which says: 'Rats be wont to make . . . a noisome crying . . . to which noise many men hearkening forthwith though it be in the dark night throw at them and kill them' (p. 320). And when Hamlet sees who it is he has stabbed he is scathing: 'Thou wretched, rash, intruding fool, farewell./ I took thee for thy better.' Far from this being a turning point for Hamlet, it merely exemplifies what we have been seeing all along, his simultaneous desire to do what his father bade him do and his inability to accept the premises, the frame, which govern that injunction, and therefore his unwillingness to carry out his father's bidding. Such ambivalence never leaves him.

Of course this act-that-was-not-an-act, this chance event, does, within the plot of the play, mark a turning point, a moment which cannot be taken back and in whose ramifications all are implicated: Gertrude, Claudius, Laertes, Ophelia, Hamlet himself. But that is for the future. In the present moment Hamlet seems

strangely unconcerned, viewing what has just happened as an
annoying interruption of the task in hand, his confrontation with
his mother. Indeed, it seems almost an excuse for a nicely turned
couplet. 'Leave wringing of your hands,' he goes on: 'sit you
down,/ And let me wring your heart.' When she angrily asks what
she has done for him to speak to her like that he finally pours out
his feelings:

> Such an act
> That blurs the grace and blush of modesty,
> Calls virtue hypocrite, takes off the rose
> From the fair forehead of an innocent love
> And sets a blister there, makes marriage vows
> As false as dicers' oaths – O, such a deed
> As from the body of contraction plucks
> The very soul, and sweet religion makes
> A rhapsody of words. Heaven's face does glow
> O'er this solidity and compound mass
> With tristful [sorrowful] visage, as against the doom [day
>   of Judgement],
> Is thought-sick at the act. (40–51)

What son of a mother who marries again has not voiced such
sentiments, or at least dreamed of voicing them? Hamlet accuses
his mother of being immodest, false, and of reducing 'to an empty
form not merely the marriage-contract but *contraction*, the very
principle of contracting solemn agreements of which the marriage-
contract is the type', as Jenkins paraphrases it (p. 321). Her act, as
Jenkins says, 'is here made to epitomize the guilt of the world'.

And all this for what? For marrying again after her first
husband's death? No wonder she responds with: 'Ay me, what act
. . .?' But Hamlet is beyond the call of reason. His only reply is to
go into a great rhetorical speech about the differences between the
two brothers, 'Look here, upon this picture, and on this . . .' The
one is a paragon of beauty, strength and authority, 'a form indeed/
Where every god did seem to set his seal/ To give the world

assurance of a man'. The other is so much his opposite that it hardly requires spelling out: 'Here is your husband, like a mildew'd ear/ Blasting his wholesome brother.'

And so, like the ghost of his father, he can move into his second round of accusations: if he is such a wretch, impossible for any woman to love, there is only one explanation for the remarriage. However, he shies away from calling it lust, for that would be to impute sexuality to her, something that he does not wish to imagine, so he settles instead for a massive failure of judgement:

> You cannot call it love; for at your age
> The heyday in the blood is tame, it's humble,
> And waits upon the judgment, and what judgment
> Would step from this to this? (68–71)

Perhaps in some devilish way Claudius 'cozen'd you at hoodman-blind', he suggests; yet he cannot quite let go of the thought that she too is responsible:

>   O shame, where is thy blush?
> Rebellious hell,
> If thou canst mutine in a matron's bones,
> To flaming youth let virtue be as wax
> To melt in her own fire; proclaim no shame
> When the compulsive ardour gives the charge,
> Since frost itself as actively doth burn
> And reason panders will. (81–7)

There is no need to try and decipher the images here; Hamlet himself probably does not fully understand what he is saying, apart from the general proposition that his mother, in marrying again, and marrying such a man, has allowed her will to overcome her reason.

Yet his impassioned words seem to have broken something in her, though Shakespeare leaves it tantalisingly vague as to what it is she feels guilty of:

> O Hamlet, speak no more.
> Thou turn'st my eyes into my very soul,
> And there I see such black and grained spots
> As will not leave their tinct. (88–91)

Hamlet takes this as licence to open his feelings up to her completely. He drops the thought that she is too old to feel desire and speaks instead his deepest horror and his deepest fascination:

> Nay, but to live
> In the rank sweat of an enseamed bed,
> Stew'd in corruption, honeying and making love
> Over the nasty sty! (91–4)

She begs him to stop, perhaps as much for his sake as for hers:

> O speak to me no more.
> These words like daggers enter in my ears.
> No more, sweet Hamlet. (93–5)

But nothing will stop him now he can at last utter what he has kept back so long, and he goes into a further diatribe about the man she has married, 'A murderer and a villain,/ A slave that is not twentieth part the tithe/ Of your precedent lord, a vice of kings . . .' 'No more,' she begs, but the image of Claudius as the devil and buffoon of the medieval theatre suddenly obsesses him. 'A king of shreds and patches,' he continues, but here he is interrupted. For the Ghost is suddenly there in the room with them.

'In his nightgown' suggests the stage direction of the First Quarto. The last time we see the Ghost, remarks Barbara Everett of this scene, he is 'a man in a dressing-gown whose wife cannot even see him', which may be a little too modern in its lack of empathy, but does catch something of the extreme oddity of the situation. Why does the Ghost choose this moment to reappear? And why (that much is clear) not in the warlike armour of his first appearance? And why is he this time visible to Hamlet alone?

Because there are as many answers to these questions as there are commentators, we should perhaps content ourselves with the observation that the play is full of such question-provoking events, which may be imputed to Shakespeare's instinct for the theatrically effective ploy, but which also serve a deeper purpose and certainly contribute to our sense of this play, more than any other, as being close to dream or nightmare.

Hamlet too has questions to ask of the Ghost, though the way he frames them suggests his own sense of why the Ghost has come:

> Do you not come your tardy son to chide,
> That, laps'd in time and passion, lets go by
> Th'important acting of your dread command?
> O say. (107–10)

Like the judge in Kierkegaard's *Either/Or*, the Ghost has always urged his son to take part in *his* play, to 'act' his command, and, like the young man in *Either/Or*, Hamlet has found himself incapable of obeying despite the fact that he knows the older man might well be right. And, like the Judge, the Ghost can only reiterate what he has said before:

> Do not forget. This visitation
> Is but to whet thy almost blunted purpose. (110–11)

This of course is the first time the nuclear family has been together on stage. And the Ghost, having admonished Hamlet, reminds him that Gertrude must be spared. She seems distracted, he says to Hamlet, speak to her. When he does so the reason for her distraction is made plain: first her son poured torrents of abuse on her, and now he speaks to thin air: 'O gentle son,' she says, 'Upon the heat and flame of thy distemper/ Sprinkle cool patience. Whereon do you look?'

This could be comic, but it is of course, after all that has just happened, anything but. Hamlet tries to get her to see what he sees, but she remains confused: 'To whom do you speak this?' When he tries to explain she repeats that there is nothing there. Again he tries in vain to explain, but the Ghost turns and vanishes. 'This,' she says, 'is the very coinage of your brain.' But that is too much for him. Her failure to see must be the result of the corruption of her soul, her total abandonment of her former husband. Please, he begs her,

> Confess yourself to heaven,
> Repent what's past, avoid what is to come;
> And do not spread the compost on the weeds
> To make them ranker. (151–4)

Like all family quarrels, which are never quite about what they seem to be about, this one starts to go round in circles. 'O Hamlet,' she cries, 'thou hast cleft my heart in twain', and again it is impossible to disentangle her horror at what has become of *him* from her sheer sense of despair at what *her* life has come to. But he is once more riding the high horse of his rhetoric: 'O throw away the worser part of it/ And live the purer with the other half.' And then, abruptly, as is his wont: 'Good night.'

Yet, exactly as in his encounter with Ophelia, he cannot bear to let go: 'But go not to my uncle's bed,' he admonishes her, and moves into a long disquisition on how if one stands fast in the face of temptation one will gradually overcome it. Again he makes to leave, again he says goodnight, and again he returns to the attack: 'And when you are desirous to be blest,/ I'll blessing beg of you.' And then, presumably seeing the dead Polonius:

> For this same lord
> I do repent; but heaven hath pleas'd it so,
> To punish me with this and this with me,
> That I must be their scourge and minister. (174–7)

Critics who study the play in the leisure of their rooms take a high moral tone here and accuse Hamlet of callousness. It seems to me to be in keeping with Hamlet's sense that the man is dead, and at his hands, and, since, strictly speaking, it is his doing, he takes full responsibility before God. At the same time he tries to see himself as playing the role of avenger and justifies whatever he might have done in terms of some higher destiny: 'heaven hath pleas'd it so'. This is not so much callousness as profound confusion.

Again he says goodnight, again he stops for one last word, as though, like Othello, he cannot let go of the images that torment him. Ostensibly warning her not to let on to the King that he is 'mad but in craft', he in fact gives way to one final cry of agony, as painful to listen to in its piling up of images one upon the other, in its mingling of sexual excitement and metaphysical torment, as Lear's rants on the blasted heath:

> Let the bloat King tempt you again to bed,
> Pinch wanton on your cheek, call you his mouse,
> And let him, for a pair of reechy kisses,
> Or paddling in your neck with his damn'd fingers,
> Make you to ravel all this matter out
> That I essentially am not in madness,
> But mad in craft . . .
> No, in despite of sense and secrecy,
> Unpeg the basket on the house's top,
> Let the birds fly, and like the famous ape,
> To try conclusions, in the basket creep,
> And break your own neck down. (184–98)

Be assured, she says, I will not breathe a word. And just as suddenly as he had launched into his exhortation, he becomes totally practical. Feeling that she has come over to his side, he tells her about the trip he must make to England with his two schoolfellows 'whom I will trust as I will adders fang'd'. He has things in control, however, he tells her,

> For 'tis the sport to have the enginer
> Hoist with his own petard, and 't shall go hard
> But I will delve one yard below their mines
> And blow them at the moon. (208–11)

It is not hard to read into the lines a kind of relief that in dealing with such matters he is dealing at last with what is clear and susceptible of resolution: foiling plots against his life is easy compared to the impossible demands of his father and the confusion inside him. As for this fellow, he concludes, taking hold of the corpse of the old courtier, 'I'll lug the guts into the neighbour room.' And then, almost jauntily, he departs with an elegantly crafted couplet:

> Mother, good night indeed. This counsellor
> Is now most still, most secret, and most grave,
> Who was in life a foolish prating knave.
> Come, sir, to draw toward an end with you.
> Good night, mother. (215–19)

FOLD ELEVEN

11.1 (IV. 1)

Hamlet has left, but the Queen remains. The Arden edition of the play I have been using starts not only a new scene here but a new act. And it does this in common with the editorial tradition at large. Jenkins, however, in his long note appended to the start of this scene, voices his discomfort with this. 'It is against all convention,' he says, 'for a character to leave the stage at the end of one scene and immediately re-enter in another' (p. 523). And he quotes Greg as saying: 'It is a disaster that editors have followed a late quarto in choosing this of all points at which to begin a new act' (p. 334). Yet editors, wedded to the division into acts and scenes with which the tradition has saddled them, seem helpless in the face of the manifest evidence of the play (the most recent Arden editors, Ann Thompson and Neil Taylor, devote an entire appendix to the problem but do not add anything that might make for a neat resolution). Directors, who have to make decisions of this kind all the time, today follow the convention of breaking the play somewhere in the middle to provide an interval for the audience to stretch their legs and spend money at the bar. But every director and every actor taking on the role of Hamlet will have his or her sense of the rhythm of the play as a whole, and all feel that somewhere around here we seem to move across the waterline of the Alpine range that is *Hamlet*, and that somewhere around here – the killing of Polonius, the open confrontation with his mother – we start, after having climbed for so long (though not always aware of it), upon the long descent. The advantage of thinking of the play in terms of a Mallarmean fan, fold on fold, is that we do not have to pinpoint precisely where, since there is clearly no precise point but only terrain as murky and difficult to decipher as the rest of the play.

What is clear is that Claudius bursts into the Queen's chamber, probably alerted by the raised voices. 'Where is your son?' he asks, all thought that Hamlet is his nephew and even, as he suggested in the opening scene, a sort of son to him, long gone. As in the narratives of the Hebrew Bible, where the way a person is described tells us how we are to stand in relation to them – Michal, for example, is described as 'the daughter of Saul' or 'the wife of David' depending on whose side she is perceived to be on in the struggle between the two men – so here Claudius places his wife firmly on the side of his problematic nephew, and thus implicitly against himself: 'Where is your son?' She responds only with the pathos of 'Ah, mine own lord, what have I seen tonight!' Trying to hold the two together in a general cry of sorrow, a cry which will recur like a leitmotif throughout the remainder of the play, she is also careful to stress her bond to Claudius.

But where is Hamlet, Claudius wants to know. He's 'Mad as the sea and wind,' she returns, and explains how, 'in his lawless fit', hearing something stir behind the arras, he

> Whips out his rapier, cries 'A rat, a rat',
> And in this brainish apprehension kills
> The unseen good old man. (10–12)

Claudius immediately realises the import of this: 'It had been so with us had we been there.' It confirms him in his belief that Hamlet, free to roam about the court, is a threat to all of them, but, consummate politician that he is, he also sees the threat Polonius's murder poses to his authority:

> It will be laid to us, whose providence
> Should have kept short, restrain'd, and out of haunt
> This mad young man. (17–19)

Brilliantly he turns the notion that something is rotten in the state of Denmark into an indictment of Hamlet, the cause of the rot:

> But so much was our love,
> We would not understand what was most fit,
> But like the owner of a foul disease,
> To keep it from divulging [becoming public], let it feed
> Even on the pith of life. (19–23)

Like all politicians, he no doubt half believes it even as he utters it.

There is still the practical problem: where is Hamlet? Gertrude, as she had promised her son, remains loyal to him. He has gone, she says,

> To draw apart the body he hath kill'd,
> O'er whom – his very madness, like some ore
> Among a mineral of metals base,
> Shows itself pure – a weeps for what is done. (24–7)

– which is a manifest untruth.

Claudius, however, has seen that in one sense Hamlet's action has played into his hands: 'we will ship him hence,' he says, and calls for Guildenstern. Inevitably, *both* Hamlet's schoolfellows appear, and Claudius explains the situation, and instructs them to find Hamlet and the body. To Gertrude he explains that it's important to counter the slander that is likely to spread throughout the country when the news of Polonius's death emerges. We have to let people know, he says, 'both what we mean to do/ And what's untimely done.' Done, that is, outside the normal process of time, a strange epithet, but suggesting that Claudius too now feels, or rather, is prepared to state explicitly, that the time is out of joint. And as he closes the scene with a rhymed couplet he sounds almost like Hamlet:

O come away,
My soul is full of discord and dismay. (44–5)

11.2 (IV. 2)

At once we are back with Hamlet and the corpse of Polonius, a corpse as fought and argued over as that of any fallen Greek or Trojan in the *Iliad*. 'Safely stowed,' mutters Hamlet, continuing, even to himself, in the matter-of-fact tone he'd adopted for talking about the old man's corpse at the end of the meeting with his mother. But now the others are calling for him, and they then rush in. 'What have you done, my lord [note the obligatory title], with the dead body?' asks Rosencrantz. But with them Hamlet is as skittish as he has always been and, when they press him, changes the subject:

Ham. Do not believe it.
Ros. Believe what?
Ham. That I can keep your counsel and not mine own. Besides, to be demanded of a sponge – what replication should be made by the son of a king?
Ros. Take you me for a sponge, my lord?
Ham. Ay, sir, that soaks up the King's countenance, his rewards, his authorities ... When he needs what you have gleaned, it is but squeezing you and, sponge, you shall be dry again.
Ros. I understand you not, my lord.
Ham. I am glad of it. A knavish speech sleeps in a foolish ear.
Ros. My lord, you must tell us where the body is and go with us to the King.

Ham. The body is with the King, but the King is not with the
     body. The King is a thing –
Guild. A thing, my lord?
Ham. Of nothing. Bring me to him. (8–28)

I have quoted practically the entirety of the scene because exchanges
like this tend to be only dimly remembered since nothing much
happens, or subsumed under the general rubric of 'Hamlet's wit',
or mined for information about Hamlet's attitude to the murder
he has just committed. But if we only dimly remember it, it nevertheless forms part of our subliminal sense of what kind of a person
Hamlet is, and its combination of riddling humour and refusal to
give his enemies any hold on him is what makes us love him and
identify with him quite as much as the metaphysical soul-searching
of his soliloquies. The image of the spy as a sponge is both wonderfully apt and profoundly insulting in its view of the two men as
mere objects, without any will of their own, while the riddle of the
King and the body identifies Claudius and Polonius, asks questions about the immortal symbol of kingship ('Denmark', as Old
Hamlet is called), as opposed to the mortal body that bears that
symbol, and seems disdainfully to make not just of his henchmen
but of Claudius himself a mere object – a thing of nothing. 'Thus
a metaphysical profundity is turned into a deliberate anticlimax,'
as Jenkins elegantly phrases it (p. 339).

11.3 (IV. 3)

And now we are with the King, who in his opening line picks up
the closing words of the previous fold: 'I have sent to seek him and
to find the body.' He goes on, however, to reiterate the need, once
Hamlet is found, to get him out of Denmark, though for a reason
not previously mentioned: 'He's lov'd of the distracted multitude'
– though since a short while later we will be told the same thing
about Laertes it may be that there is an element of paranoia at
work here: for a king who has killed to get the throne, whether it
be Bolingbroke, Macbeth or Claudius, there will always be the

fear that at any moment one of his subjects will enlist 'the people' to help topple him in turn.

Hamlet is brought in, but is as little willing to satisfy the King as he was to give a straight answer to Rosencrantz and Guildenstern. Now, however, he is before a superior, and probably under guard – more like Christ before Pilate than like Socrates with his students. In answer to the question of where Polonius is, he answers: 'At supper.' The King is puzzled: 'At supper? Where?' 'Not where he eats,' explains Hamlet, 'but where a is eaten. A certain convocation of politic worms are e'en at him.' And he proceeds to turn rhetorical somersaults on this common late medieval theme, playing on the name of the famous meeting in Worms presided over by the Emperor, at which Luther was excommunicated, the Diet of Worms (still good material for comedy three centuries later in *1066 and All That*), and ending with a series of dazzling paradoxes, quite as startling as those the earlier Middle Ages loved to explore concerning Christ as both creator of the world and son of his mother: 'A man may fish with the worm that hath eat of a king, and eat of the fish that hath fed of that worm' (27–9).

The King tries to stem the flow, first with an 'Alas, alas', presumably believing, or pretending to believe, that Hamlet is far gone, but then returning to his blunt: 'Where is Polonius?' In his response to this Hamlet seems to veer wildly off course again, though we dimly feel that there is indeed method in his madness; then abruptly he gives Claudius what he wants:

> In heaven. Send thither to see. If your messenger find him not there, seek him i'th'other place [Hell] yourself. But if indeed you find him not within this month you shall nose [smell] him as you go up the stairs into the lobby. (32–7)

While waiting for the body to be found Claudius informs Hamlet that, for his own safety, he is sending him to England. To England? Hamlet asks, as if this is the first he's heard of it, then appears to resign himself: 'But come, for England. Farewell, dear mother.'

The effect on the audience of this insistence on England, as with the earlier appearance of the players talking of the problems afflicting the contemporary English stage, is like that of having the Ghost stamp around under the stage: it acts as a reminder that this is not 'reality', that we are not really in Denmark but in an English play being performed in London. This is not to say that we lose all belief in what we are seeing on the stage, in Hamlet's felt entrapment both within the court and in the call of his murdered father for vengeance. On the contrary, it shows us how easy it is both to believe and not believe at the same time, and thus develops one of the central themes of the play.

Hamlet's reply is by no means odd. Even though his mother is not present she is always in his thoughts; it was her plea that had led to his staying in Denmark in the first place, and now he ignores Claudius, who stands before him, and says an internal goodbye to her. Claudius takes this as a snub, which perhaps it is, and seeks to correct him: 'Thy loving father, Hamlet.' That is always a dangerous thing to do with this man who is never short of words: 'My mother,' Hamlet insists. 'Father and mother is man and wife, man and wife is one flesh; so my mother. Come, for England' (53–5).

He rushes out and Claudius immediately sends his men after him with instructions to get him on board the ship at once. Left alone, Claudius makes it clear to us that if the King of England follows his instructions, which as his vassal he is bound to do, Hamlet will soon be dead. 'Do it, England,' he concludes; 'For like the hectic in my blood he rages/ And thou must cure me.'

11.4 (IV. 4)

The portion of this fold designated Act IV, scene 4 by the editorial tradition (both Quarto and Folio have long given up divisions into acts and scenes by this stage) is the prime example for those, like me, who believe the Folio text represents Shakespeare's final corrections as he helped prepare the play for the stage. In the Folio it consists of eight lines: Fortinbras enters 'with his Army', and instructs an officer to inform the Danish king that he is here, as previously agreed, to cross this corner of his land in peace on his way to Poland, and, before he does so, to 'express our duty in his eye [face to face]'. This is the kind of scene Shakespeare was to perfect in the years to come, culminating in the hectic criss-crossing of armies on stage in *Antony and Cleopatra* a few years later, and it was to have an important influence on Brecht and his followers in the twentieth century.

We have heard of Young Fortinbras at intervals throughout the play, how hot-headed he is, how he sought, against his father's wishes, to regain from Denmark the lands Old Hamlet had conquered, how he had been overruled but wished now to cross Denmark on his way to conquer other lands. And now we see him, briefly, fully engaged in what he is doing, with no time for thought or banter. 'I will do't, my lord,' says the officer, and Fortinbras replies: 'Go safely on.'

In the Quarto what he says is: 'Go softly on', but Shakespeare must have realised that such language was Hamlet's and that it would dilute our sense of his hero if he used the phrase indiscriminately. On the other hand it is easy to see why he should have done so in the first place, Hamlet spreading his 'mood music' over the play as surely as Kierkegaard suggested Don Giovanni did his over Mozart's opera. But it is out of words that literature is made and a whole raft of such minute changes, as John Jones has shown in *Shakespeare at Work*, results in the Folio being, for many of us, on the whole a finer thing than the Quarto.

The second change Shakespeare made to this scene had to do not with the alteration of one word but with the excision of almost sixty lines, including one of Hamlet's best-loved soliloquies, 'How all occasions do inform against me'. This is too much for editors to bear and, until recently, they have given it all to us, as have most directors in the theatre. But I am sure John Jones is right in his view that the soliloquy only repeats what had been said better in the soliloquy Hamlet utters after he has heard the Player, 'O what a rogue and peasant slave am I!' (II. 2. 544ff.). There he tormented himself with the thought that the actor could shed tears for a fictional heroine while he, whose own father had been killed and whose mother was either implicated in the murder or at least had with undue haste married the murderer, seemed hardly able to feel a thing. Here, after a conversation with the Captain, who explains what this army is, and that it is off to fight for a barren strip of land of no interest to anyone, Hamlet meditates on the folly of men and, in lines whose grammatical confusion only expresses his own confused feelings, draws a similar conclusion:

> Rightly to be great
> Is not to stir without great argument,
> But greatly to find quarrel in a straw
> When honour's at the stake. How stand I then,
> That have a father kill'd [who has been killed], a mother
>   stain'd . . .
> And let all sleep, while to my shame I see
> The imminent death of twenty thousand men
> That, for a fantasy and trick of fame,
> Go to their graves like beds . . . (53–62)

Shakespeare had known from very early on that he had no shortage of the primary skill of the maker, *inventio*, but that his very facility meant that he was prone to let language run away with him. One can see him, in play after play, seeking means to harness this to his true purposes, and in *Hamlet*, as one compares Quarto 2 and Folio, one can see that what he chiefly does is cut, not fill out. Here he dares to sacrifice some good but redundant lines for the good of the whole. Picasso, who faced the same temptations and dealt with them in much the same way, and who once said, 'kill the local beauty for the sake of the larger truth', would have approved. What is needed at this point in the play is a series of short scenes, hurrying the action on, after the long-drawn-out scenes of the opening half and the even longer scenes with which it will end: eight lines, a first glimpse of Fortinbras, that is quite enough.

The existence of two versions, one short, one long, brings out clearly what Margreta de Grazia has so acutely noted, the extreme oddity of this play, which seems less, like *Lear*, to consist of two very different approaches to the same material, and more to possess a kind of infinite flexibility of length – a quality, though she does not say this, which links it to works of prose fiction like those of Rabelais and Sterne, which do not really end and seem able to stretch or contract without too much damage to their essential qualities, more than to drama of any kind, certainly to drama as it is found in the classical tradition of the West from Aeschylus to Chekhov.

FOLD TWELVE

12.1 (IV. 5. 1–73)

Now Ophelia, so long in the shadow of her father and of Hamlet, is about to have her day.

This is another of those scenes, like that of the Player's speech, which is at once wholly unexpected, not strictly necessary, and yet an essential element in our sense of this play. Even more than that earlier scene, though, it has detached itself from the play in which it is embedded and, in the subsequent centuries, taken on a life of its own. All the more reason then to see how it unfolds here.

It begins *in medias res*. 'I will not speak with her,' says the Queen. A courtier tells her that Ophelia is importunate, distracted: 'Her mood will needs be pitied.' She talks much of her murdered father, it seems, yet it is difficult to make out quite what it is she says:

> Her speech is nothing,
> Yet the unshaped use of it doth move
> The hearers to collection. They aim at it,
> And botch the words up fit to their own thoughts,
> Which, as her winks and nods and gestures yield them,
> Indeed would make one think there might be thought,
> Though nothing sure, yet much unhappily. (7–13)

Well then, says the Queen, let her come in. But before Ophelia does so Gertrude confesses to a heavy heart, a 'sick soul', and to her feeling that each little thing 'seems prologue to some great amiss'. In witnessing Ophelia's distress, then, we will be in a sense witnessing that of both the women at the centre of Hamlet's thoughts and of this play.

Ophelia enters, and what follows will give director and actor ample information, allowing them to decide how she is to be dressed and how she is to be played. For what we now have is one of those horrifying scenes, of which Cassandra's at the end of the *Agamemnon* is the prototype, where a woman appears before us who no longer knows the proper conventions of behaviour and who is, for those who witness her both on stage and in the audience, an object of pity and horror.

And just as Cassandra keens, howls and prophesies, so Ophelia sings. These snatches of old ballads, some of which survive, speak both of death and of a woman abandoned by her lover, thus binding together the two men who seem to have been central to her life, her father and Hamlet. But it is quite wrong to seek to pin specific meanings to each of her utterances. What we sense as we see and listen is that the two men, whose conflicting demands on her must already have been difficult to bear, now that she knows that one killed the other, creates in her just such a knot, such an unresolvable conflict, as Hamlet had experienced in trying to reconcile his mother with Claudius's wife. And as that knot drove Hamlet close to madness, so this one seems to have driven Ophelia right into it.

The horror, for us, comes from the sweetness of her voice and the fact that the conventional music and words so clearly hide a terrible darkness which cannot be directly uttered:

> *How should I your true love know*
> *From another one?*
> *By his cockle hat and staff*
> *And his sandal shoon.* (23–6)

An innocuous old song or saying is suddenly filled with a new and threatening life when yanked out of its context and inserted into a new one, as with 'Why, let the strucken deer go weep' (III. 2. 265); and a quoted text is given a new twist by being commented upon by others, as we have seen in the case of Hamlet's letter to Ophelia, read and commented upon by Polonius to the King and Queen, and of the Player's speech, commented upon by Polonius and Hamlet (in all this again very like Rabelais, Cervantes and Sterne). Now the Queen interrupts with: 'Alas, sweet lady, what imports this song?' But Ophelia is not in a state to explain: 'Say you?' she responds, then goes her way: 'Nay, pray you mark.' And she sings again:

> *He is dead and gone, lady,*
> *He is dead and gone,*
> *At his head a grass-green turf,*
> *At his heels a stone.* (29–32)

The Queen interrupts once more, but again Ophelia overrides her with a 'Pray you mark.' But now, as she picks up again, the King enters. He listens a while and then interrupts: 'How do you, pretty lady?' 'Well,' she answers, 'good dild you [God yield you].' And then she is off, not in verse this time but in prose, her words as clear and as opaque as Hamlet's in his replies to the King and his courtiers. It is as if Shakespeare, having seen how far language can go before it descends into the pure scream or laugh, wishes to test it yet further – a form of theatre he carries to breaking point in *Lear* and which helps to explain the hold he has had on directors searching for an ever more visceral and physical theatre, from Artaud to Peter Brook: 'They say the owl was a baker's daughter. Lord, we know what we are, but know not what we may be. God be at your table' (42–4).

Claudius is convinced she is talking about her father, but Ophelia – rather like Hamlet asking Rosencrantz and Guildenstern what right they have to try to play upon him as they would upon a pipe – answers firmly, clear in her madness: 'Pray, let's have no words of this, but when they ask you what it means, say you this:

Tomorrow is Saint Valentine's day,
*   All in the morning betime,*
And I a maid at your window,
*   To be your Valentine.*
Then up he rose, and donn'd his clo'es,
*   And dupp'd [opened] the chamber door,*
Let in the maid that out a maid
*   Never departed more.* (48–55)

The meaning is in the song. Do not ask what it is, just listen.

How long has she been like this? asks the King, but instead of the Queen it is Ophelia who speaks again, in prose now. This is even more painful to take, for her words purport to be sensible and rational and yet she remains locked in a world of her own, unable ever to untie the knot of contradictions which has brought her to this state:

I hope all will be well. We must be patient. But I cannot choose but weep to think they would lay him i'th' cold ground. My brother shall know of it. And so I thank you for your good counsel. Come, my coach. Good night, ladies, good night. Sweet ladies, good night, good night. (68–73)

12.2 (IV. 5. 74–216)

No sooner is she gone than Claudius unburdens himself of his many anxieties to his wife: 'O Gertrude, Gertrude,/ When sorrows come, they come not single spies,/ But in battalions.' There is Ophelia's descent into insanity, her father's death, 'your son gone', the people muttering about Polonius's death and the undue secrecy and haste with which he has been buried and, on top of all that, Laertes, it seems, has returned in secret from France, and is being fed all sorts of rumours about his father's murder. 'O my dear Gertrude, this,/ Like to a murd'ring-piece, in many places/ Gives me superfluous death' – that is, like a scattergun which can kill many people at once, this has killed me many times over.

There is no doubt that Claudius believes what he says, no suggestion that he is play-acting before Gertrude. Like many tyrants, he is prone to self-pity and careful to avoid taking the blame. It is fascinating, though, how the accidental death of Polonius seems to have led almost everyone to feel that they are caught in a trap not of their own making and from which they cannot escape.

And, indeed, no sooner has Claudius unburdened himself of his fears and doubts than there is 'a noise within', and a messenger enters with the news that Laertes, like an avenging angel and buoyed up by the cries of the populace shouting 'Laertes shall be king', is fast approaching. Just as the King cries out: 'The doors are broke', Laertes enters; 'with followers', says the Quarto, though the Folio has him enter, like Ophelia in the previous scene, alone.

Like her, he takes centre stage. It is his moment (as, perhaps, she dimly knew that was *her* moment):

> O thou vile king,
> Give me my father. (115–16)

Laertes is in his element in the world of revenge tragedy, more than happy to play his part, as Hamlet emphatically was not. When the King begs him to keep calm, he does not, like Hamlet, deploy wit to find another meaning for 'calm', but throws the word back in his face:

> That drop of blood that's calm proclaims me bastard,
> Cries cuckold to my father, brands the harlot
> Even here between the chaste unsmirched brow
> Of my true mother. (117–20)

This is the first we've heard of Mrs Polonius, and indeed she is only brought in, in all her other-worldly purity, to lend force to Laertes's claim that he would be besmirching both his parents' memory if he stayed calm in the face of what has happened.

Claudius responds with a show of regal confidence and dignity. Let him go, he orders Gertrude, who must have tried to hold him back: no one would dare attack a divinely ordained monarch (this is the first and last we hear of such practices in Denmark). Tell me, he orders Laertes, what is your grievance? 'Where is my father?' 'Dead.' 'But not by him,' interjects Gertrude. 'How came he dead?' presses Laertes, ignoring her, and then, once more, his righteous anger bursts forth:

> I'll not be juggled with.
> To hell, allegiance! Vows to the blackest devil!
> Conscience and grace, to the profoundest pit!
> I dare damnation . . .
> Let come what comes only I'll be reveng'd
> Most thoroughly for my father. (130–5)

The imperative of revenge for a murdered father, in other words, trumps the danger of the avenger ending up damned in hell.

Slowly, though, Claudius succeeds in calming him down. Are you really determined to avenge your father? Yes. Whoever it was who did it? Yes. Then let me tell you that I am guiltless and can give you a full account of the man who did it.

But before he can do so there is, again, 'a noise within', and Ophelia makes a second entry.

However she is dressed, whatever her movements, whether she comes in singing or starts to sing once she is on stage, her effect on her brother is instantaneous:

> O heat, dry up my brains. Tears seven times salt
> Burn out the sense and virtue of mine eye.
> By heaven, thy madness shall be paid with weight
> Till our scale turn the beam. (154–7)

But just as Ophelia was forced out of her private universe by the sight of Hamlet mad, so here Laertes is by the sight of her. The

brother and sister share an appealing innocence and a generous
spirit. He goes on:

> O rose of May!
> Dear maid – kind sister – sweet Ophelia –
> O heavens, is't possible a young maid's wits
> Should be as mortal as an old man's life? (157–60)

Locked in her private world now, she goes on singing, interrupting her songs with her own commentary. Though 'Fare you
well, my dove' in what follows is printed as part of the song in F:

> *They bore him bare-fac'd on the bier,*
> *And in his grave rain'd many a tear –*
> Fare you well, my dove. (164–6)

Laertes can only say: 'Hadst thou thy wits and didst persuade
revenge,/ It could not move thus.'

As they listen she starts to talk again of 'hapless maidens and
deceits in love', as Jenkins puts it (p. 395), and then proceeds to
hand them all imaginary flowers: 'There's rosemary, that's for
remembrance – pray you, love, remember. And there is pansies,
that's for thoughts.' As Jenkins notes, by asking her brother to
remember, Ophelia plays the same role in his life as the Ghost does
in Hamlet's. But of course rosemary is normally exchanged by
lovers, thus setting up a counter-current and suggesting that at this
moment Laertes is actually standing in for Hamlet in her disor-
dered imagination. And, like Hamlet with the dumb-show, Laertes
here acts the chorus: 'A document in madness: thoughts and
remembrance fitted.' Oblivious, she goes on, returning to her
father at the end: 'I would give you some violets, but they withered
all when my father died. They say a made a good end.' Violets
were traditionally given to lovers, bringing out clearly that just as
Hamlet could not keep Ophelia and his mother from merging
into the single figure of the betraying woman, so Ophelia cannot
keep the loss of her father and of her lover from merging into one,

which is even more pitiful, given that the one is responsible for the death of the other: '*For bonny sweet Robin is all my joy*,' she sings, and then:

> *And will a not come again?*
> *And will a not come again?*
>   *No, no, he is dead,*
>   *Go to thy death-bed,*
> *He never will come again.* (187–91)

'*God a mercy on his soul*,' she ends, and adds, 'And of all Christian souls. God buy [be with] you.'

Claudius wastes no time in keeping up the pressure on Laertes. Come, he says to him, I'll prove to you I am not guilty of your father's murder. But now Laertes wants to know why his father was so hurriedly and obscurely buried, 'no noble rite, nor formal ostentation' – in other words, no proper funeral. I will explain it all, Claudius assures him, concluding with one of the gnomic invocations of doom to come which have always formed part of the language of tragedy: 'And where th'offence is, let the great axe fall.'

Why was Polonius in fact not given a proper funeral? Why does Claudius seem to collude with Hamlet in, so to speak, attempting to wipe the loquacious old councillor from memory? Scholars have racked their brains to explain it, but it remains one of the many dark areas of this mysterious play. Is it because Claudius wanted the death hushed up in order to protect Hamlet, and thus, in the end, himself? Is it that he somehow hoped Laertes would not hear of it, for a while at least? Enough to say that that is how it is, and it is a major cause of Laertes's anger, hypersensitive as he is to questions of honour and protocol.

FOLD THIRTEEN

(IV. 6)

Another brief episode, another letter to be perused and deciphered. It is from Hamlet, brought to Horatio by certain sailors. In it Hamlet tells his trusted friend what has happened to him at sea. Not two days out from port they were attacked by pirates, and in the *mêlée* Hamlet managed to get on board the pirate vessel while the ship, with Rosencrantz and Guildenstern still in it, escaped, and is on its way to England. Now the pirates seek to ransom him. All he can say at the moment is: 'I have words to speak in thine ear [the ear again!] will make thee dumb', and he asks that Horatio go with the sailors, who will bring him to Hamlet.

Thus does Shakespeare deftly lock the varied elements of his plot into place.

FOLD FOURTEEN

14.1 (IV. 7. 1–161)

Back then to Claudius and Laertes. The latter has calmed down enough to raise a few questions about the King's version of his father's death. But why, he asks, if Hamlet in effect attempted a coup, did you not take action? Two reasons, returns the King. First, to spare his mother, who adores him; and then because of the love the common people have for him. Laertes takes this in:

> And so I have a noble father lost,
> A sister driven into desp'rate terms,
> Whose worth, if praises may go back again,
> Stood challenger on mount of all the age
> For her perfections. But my revenge will come. (25–9)

'Break not your sleeps for that,' the King reassures him. 'I lov'd your father,' he goes on, 'and we love ourself', and for both those reasons I have made certain plans, which I will lay out before you in good time.

But this is not a play where time is idle. A messenger enters, with letters brought by certain sailors. Again, a letter of Hamlet's is read out loud and we are reminded of all the scenes within scenes in this play, all the letters read out, the apparitions, the plays performed, or partly performed. The life of this play is thick with ghostly presences.

> *High and mighty, you shall know I am set naked on your kingdom.*
> *Tomorrow shall I beg leave to see your kingly eyes, when I shall,*
> *first asking your pardon, thereunto recount the occasion of my*
> *sudden and more strange return. Hamlet.* (41–6)

Again, Claudius, and we, know more than anyone else and we can gauge the degree of bewilderment and anxiety with which he responds to this: 'What should this mean? Are all the rest come back?/ Or is it some abuse, and no such thing?' (Is it a joke of some sort and not really the case?)

They proceed to try and decipher the enigma. Is it Hamlet's handwriting? asks Laertes. It is, says the king. 'Naked,' he reads out, and adds, mysteriously, since we thought he had read out the whole letter: 'And in a postscript here he says "Alone".' What can it mean?

'I am lost in it, my lord,' responds Laertes,

> But let him come.
> It warms the very sickness in my heart
> That I shall live and tell him to his teeth,
> 'Thus diest thou.' (53–6)

Not very good at working things out, Laertes is in his element when it comes to questions of honour. His father, who had, we recall, had serious doubts about him, would have been proud of him had he been alive to see him at this moment. But Claudius knows that if he is to get his way he has to control his impetuosity, so he now hints that he has a scheme to get rid of Hamlet which will leave no trace of blame on anyone, and even his mother will have to accept that it was nothing but an accident.

To Laertes, he explains further. Hamlet, he says, is extremely competitive, and your skill at fencing has been highly touted, in particular by a Frenchman who was here recently, a certain Lamord (the Folio, we remember, has Lamound); so much so that Hamlet was impelled to say that he wished you would quickly return from Paris so that he could take you on. And so? asks Laertes, which gives Claudius the chance, Iago-like, to pull him close into his orbit by a sudden shift of direction:

> Laertes, was your father dear to you?
> Or are you like the painting of a sorrow,
> A face without a heart? (106–8)

And when Laertes, as expected, protests, Claudius presses home his advantage: of course I know you loved your father, but time has a habit of blunting these passions. He then meanders off into a long, abstract speech about how, wanting to do things very much, we nevertheless make excuse after excuse and end up not doing anything. Shakespeare wisely cut this in the Folio version, and it is found only in the Quarto (113–22). Evidence that he felt even as he was writing that he was not getting anywhere – which would have been fine had Polonius been speaking, since not getting anywhere was central to Shakespeare's conception of his character, but is clearly wrong for the politically astute and highly manipulative Claudius – is found in the way he closes (which is where the Folio picks up):

> But to the quick of th'ulcer:
> Hamlet comes back; what would you undertake
> To show yourself in deed your father's son
> More than in words? (122–5)

Laertes needs no prompting: 'To cut his throat i'th' church,' he responds, taking us back to the moment when Hamlet hesitated to do just that with Claudius, who, of course unaware of the irony, merely compounds it:

> No place indeed should murder sanctuarize;
> Revenge should have no bounds. (126–7)

That, however, will not be necessary, Claudius goes on, and
explains his plan: to arrange a fencing match between Hamlet and
Laertes, and then, since

> He, being remiss,
> Most generous, and free from all contriving,
> Will not peruse the foils, so that with ease –
> Or with a little shuffling – you may choose
> A sword unbated [whose end is not covered], and in pass
>   of practice
> Requite him for your father. (133–8)

Claudius is so deeply imbued with the ethics of self-preservation at
all costs, if ethics it can be called, that he quite unselfconsciously
invokes Hamlet's very openness and generosity of spirit as the
means by which they may do away with him. And a sign of how
deeply Laertes has now been sucked into this world, or perhaps
only of how little the ethic of revenge retains its old link to honour
in all its forms, is that we find him eagerly developing this scenario:
he will not only contrive to stab Hamlet with an 'unbated' sword,
he will 'anoint' it (the religious connotations are surely meant by
Shakespeare, though the word was often used simply to mean
'wet') with a deadly poison bought by him 'of a mountebank', and
so make doubly sure of Hamlet.

Claudius manages to cap even this: to make the whole thing
absolutely fool-proof, he says, I will prepare a poisoned drink,
which I will offer Hamlet in the course of the bout,

> whereon but sipping,
> If he by chance escape your venom'd stuck [sword-thrust],
> Our purpose may hold there. (159–61)

There is something melodramatic and excessive about the whole
scene, as there is indeed about the whole play. Scholars have
fastened on the name of the Frenchman who has come to Elsinore
with reports of Laertes's fencing skill, Lamord, and argued that he

is none other than La Mort, Death. This is what this play does to you: everything starts to seem both meaningful and, at the same time, quite meaningless. What is clear is that such a contrived scene fits in perfectly with what we have seen of the machinations of Claudius and his henchmen Polonius, Rosencrantz and Guildenstern. For them spying – acting in such a way as to influence events while making it seem that it is simply nature taking its course, seeking to 'uncover' the 'secrets' they believe reside in each man's heart, all in the name of security – all of this is so much a way of life that they accept it as natural. Hamlet and Ophelia are clearly on the other side of this divide, while Gertrude ambiguously hovers between the two worlds, and Laertes, who had seemed as honest and innocent as his sister, shows how easy it is to cross over from the one to the other.

But there are, of course, other divides, equally clear, equally easy to blur, such as the one between sanity and madness. It is this with which we are now confronted.

14.2 (IV. 7. 162–93)

In Grand Opera, the saying goes, the show is not over till the fat lady sings – till the heroine's final lament, that is, often a *Liebestod* or song of love and death, brings the whole thing to an end. In very pre-Romantic fashion Shakespeare brings forward the heroine's last song to a point about four-fifths of the way through (the editorial tradition places it at the end of the fourth act, though as I have said there are no acts or scenes signalled in the Quarto or Folio after the first half of the play), and, more to the point, he makes of it not her song but a dirge – a song by someone else describing her end.

And this is right, for Ophelia, like Hamlet, has never felt at ease in any of the roles she has been asked to play: daughter, lover or member of Claudius's court. Like Hamlet she felt – and Shakespeare has made us feel her feeling – that there were no words and no modes of discourse appropriate to her condition, and, by the end, that there was a terrible knot at the heart of her affective life, the knowledge that the man she loved and admired had killed the father she had unquestioningly obeyed, if not revered, all her life.

It has to be the other woman at the heart of this play, Gertrude, who utters the dirge, and, in doing so, merges momentarily with her. She rushes in, interrupting the plotting of Claudius and Laertes:

> One woe doth tread upon another's heel,
> So fast they follow. Your sister's drown'd, Laertes. (162–3)

'Drown'd?' the poor man says. And then, in the way one does, asks a question at once pertinent and essentially meaningless: 'O, where?' which allows Gertrude to speak her piece:

> There is a willow grows askant [F: aslant] a brook
> That shows his hoary leaves in the glassy stream.
> Therewith fantastic garlands did she make
> Of crow-flowers, nettles, daisies, and long purples . . .
> There on the pendent bows her crownet weeds
> Clamb'ring to hang, an envious sliver broke,
> When down her weedy trophies and herself
> Fell in the weeping brook. Her clothes spread wide,
> And mermaid-like awhile, they bore her up,
> Which time she chanted snatches of old lauds
> As one incapable of [insensible to] her own distress,
> Or like a creature native and indued
> Unto that element. But long it could not be
> Till that her garments, heavy with their drink,
> Pull'd the poor wretch from her melodious lay
> To muddy death. (165–82)

Like Ophelia's mad scene, this one has spawned its own posterity, so much so that Millais's Pre-Raphaelite painting of Ophelia floating in the river, surrounded by rich vegetation, is said by the Tate to be the picture most viewed in its entire collection. Even if the detailed meaning of the speech passes one by, its sound and rhythm carry one along from the opening 'There is a willow' to the end, 'To muddy death'. But that detailed meaning is of considerable interest. Our last glimpse of Ophelia had been of her handing out imaginary flowers to those around her. Now she becomes one with the vegetable world. The willow had always been associated with sadness ('weeping' refers to the way its branches fall). Fuller, in his *Worthies of England* (1662), called it 'a sad tree, whereof such who have lost their love make their mourning garlands'. All the other flowers and herbs mentioned are ill-omened – they are, says Jenkins, 'useless or noxious weeds, associated with pain, poison or . . . betrayal' (p. 545). But it is the way Shakespeare gives the landscape its own life ('an envious sliver broke') while robbing Ophelia of human agency – her clothes bear her up for a while yet it is the clothes which drag her down, though by then she has merged with water, trees and flowers ('like a creature native and indued/ Unto that element') – that makes one simultaneously want to applaud the brilliance of the rhetoric and weep at what that rhetoric unfolds.

Like so much else in this play, this is strictly speaking both unnecessary (a brief account of her death would suffice to keep the plot ticking over) and a fundamental part of the whole texture of the work. For the question no one asks here, but that will be debated in the very next scene, is of course one that will hang over Hamlet himself: was this an accident or was it deliberate? Is this death natural or is it suicide? Or was it, in a sense, neither and both, the result of her inability to undo the knot at the heart of her being, partly willed and partly submitted to?

The result, though, is not in doubt. 'Drown'd, drown'd,' intones Gertrude. Laertes makes a vain attempt to speak some appropriate words, but, though he firmly says 'I forbid my tears', he nevertheless gives way to them, before stomping out with:

Adieu, my lord,
I have a speech o' fire that fain would blaze
But that this folly douts [Q: drownes] it. (187–9)

FOLD FIFTEEN

15.1 (V. 1. 1–64)

Shakespeare is fond of introducing an almost emblematic scene, one that would not be out of place in a late medieval play and that could almost be taken as a two-dimensional medieval image, three-quarters of the way through his plays. In *Richard II*, for example, the action suddenly halts and we find ourselves in the presence of two gardeners, who proceed to talk about the state of the country in terms of plants and gardens. In *Hamlet*, after the trauma and pathos of Ophelia's mad scene and then Gertrude's heart-rending announcement of her death and how it came about, the play abruptly switches to just such a scene, a *memento mori* this time, the common trope of the meditation on death by the contemplation of a skull. Except that, *Hamlet* being *Hamlet*, it is a scene which rethinks, reanimates, and finally subverts the trope.

The scene in *Richard II* had two gardeners, low-class characters, commenting in an earthy vernacular on the state of England, conceived as a garden grown full of weeds. They stand, we are made to feel, for sturdy English common sense, at one with tradition. Here we also have two low-born characters. 'Enter two Clowns,' says the stage direction, but it is at once clear that one and perhaps both are gravediggers. The word 'clown', in Elizabethan times, meant both 'low-born' and 'comic', so that in *As You Like It*, for example, Shakespeare, when talking about Touchstone, can play on the dual meaning. They have come, it turns out, to dig a grave for a woman who may or may not have committed suicide, and whose burial in a Christian churchyard is therefore problematic. 'Is she to be buried in Christian burial, when she wilfully seeks her own salvation?' asks the first, preparing us for the tone of the scene by confusing 'salvation' and 'damnation'. 'I tell thee she is,' answers the other, 'therefore make her grave straight. The crowner hath sat on her and finds it Christian burial.' The coroner, who had to give a warrant for burial, has considered her case, it seems, and determined that it was not suicide. Though 'sat on her' can easily be understood, it does nonetheless conjure up the ridiculous image of the man of law actually sitting on the poor deceased, and the response of the first clown maintains this curious balancing act between the ludicrous and the commonsensical: 'How can that be,' he says, 'unless she drowned herself in her own defence?' The other is noncommittal: 'Why, 'tis found so.' This leads the first into a long meditation which would not be out of place amidst the more bizarre legal wranglings in Rabelais, though it also picks up Polonius's fondness for breaking events down into their constituent parts:

> It must be *se offendendo*, it cannot be else. For here lies the point: if I drown myself wittingly, it argues an act, and an act hath three branches – it is to act, to do, to perform; argal, she drowned herself wittingly . . . Here lies the water – good. Here stands the man – good. If the man goes to this water and drown himself, it is, will he nill he, he goes, mark you that. But if the water comes to him and drown him, he drowns not himself. Argal, he that is not guilty of his own death shortens not his own life. (9–20)

'But is this law?' asks the other. 'Ay, marry is't,' comes the response, 'crowner's quest law.' The other is cynical: 'Will you ha' the truth an't? If this had not been a gentlewoman, she should have been buried out o' Christian burial.'

The first clown begins by confusing *se offendendo* and *se defend-endo*, showing off his legal Latin to the other but only revealing his ignorance. Then he tries to prove that a person can only be said to have drowned accidentally if he is overwhelmed by water, but that if he throws himself *into* the water then it is clearly suicide. The other cuts through all this by the simple assertion that the dead woman is really being buried in consecrated ground only because she is a gentlewoman, not because a good legal case can be made out for her *not* having committed suicide.

But the effect of breaking down an action into its constituent parts, in the kind of logic-chopping that was associated in the late Middle Ages with the schoolmen, is not just comic; it makes the action take on a dream-like slow-motion quality, which mirrors in comic mode the description we have just been given, in tragic mode, of Ophelia's actual death. What both descriptions do is precisely to blur the line between suicide and involuntary death, and to make us aware of the fact that this is a more complex busi-ness than we might have supposed or that a court of law has the means to consider. Ophelia very definitely went to the water, but in what sense was she a free agent when she did so? How much did she *will* her death and how much did she simply succumb to it? And while it is true that 'he that is not guilty of his own death shortens not his own life', in real life as opposed to a court of law and a university course in logic it is rather less easy to know whether someone is or is not guilty of their own death, or if the word 'guilt' is ever an appropriate one.

What is undeniable, however, is that there is one law for the rich and one for the poor. The two clowns are agreed on that, and it leads to an exchange in which the first clown, upturning the old revolutionary adage, 'When Adam delved and Eve span, Who was then the gentleman?' with its implication that in the first days of the human race there were no class distinctions, proves that Adam was the first gentleman: since we are told that Adam 'digged', that one needs arms to dig, and that since arms (a coat of arms) are a sign of a gentleman, Adam must have been one. Here Shakespeare is perhaps wryly commenting on his own recent purchase of a coat of arms. They exchange some more jokes of the same kind, ending in the 'proof' that a gravedigger 'builds stronger' than a mason, a shipwright or a carpenter, for the house he builds lasts 'till doomsday'. Upon which the second clown departs, leaving the first alone to get on with his digging. As he does so he sings a popular love song that, as Jenkins notes, picks up many of the themes of Ophelia's songs:

> In youth when I did love, did love,
> Methought it was very sweet . . . (61–2)

15.2 (V. 1. 64–210)

It is at this point that Hamlet and Horatio enter and stand, unseen, commenting on what they see and overhear in a manner that we have become used to in this play where nearly everything is framed.

Hamlet seems shocked at the man's callousness in the face of death, but Horatio reminds him that 'custom hath made it in him a property of easiness'. True, says Hamlet, but when the gravedigger throws up a skull Hamlet shows that his mind is, as ever, focused on the strangeness of human life:

> That skull had a tongue in it, and could sing once. How the knave jowls [dashes] it to th' ground, as if 'twere Cain's jawbone, that did the first murder. This might be the pate of a politician which this ass now o'er-offices [lords it over], one that would circumvent God, might it not? . . . Or of a courtier, which could say, 'Good morrow, sweet lord, How dost thou, sweet lord?' . . . Why, e'en so, and now my Lady Worm's, chopless, and knocked about the mazard with a sexton's spade. Here's a fine revolution and we had the trick to see't. Did these bones cost no more the breeding but to play at loggets with 'em? Mine ache to think on't. (74–91)

This is common *memento mori* discourse: look what they have come to, they who thought so well of themselves in their lifetime!

Commentators have picked on 'Cain's jawbone' to remind us that Claudius himself earlier referred to the murder of Abel by his brother Cain by saying that his own crime had 'the primal eldest curse upon 't' (III. 3. 37), but equally interesting is Hamlet's immediate thought that the 'skull had a tongue in it, and could sing once', which suggests that Hamlet is not in the first place thinking of the inevitable and dreadful end of those who in their lifetime thought only of themselves, but rather of the horror of death silencing what was once alive and singing – a general lament rather than a bit of moralising satire. It is as though he is starting to see himself as already dead and tries to understand what it is that he will then have lost.

Oblivious to his visitors, the clown/gravedigger goes on singing and digging. He throws out another skull and Hamlet proceeds to moralise on that. Finally, he addresses the gravedigger, who seems quite unfazed by the discovery that two strangers are standing beside him:

> *Ham.* Whose grave's this, sirrah?
> *Grave.* Mine, sir. (*Sings*) *O a pit of clay for to be made* –
> *Ham.* I think it be thine indeed, for thou liest in't.
> *Grave.* You lie out on't, sir, and therefore 'tis not yours. For my part, I do not lie in't yet it is mine.
> *Ham.* Thou dost lie in't, to be in't and say 'tis thine. 'Tis for the dead, not for the quick [living]: therefore thou liest.
> *Grave.* 'Tis a quick lie, sir, 'twill away again from me to you.
>   (115–25)

Something extraordinary has happened here. Hamlet has taken the place of the second clown. For it does not matter if we don't get all the double entendres of this exchange, it is clear that a bantering match is taking place before our eyes. Hamlet, who, we have seen, had quite naturally taken on the role of court jester both to hide his real feelings, even from himself, and to force those around him out of their complacency, has here met his match.

Who is it you are digging the grave for? he asks, but the gravedigger persists in his banter: it's not a man and not a woman either. Who then? asks Hamlet, baffled. 'One that was a woman, sir; but rest her soul, she's dead.' And as so often happens when one of the upper classes tries to engage a clown in banter (as in the exchanges between Olivia and her fool Feste in *Twelfth Night*), they soon tire of the game when they find the other is too quick for them. 'How absolute the knave is,' grumbles Hamlet to Horatio. 'We must speak by the card or equivocation will undo us.' It just shows, he goes on, that class barriers are eroding all round us that now even peasants have the finicking art of courtiers – a sure sign that he has been rattled, since it is he who began the contest.

He decides to try another, more direct route. How long have you been a grave-maker? he asks, and the man gives a surprising answer that suddenly brings us back to the present moment of Shakespeare's play:

Grave. Of all the days i'th'year I came to't the day that our last
        King Hamlet o'ercame Fortinbras.
Ham. How long is that since?
Grave. Cannot you tell that? Every fool can tell that. It was
        that very day that young Hamlet was born – he that is
        [F: was] mad and sent into England.
Ham. Ay, marry. Why was he sent into England?
Grave. Why, because a was mad. A shall recover his wits there.
        Or if a do not, 'tis no great matter there.
Ham. Why?
Grave. 'Twill not be seen in him there. There the men are as
        mad as he.
Ham. How came he mad?
Grave. Very strangely, they say.
Ham. How 'strangely'?
Grave. Faith, e'en with losing his wits.
Ham. Upon what grounds?
Grave. Why, here in Denmark. I have been sexton here, man
        and boy, thirty years. (139–57)

The quip about the English was of course meant to be funny, a joke reaching out to the audience of the Globe from within the confines of the play, as often happens in Elizabethan drama. But here it is part of a pattern we have been tracing, of Shakespeare constantly reminding us that what we are watching is only a play, a pattern, we have noted, that has the surprising effect of strengthening rather than weakening the hold the play has upon our imaginations. It also, as Margreta de Grazia has shown, reinforces our sense of the geopolitical dimension of the play and makes sure we do not see it as simply about Hamlet. Fortinbras, the son of the Norwegian king and therefore belonging to Hamlet's generation, has just been seen crossing the stage with his army bound for Poland, and he will reappear at the climax. He is evoked here as the Gravedigger recalls what was obviously an important day in the national memory of both Denmark and Norway, a day described in the opening scene of the play, when Old Hamlet overcame Old Fortinbras in hand to hand combat and thus single-handedly enlarged Denmark's boundaries at the expense of its northern neighbour. In addition the exchange gives us a precise age for Hamlet, thirty, which those raised on the image of Hamlet as a Shelleyan youth find hard to swallow, and with some reason, since Shakespeare is, as ever, opportunistic, and it is the youthful Hamlet who seems to inhabit the earlier part of the play, the middle-aged Hamlet, 'fat and scant of breath' as his mother will call him (V. 2. 290), the later. Finally, though, it brings Hamlet face to face with himself as seen by others, and we feel that his persistent questioning of the Gravedigger as to why he (Hamlet) is thought mad is neither simple curiosity nor the result of a desire to see how the land lies as he tries to formulate his plans, but stems from a real need to be told this in order to help him understand himself.

The dialogue moves on to the question of how long a man will lie in the earth before he rots, and in the course of his answer the Gravedigger produces another skull as evidence. This one, he says, has lain in the earth for twenty-three years. Hamlet is intrigued: 'Whose was it?' 'A whoreson mad fellow's,' responds the other. But whose? presses Hamlet:

Grave. A pestilence on him for a mad rogue! A poured a flagon
of Rhenish wine on my head once. This same skull, sir,
was Yorick's skull, the King's jester.

Ham. This?

Grave. E'en that.

Ham. Alas, poor Yorick. [F: Let me see. Alas . . .] I knew him,
Horatio, a fellow of infinite jest, of most excellent fancy.
He hath bore me on his back a thousand times, and
now – how abhorred in my imagination it is. My gorge
rises at it. Here hung those lips that I have kissed I know
not how oft. Where be your gibes now, your gambols,
your songs, your flashes of merriment, that were wont
to set the table on a roar? Not one now to mock your
own grinning? Quite chop-fallen? Now get you to my
lady's chamber and tell her, let her paint an inch thick,
to this favour she must come. (172–88)

Among the numerous studies of how Shakespeare was seen in the
seventeenth, eighteenth and nineteenth centuries there is hardly
ever any mention of Sterne, and yet, it seems to me, Sterne understood this play better than almost anyone before or since. It is in
Chapter X of Volume I of *Tristram Shandy*, in the course of
discussing midwives and hobby-horses, that Tristram comes to talk
of the local parson and his horse, the latter, he says, a veritable
brother to Don Quixote's nag, Rosinante; and it is only at the start
of the following chapter that he reveals (or hits upon the idea) that
the parson's name was Yorick. I say 'hits upon the idea' because
though Sterne is of course describing and dramatising the haphazard
nature of Tristram's mind as he seeks to write the story of his life,
there is no doubt that this mirrors Sterne's own mind as he seeks to
write his novel. The parson's name, we are told, was Yorick, and this
allows Sterne to invent a comic genealogy for him, informing us

that the family was originally of *Danish* extraction, and had
been transplanted into *England* as early as in the reign of
Horwendillus, king of *Denmark*, in whose court it seems, an

ancestor of this Mr. *Yorick*'s, and from whom he was lineally descended, held a considerable post to the day of his death. Of what nature this considerable post was, this record saith not; – it only adds, That, for near two centuries it had been totally abolished as altogether unnecessary, not only in that court, but in every other court of the Christian world.

It has often come into my head, that this post could be no other than that of the king's chief Jester; – and that *Hamlet*'s *Yorick*, in our *Shakespear*, many of whose plays, you know, are founded upon authenticated facts, – was certainly the very man.

I have not the time to look into *Saxo-Grammaticus*'s *Danish* history, to know the certainty of this; – but if you have leisure, and can easily get at the book, you may do it full as well yourself. (Vol. I, Chapter VI)

Sterne jokingly authenticates his own narrative by reference to another work of fiction, Shakespeare's *Hamlet*, and shows he is quite au fait with *Hamlet* scholarship, which informs us that Shakespeare's source for the Hamlet story is to be found in Saxo Grammaticus's *Gesta Danorum* (*c*. 1200), where Hamlet's father is called Horwendillus. A further learned joke is that no Yorick is ever mentioned there.

Sterne has Tristram go on to assert that 'by what I can remember of him, and by all the accounts I could ever get of him, [Yorick] seem'd not to have had one single drop of *Danish* blood in his whole crasis; in nine hundred years, it might possibly have all run out.' Fascinatingly, Sterne soon began to identify with this invented figure based on another invented figure and when he came to publish his sermons did so under the name of Mr Yorick, as well as using the name for the protagonist of *A Sentimental Journey*. (This is even more extraordinary, and a tribute to Shakespeare's ability to conjure life out of a few words, when we recall that Yorick never actually appears in Hamlet but is only evoked here, first by the gravedigger and then by Hamlet.) And we can, I think, see the genesis of this identification in what follows in Chapter XI:

The fact was this: – That instead of that cold phlegm and exact regularity of sense and humours, you would have look'd for, in one so extracted [i.e. of Danish descent], – he was, on the contrary, as mercurial and sublimated a composition, — as heteroclite a creature in all his declensions, – with as much life and whim, and *gaité de coeur* about him, as the kindliest climate could have engendered and put together . . . For, to speak the truth, *Yorick* had an invincible dislike and opposition in his nature to gravity; – not to gravity as such; – for where gravity was wanted, he would be the most grave or serious of mortal men for days and weeks together; – but he was an enemy to the affectation of it, and declared open war against it, only as it appeared a cloak for ignorance, or for folly; and then, whenever it fell in his way, however sheltered and protected, he seldom gave it much quarter.

This is a figure clearly more tenderly conceived than Shakespeare's Yorick who, it seems, was prepared to pour a jug of wine on the poor gravedigger's head for who knows what perceived offence; but this is part of Sterne's peculiar genius – he sentimentalises and then shows us that he is fully aware of the fact that he is doing so, thus managing, like Shakespeare, to have his cake and eat it. And this emerges clearly in what follows in the novel, which will bring us back to Shakespeare.

In brief, Yorick dies. And, Sterne tells us,

He lies buried in a corner of his church-yard, in the parish of ——, under a plain marble slab, which his friend *Eugenius*, by leave of his executors, laid upon his grave, with no more than these three words of inscription, serving both for his epitaph and elegy:

| Alas, poor YORICK! |

Ten times a day has *Yorick*'s ghost the consolation to hear his monumental inscription read over with such a variety of

plaintive tones, as denote a general pity and esteem for him; –
a footway crossing the church-yard close by the side of his
grave, – not a passenger goes by without stopping to cast a look
upon it, – and sighing as he walks on,

Alas, poor YORICK! (I.XII)

And, as if this weren't enough, it is followed by the famous all-
black page, an emblem of what awaits each one of us.

A funerary monument is meant to outlast its immediate occasion. That is why it is set up, why it is usually in stone, and why
any words that appear on it are chiselled into the stone. It stands
in stark opposition to the immediate outpourings of grief that
greet the death of a loved person. Yet Sterne here tries, or pretends
to try, to conflate the two. The result is, interestingly, something
that does not succeed in evoking either the grief of the bereaved or
the dignity of traditional memorials. That the meaningfulness of
tombstones depends on shared systems of belief and that these
systems were starting to be obscurely felt to be under threat is seen
in the new awareness of the significance of traditional graveyards
attested to by Gray's *Elegy* and Wordsworth's beautiful essay on
epitaphs. It is no surprise to find Sterne there as well. The pages on
Yorick's death and burial bring out clearly what is involved. Instead
of a simple acceptance of the monument there comes the fear that
feeling will disappear in the impersonality of the stone inscription.
Hence the attempt to counter that by making the inscribed phrase
as much like utterance as possible, starting with 'alas' and ending
with an exclamation mark.

Of course with Sterne there is the added sense that not just a
stone monument but print itself will fatally divorce utterance from
the utterer – hence his comic attempts to compensate, throughout
Tristram Shandy, with dashes of varied lengths, black pages,
pointing hands in the margins and all the rest.

This, we might think, is not an issue that would affect a playwright, for in the theatre the words in the script are being uttered
by a living person. And yet a little reflection will show us that this
is merely pushing the issue back one stage. For this living person is

not the playwright but an actor, who speaks the lines by rote, night after night, and, who, if, like *Hamlet*, the play survives, will go on doing so long after the playwright is dead.

So Sterne can help us here too. For behind the anxiety about funerary monuments and even about print, he is probing an anxiety about the human expression of emotion as such. The sense that comes through the whole episode of the death of Yorick in *Tristram Shandy* is that all expressions of feeling are a betrayal of feeling. That is the effect of making what should ostensibly be a moving personal moment be flagged up as nothing but the iteration of a famous line in literature (I have the feeling that Shakespeare's line came first to Sterne and the character of his Yorick, with all its enormous ramifications for his art and life, followed).

Thus Sterne's play with exclamation marks has something to tell us about *Hamlet*. It asks us at least to consider the possibility that when Hamlet utters his famous phrase he is himself to some extent play-acting. Perhaps that does not emerge in performance, for there are as many ways of uttering the phrase as there are great Hamlets. But the phrase does come a little too pat, and in doing so reminds us of Hamlet's perpetual problem: hardly anything he says is completely natural, nearly everything has a faintly rhetorical, second-hand quality – and he is aware of it. As we have seen, Shakespeare plays on this no less than Sterne, continuously framing scenes, having letters read out by those other than the author, setting spies to watch unseen. Everybody in this play is acting, but only Hamlet appears aware of it, and of course he does it better and in more varied ways than anyone else. Thus, shown a skull and told who it once belonged to, he is more than likely to strike a pose. And yet the quickening rhythm of what follows, like the quickening rhythm of 'He that plays the king shall be welcome' at II. 2. 318ff. (pp. 97ff. above) gives us a powerful sense that any pose he might have adopted can quickly drop away if he is sufficiently engaged. As he is here, as the memory of the old jester starts to flood into him: 'I knew him, Horatio, a fellow of infinite jest, of most excellent fancy. He hath bore me on his back a thousand times . . .' Both the gravedigger and Hamlet have strong memories of Yorick, and they are both strong *physical* memories – the gravedigger's of Yorick pouring the jug of Rhenish wine on his head, and Hamlet of Yorick carrying him on his back. Is it too much to suggest that Hamlet in that moment recalls Yorick as the loving playful father he never had, a man different from both the austere and warlike Old Hamlet and the Machiavellian uncle who has taken his place? (Gertrude too does not strike one as the kind of parent who would enjoy playing with her child.)

And it is not just that Hamlet recalls a physical action of Yorick's; he seems at this moment to feel in his body the sensation of being carried by the jester. He 'remembers' too his 'gambols', his songs, his 'flashes of merriment, that were wont to set the table on a roar'. True, this is all offset by the sense of what he has come to 'now', but the effect of the whole is very similar to the one I suggested earlier was to be had by hearing the singing of 'For O, for O, the hobby-horse is forgot!' – it is the rollicking air we take away from that, linked to the hobby-horse, and 'is forgot' tends to drop away – the imagination, said Freud, does not know negatives – so that, though the phrase tells us the hobby-horse is forgot, we register it as a reminder of the hobby-horse and its power, of mumming and morris dancing and their power. So here. We see the skull, but instead of the living Yorick being annihilated by the skull, the opposite happens: the skull evokes a person and a way of life, one which Hamlet, twenty-three years later, can still feel in his body as the living Yorick comes back to him in the wake of the gravedigger's utterance of his name. And this does not really surprise us, for, despite his melancholy, despite his anguish, something of the actor's delight in performance, as well as of the jester's speed of thought and language and delight in his own dexterity, makes him, like Sterne, a true descendant of Yorick.

And though the talk now turns to the familiar trope of the levelling effect of death, Hamlet seems to have been buoyed up by his encounter with Yorick, as we might put it, and returns to his jesting with renewed gusto: 'To what base uses we may return,

Horatio!' he exclaims. 'Why, may not imagination trace the noble dust of Alexander till a find it stopping a bung-hole?' And then, as at the conclusion of *The Mousetrap*, not satisfied with prose, he turns to verse to express his combination of horror and high spirits:

> Imperious Caesar, dead and turn'd to clay,
> Might stop a hole to keep the wind away.
> O that the earth which kept the world in awe
> Should patch a wall t'expel the winter's flaw [wind].
> (206–9)

15.3 (V. 1. 210–88)

Now the mood abruptly changes, heralded by that word, 'soft', and that fondness for repetition, to which John Jones has drawn our attention: 'But soft, but soft awhile. Here comes the King.'

And the King, Queen, Laertes and attendants appear, with a priest and men bearing a coffin. Hamlet, presumably concealed, turns commentator:

> Who is this they follow?
> And with such maimed rites? This doth betoken
> The corse they follow did with desp'rate hand
> Fordo its own life. (211–14)

He does not know, of course, that Ophelia is dead. The 'maimed rites' are the burial rites which a contemporary would have recognised as being more spare or limited than usual, because, as we know, a question hangs over the cause of her death. And this the priest goes on to explain, as Hamlet and Horatio look on, unseen:

> Her death was doubtful;
> And but that great command o'ersways the order,
> She should in ground unsanctified been lodg'd
> Till the last trumpet. (220–3)

Laertes is appalled: 'Must there no more be done?' he asks. 'No more be done,' responds the priest,

> We should profane the service of the dead
> To sing sage requiem and such rest to her
> As to peace-parted souls. (229–31)

'Psalms and masses for suicides were explicitly forbidden in canon law,' Jenkins tells us (p. 389), but what he does not say, in commenting on this scene, is how this relates to all the other references to the afterlife which run through the play, from the Ghost's description of the Purgatory from which he has been briefly released to Hamlet's meditations on 'the undiscovered country, from whose bourn/ No traveller returns', to his anguished uncertainty over whether or not to make an end of Claudius while he is at prayer. Whatever the doctrinal and legal changes taking place in the course of his life, Shakespeare is always opportunistic, picking from the common stock of attitudes what will suit him, when it suits him.

But Laertes can control himself no longer:

> I tell thee, churlish priest
> A minist'ring angel shall my sister be
> When thou liest howling. (233–5)

Suddenly, Hamlet understands: 'What, the fair Ophelia!' But already the Queen is scattering flowers over the grave and in the process making clear both who is being buried and her own now thwarted wishes:

> Sweets to the sweet. Farewell.
> I hop'd thou shouldst have been my Hamlet's wife:
> I thought thy bride-bed to have deck'd, sweet maid,
> And not have strew'd thy grave. (235–9)

Does Hamlet recall his father's account of his own death taking place in a flowery orchard, which he sought to replicate in the mime and play he had the Players perform? Again, the images fold in upon themselves; but what is happening in present time is too tumultuous to give anyone – the audience, Hamlet, the reader – time to sort them out. For Laertes is now in his element, as he cries out:

> O, treble woe
> Fall ten times treble on that cursed head
> Whose wicked deed thy most ingenious sense
> Depriv'd thee of. – Hold off the earth awhile,
> Till I have caught her once more in my arms.
> *(Leaps in the grave.)* [not in Q2]
> Now pile your dust upon the quick and dead,
> Till of this flat a mountain you have made
> T'oertop old Pelion or the skyish head
> Of blue Olympus. (239–47)

But this is more than Hamlet can stand, or perhaps just the spur for which he has so long been waiting. Now at last he finds the rhetoric of the Player's speech, the heroic and defiant Marlovian rant, springing to his lips:

> What is he whose grief
> Bears such an emphasis, whose phrase of sorrow
> Conjures the wand'ring stars, and makes them stand
> Like wonder-wounded hearers?

Now at last he can take on the mantle of his father and call himself 'The Dane':

> This is I,
> Hamlet the Dane.

And, in another nightmarish tableau, the two grapple over or perhaps inside the newly dug grave (see Jenkins, p. 391). Pandemonium ensues. The King calls out for them to be separated, while the Queen can only repeat her son's name, either in anguish or reproof: 'Hamlet! Hamlet!'

They are no longer fighting over a father's death. In a further twist to the already twisted affects loose in the play, they are fighting over who loved Ophelia more, the brother or the lover. At any rate Hamlet is, for from now on Laertes is silent:

> I lov'd Ophelia. Forty thousand brothers
> Could not with all their quantity of love
> Make up my sum. What wilt thou do for her? (264–6)

The others try to intervene but now he has at last found his voice he is not to be silenced:

> 'Swounds, show me what thou't do.
> Woo't weep, woo't fight, woo't fast, woo't tear thyself,
> Woo't drink up eisel, eat a crocodile?
> I'll do't. Dost come here to whine,
> To outface me with leaping in her grave?
> Be buried quick with her, and so will I.
> And if thou prate of mountains, let them throw
> Millions of acres on us, till our ground,
> Singeing his pate against the burning zone,
> Make Ossa like a wart. (269–78)

But that word 'prate' starts to give the game away, and he ends with an assertion of intent that demonstrates the opposite of what it says: 'Nay, and thou'lt mouth,/ I'll rant as well as thou.' No one who really believed in what they were saying would describe it as a 'rant'.

For Laertes what *he* said was no prating or ranting but a natural mode of expression. For Hamlet to live with Laertes (in the sense of an athlete 'living with' a rival over five or ten thousand metres) the ranting vein would have to come to him as naturally as it does to his rival. And there's the rub. Hamlet loves 'Ercles' vein' (*MND*, I. 2. 23–34) but he is not himself capable of it. The voice Hamlet has found is no more 'his', it turns out, than any of the others he has tried out in the course of the play. There is something in him that makes him see it for what it is, 'prating', 'ranting', and that is not surprising, and to be applauded, given his awareness of the nuances of language, given his wit and his humour. He may try to out-Laertes Laertes, but, as with Dr Johnson's friend, a sense, if not of cheerfulness, then at least of the absurdity of the situation and of his words, keeps breaking in.

The scene is directly parallel to that of the killing of Polonius. There Hamlet both wants and does not want to fulfil his father's injunctions, and he acts hoping to kill Claudius yet hoping to absolve himself of that responsibility and instead kills the doddering old councillor, the father of the woman he loves. He acts in bad faith and the result is an unintended disaster. Here he is driven by Laertes's histrionics to reveal himself and to proclaim that he and only he truly loved Ophelia, but even as he speaks he starts to feel that this is the wrong tone, that it is not thus that he can show, if he can ever show, his love. In both cases he causes mayhem and confusion by his decision to play a role assigned him, though (or perhaps because) deep down he is unable or unwilling to commit himself fully to that role.

His mother sees through him, as well as trying to protect him from himself: 'This is mere madness,' she says. Let the fit work itself out and then you'll see he'll become again 'as patient as the female dove', she insists. And, indeed, Hamlet seems to have exhausted his fund of Marlovian rhetoric. 'Hear you, sir,' he says to Laertes, in one of those quiet utterances which Shakespeare manages to make so devastating, coming as they so often do immediately after an unduly rhetorical one:

> Hear you, sir,
> What is the reason that you use me thus?
> I lov'd you ever. But it is no matter.
> Let Hercules himself do what he may,
> The cat will mew, and dog will have his day. (283–7)

And with this familiar-sounding proverb to clinch the couplet which defines closure, or attempted closure, Hamlet leaves the stage, followed by Horatio.

15.4 (V. 1. 289–94)

Despite all that has gone on Claudius has not forgotten his main objective, which is winning Laertes over to his plan. He reminds him now of their talk the night before, urges Gertrude to 'set some watch over your son' (he has taken to using this locution more and more as he seeks to distance himself from Hamlet, now that his efforts at some sort of reconciliation have obviously broken down for good), and, with the ambiguous phrase, 'This grave shall have a living monument' (a mysterious line which could be taken in a variety of ways), and the by now almost obligatory couplet, the long scene draws to a close.

FOLD SIXTEEN

16.1 (V. 2. 1–80)

Shakespeare has held back the full explanation of how Hamlet escaped from the ship that was conveying him to England and his death, even though realistically it would have been the first thing Hamlet would have said to Horatio once they met again, because he wanted the emblematic Gravedigger scene to follow directly on Gertrude's account of Ophelia's death. Now that that fold has been thoroughly developed he can use Hamlet's account of what occurred as an emotional pause before the rush to the climax.

And what emerges, as Hamlet relates his story to Horatio, is that, when he has to, Hamlet can be as decisive and resourceful as anyone. Critics have fastened on this to say that the unexpected killing of Polonius marks a turning point in his attitude to the world, that now he has taken himself in hand and shown his true character. But that tells us more about the critics' desire for decisive turning points than it does about the play.

Certainly we have evidence here of decisive action. Hamlet tells Horatio how on the voyage to England he lay in his bunk, unable to sleep, turning all sorts of things over in his mind, then got up, entered the cabin of Rosencrantz and Guildenstern, found the 'packet' containing the letter to the King of England, crept back into his own cabin, unsealed it and read to his horror and amazement of the instructions to the English King that he have Hamlet's head chopped off. Yet he at once sat down and counterfeited a fresh letter, ordering the King to put the bearers 'to sudden death,/ Not shriving-time allowed' (46–7) (that theme again). But how, asks Horatio, did you seal it? Even there, replies Hamlet, he was in luck, for he had his father's signet ring with him, which was the exact likeness of the seal of Denmark. So he folded the letter, put it in the envelope, sealed it, and quietly replaced it where he had found it. The next day the pirate vessel attacked them and the rest is known. 'So Rosencrantz and Guildenstern go to't,' exclaims Horatio. 'Why, man,' replies Hamlet,

> they did make love to this employment.
> They are not near my conscience, their defeat
> Does by their own insinuation grow. (57–9)

They are riff-raff, he says, not worth a thought (just as he had felt the death of Polonius was not worth a thought), so in love with their role as spies that they deserved everything they got. But when Horatio exclaims at the baseness of what Claudius has tried to do Hamlet is all too ready to give vent to all his old obsessions:

> He that hath kill'd my king and whor'd my mother,
> Popp'd in between th'election and my hopes,
> Thrown out his angle for my proper life
> And with such coz'nage [deception] – is't not perfect
>   conscience
> To quit him with this arm? And is't not to be damn'd
> To let this canker of our nature come
> In further evil? (64–70)

'Killed my king' is a curious phrase, neither 'killed the king' nor 'killed my father', as though Hamlet had difficulty deciding between the two and ended up with neither. And once again killing and whoring are lumped together, followed by 'popped in between', which would suggest 'popped in between her sheets', then at the last moment Hamlet veers off into the completely unfounded accusation that Claudius has somehow wrongfully deprived him of his rightful inheritance, an idea he has floated before, but which, we have seen, is wide of the mark since kingship in Denmark was not hereditary. However, to add to his previous grievances he now has another and decisive one, the attempt on his life.

Horatio, though, is, as always, the realist. Do you realise that what you've done will be known as soon as news comes back from England? he asks. Hamlet acknowledges this. 'It will be short. The interim is mine.' As for Laertes, he admits the fault was his own – not the killing of his father, which he never seems to want to acknowledge, but insulting him in the churchyard. I see myself in him, he says, meaning perhaps nothing more than that he recognises Laertes's inherent nobility of spirit and his freedom from the ethos of selfishness and spying which characterises the court, and this makes him feel like a kindred spirit; but we cannot help noting that Laertes seeking revenge on Hamlet for the killing of his father is a mirror image of Hamlet in more crucial ways too, though Hamlet will never have the beautiful simplicity of spirit of Ophelia's brother, as the last lines of this speech suggest:

> But sure the bravery of his grief did put me
> Into a tow'ring passion. (78–9)

What is an aspect of Laertes's 'spirit' is, in Hamlet, an unnatural condition, brought on by circumstances, and now past.

It is extraordinary how much comment there has been on this brief episode. Critics have even suggested that Hamlet's account of how he got hold of the letter –

> in the dark
> Grop'd I to find out them, had my desire,

Finger'd their packet, and in fine withdrew
To mine own room again (13–16)

– is an account of Hamlet's imagined rape of his old schoolfellows, which has the merit at least of bringing out the sensual nature of Hamlet's description, but deflects attention from what is really going on here. What that is has been seen by the bulk of critics as exemplifying Hamlet's new-found confidence. After all, he says when speaking of his inability to sleep on the boat:

There's a divinity that shapes our ends,
Rough-hew them how we will – (10–11)

And, later, talking about having his father's ring in his bag, 'Why, even in that was heaven ordinant,/ I had my father's signet in my purse . . .' – does this not show that Hamlet, after all his uncertainty as to the rightfulness of his cause, is now sure that Heaven is with him in an act of just revenge? Or, as Jenkins, speaking for the bulk of commentators, puts it: 'The present passage shows Hamlet recognising a design in the universe he had previously failed to find' (p. 557).

I am not so sure. It seems to me that in this episode Hamlet emerges mainly as an efficient theatre director (which clearly he aspired to be). Shakespeare was fascinated by such figures, and in *Othello* he creates his greatest example – not Othello, of course, but Iago. The type reappears in *King Lear*; again, not Lear or Cordelia but Edmund. Such figures, in other words, are associated in Shakespeare's mind with the manipulative egoists who seek to destroy the noble but vulnerable hero, and usually succeed. Claudius is such another, and what we are seeing here is Hamlet outdoing Claudius at his own game.

In *The Play Called Corpus Christi* V. A. Kolve describes a figure who appears in the Chester cycle as the Expositor:

The Chester *Expositor* really does control the game – hurrying here, moralizing there, now briefly narrating a story that cannot, because of time, be played, and occasionally stepping forth to address the audience directly on what they have been watching together. The French medieval drama often used a *meneur* (or *maître*) *du jeu*, and we know from a miniature by Jean Fouquet that he could be in the very middle of the action, holding the playbook in one hand and a baton in the other, conducting the game.

This is a benign figure because what had to be shown in play and game in these plays was something in a sense already known, authors and spectators sharing a general theological view of the world but the audience needing to be led into it, or reminded of it, by the drama. That commonly accepted view no longer exists by Shakespeare's time and those who would instruct and direct tend now to be seen as fanatics and falsifiers. They are the ones who want to control, and their control, in Shakespeare's plays, is nearly always malignant.

Thus Hamlet's brief impersonation of a *meneur de jeu* is no more 'in character' than Hamlet the Avenger or Hamlet the Lover. In each case he puts a certain 'disposition' on, in the hope that it will stick, but, alas, it never does. His heart is not in it. He stabs out at a noise behind the arras, hoping thereby to pay his debt to his father, only to find that he has killed the wrong man; he is driven by his discovery that Ophelia is dead to leap into her grave and outdo her brother in his protestations of love but he soon realises that all he is doing is ranting; and he is driven by fear for his life to act in ways he would normally find abhorrent. In each case the action is impulsive and undertaken on the spur of the moment. His justification for it here does not smack to me of a new kind of understanding of his role in the world but rather seems a vain attempt to justify his actions. He had already said of Polonius's death, 'heaven hath pleas'd it so' (III. 4. 175). Now he elaborates on this thought:

> Rashly –
> And prais'd be rashness for it: let us know

> Our indiscretion sometime serves us well
> When our deep plots do pall; and that should learn us
> There's a divinity that shapes our ends,
> Rough-hew them how we will – (6–11)

Hamlet seems here to be trying to persuade himself that rashness, impulsiveness, does sometimes seem to be a sign that we are really acting according to some deeper purpose, unseen by us but meaningful all the same. Yet we cannot help but recall his comments at the time of Polonius's death, when he dismissed the old councillor as a 'rash intruding fool' and Gertrude reacted, horrified, with: 'What a rash and bloody deed is this?' However, he does his best to persuade himself here, even going on to argue that the whole episode must have been engineered by a gracious God because how else to explain the chance presence in his bag of a seal identical to the one he has just broken. Surely, he says, this can't all have been coincidence or luck? Providence must have been at work, a divinity that shapes our ends, even if we cannot discern it. This seems to me to be a perfect example of Eliot's contention that Shakespeare's heroes use their fine rhetoric quite often merely to 'cheer themselves up'. For Hamlet's heart is heavy, and the new disposition he is trying on here sits as uneasily upon him as do all the others.

By responding to the play we can grasp more fully (even if we find it difficult to express in words) just what Hamlet is going through at this point. In their fascinating book, *Shakespeare in Parts*, Simon Palfrey and Tiffany Stern attempt to bring out how actors learning their lines in Elizabethan England would only have had their own parts and the most minimal cues to work with. Talking of how the half-lines which often close speeches in Shakespeare's plays help to keep actors on their toes, open to the possibilities of the moment, they say:

> It is a classic example of how working in parts pre-empts what
> might be construed as the metaphysical presumptuousness
> of the complete play: the sense that everything has been

pre-written, masterminded to the last detail. The various
lonely spaces in parts – epitomized in the speech-closing half-
line – show that more than one mind and more than one
choice, goes to make a moment.

This kind of argument of course appeals to our age, which is
deeply suspicious of master narratives and tends to favour a Zen-
like attitude of openness to the world. But whether or not they are
right to hang such large claims on technical details (I find their
arguments often quite compelling), what such a formulation does
is help us to grasp what is going on at this point in *Hamlet*. Hamlet,
we could say, is desperate (as in a sense we all are) to believe that
'everything has been pre-written, masterminded to the last detail'.
And Calvinists in the audience would certainly not have seen this
as 'metaphysical presumptuousness', but as the simple truth. Yet
Hamlet is also too sceptical, too ironic, to accept for long any such
notion as operative in his life. What we see in the closing stages
of the play is the struggle between his need to believe in an over-
arching Providence and his profound sense that life is not like
that, that it is indeed open at every moment, random and
contingent.

16.2 (V. 2. 81–220)

Their conversation is interrupted by Osric, a courtier.

Polonius, Rosencrantz and Guildenstern are all dead, but
Hamlet still needs a courtly foil. Shakespeare, whose powers of
invention are such that he is always able to create a new and unique
character to fulfil even a minor role, is not going to fall down at
this moment. Osric is both more extravagant than the other three
and thinner, almost paper-thin – and yet he never becomes a
Jonsonian type, he is too closely tied in to the central concerns of
the play.

His first words give nothing away: 'Your Lordship is right
welcome back to Denmark.' Does he know Hamlet was not meant
to return? Or is his greeting genuine? Hamlet responds in kind: 'I

humbly thank you sir' – but then in his sotto voce words to Horatio tells us how we should view this man, and of course tells the actor how Shakespeare wants him to project himself: 'Dost know this waterfly?' he asks. When Horatio says he doesn't (his relation to the court, as we have seen from the start, is curiously porous: a complete outsider at moments yet apparently close friends with the guards and with Hamlet), Hamlet fills him in: 'Thy state is the more gracious, for 'tis a vice to know him . . . 'Tis a chuff, but, as I say, spacious in the possession of dirt' (a dismissive way of saying 'owning much land') (83–9).

The man is clearly a rich fop, a ridiculous dresser, and Hamlet the prince has all the disdain of the aristocrat for the parvenu. The dialogue proceeds in the form made familiar by the encounters with Polonius and Rosencrantz and Guildenstern, surface politeness and unspoken jockeying for position:

> *Osr.* Sweet lord, if your lordship were at leisure, I should impart a thing to you from his Majesty.
> *Ham.* I will receive it, sir, with all diligence of spirit. Your bonnet to his right use: 'tis for the head.
> *Osr.* I thank your lordship, it is very hot.
> *Ham.* No, believe me 'tis very cold, the wind is northerly.
> *Osr.* It is indifferent cold, my lord, indeed.
> *Ham.* But yet methinks it is very sultry and hot for my complexion.
> *Osr.* Exceedingly, my lord, it is very sultry – as 'twere – I cannot tell how. (90–100)

Finally he succeeds in bringing out what he had come to say, though Hamlet keeps interrupting him to urge him to put on his hat: the King wishes to inform Hamlet that he has made a bet with Laertes that Hamlet will beat him in a fencing bout. As I pointed out in the Introduction, the precise terms of the bout are far from clear, probably deliberately, possibly because Shakespeare kept changing his mind. Signs that he had trouble catching precisely the tone he wanted this scene to have are to be found in the fact that the Folio drops about thirty lines here, mainly a Polonius-like ramble on Osric's part about the qualities and virtues of Laertes. Shakespeare clearly wanted everything to slow down at this point, purpose and direction to drown, as it so often does in this play, in a plethora of words that seem utterly beside the point and yet, like the digressions in *Tristram Shandy*, never are, quite. That he eventually dropped what amounted to a third of the episode suggests that he felt he could achieve his purpose more economically, and perhaps that Osric's praise of Laertes was in fact *too* reminiscent of Polonius.

Osric's way with language makes it difficult to grasp much about the wager except that Claudius has backed Hamlet and hopes he will agree to take part:

> *Osr.* The King, sir, hath wagered with [Laertes] six Barbary horses, against which he has impawned, as I take it, six French rapiers and poniards, with their assigns, as girdle, hanger, and so . . . The King, sir, hath laid, sir [F omits the second 'sir'], that in a dozen passes between yourself and him he shall not exceed you three hits; he hath laid on twelve for nine. And it would come to immediate trial if your lordship would vouchsafe the answer . . .
>
> *Ham.* Sir, I will walk here in the hall. If it please his Majesty, it is the breathing time of day with me. Let the foils be brought, the gentleman willing, and the King hold his purpose, I will win for him and I can; if not, I will gain nothing but my shame and the odd hits.
>
> *Osr.* Shall I deliver you so?
>
> *Ham.* To this effect, sir, after what flourish your nature will.
>
> (144–78)

We understand the substance of what is going on even if much of the detail escapes us. This is almost the norm in Rabelais but rare in Shakespeare – *Hamlet* is the most Rabelais-like of his plays. Shakespeare creates for *Hamlet* an atmosphere in which at one and the same time nothing happens and everything happens, in which the protagonist feels himself to be drowning in a sea of words ('What are you reading, my lord?' 'Words, words, words') yet being pulled inexorably towards a conclusion he both desires and does not believe in. And we warm to him in great part because that seems also to be our common experience of life: we are bombarded with information and with reading matter but know obscurely that regardless of how we react to this a common fate awaits us all. Underneath all the stories we may tell ourselves, 'something is taking its course', as Beckett's most Hamlet-like hero, Hamm, reflects.

With Osric gone, Hamlet and Horatio discuss the encounter. 'This lapwing runs away with the shell on his head,' remarks Horatio (the lapwing was the proverbial type of juvenile pretension, explains Jenkins (p. 405)). Hamlet, as we would expect, is more expansive:

> A did comply with his dug before a sucked it. Thus has he –
> and many more of the same bevy that I know the drossy age
> dotes on – only got the tune of the time and, out of an habit
> of encounter, a kind of yeasty collection, which carries them
> through and through the most fanned and winnowed opin-
> ions; and do but blow them to their trial, the bubbles are out.
> (184–91)

And yet another cog has, in the course of all these bubbles, been locked into place.

The Folio now drops another twelve lines that are in the Quarto, and cuts to the quick:

> *Hor.* You will lose, my lord.
> *Ham.* I do not think so. Since he went into France, I have
>   been in continual practice. I shall win at the odds.
> (205–7)

And then, devastatingly, in the same matter-of-fact tone: 'Thou wouldst not think how ill all's here about my heart; but it is no matter.' This is a world away from 'there's a divinity doth shape our ends', but also from the rhetorical self-consciousness of: 'I have that within which passes show.' Coming as it does after so much action and so much talk it feels as though a space, a pool of silence, has been created precisely for it to drop into.

Horatio tries to remonstrate with him: 'Nay, good my lord.' But Hamlet waves this away: 'It is but foolery, but it is such a kind of gaingiving [misgiving] as would perhaps trouble a woman.' Horatio, ever sensible, urges him: 'If your mind dislike anything, obey it.' But Hamlet is too far in to pull back now, neither fully behind what he is about to do nor willing to step back from it. It may be that the death of Ophelia has brought about a kind of lassitude in him, a sense that nothing matters any more, or it may be that, like her, he is half-consciously happy to allow the stream to carry him where it will. Whatever it is, he rallies, and once again tries to cover his sense of unease with an appeal to Providence:

> Not a whit. We defy augury. There is special providence in the fall of a sparrow. If it be now, 'tis not to come; if it be not to come, it will be now; if it be not now, yet it will come. The readiness is all. Since no man, of aught he leaves, knows aught, what is't to leave betimes? (215–20)

This is the Quarto (with 'ought' emended to 'aught'), once again favoured by Jenkins, who glosses it: 'Since no man has any knowledge of anything he is leaving, what signifies an early death?' (p. 407). But what does 'knowledge' mean here? The Folio has: 'Since no man ha's ought of what he leaves, what is't to leave betimes?' which makes more sense: since we take nothing away with us from this life, why not die now rather than later?

This passage has elicited a huge amount of commentary, mainly from scholars wishing to show that Hamlet has here arrived at a new-found wisdom and made a kind of peace with himself. That is not how it strikes me. Compare these lines from *2 Henry IV*, in which a certain Feeble, the only one of the men Falstaff is seeking to conscript who does not try to get out of it, justifies his position:

> A man can die but once. We owe God a death. I'll ne'er bear a base mind. And't be my destiny, so. And't be not, so. No man's too good to serve's Prince. And let it go which way it will, he that dies this year is quit for the next. (III. ii. 221–5)

Feeble may be uttering a string of clichés, but they are clearly ideas he believes in wholeheartedly. His simple life is governed by two central tenets, belief in God and loyalty to King and Country. Hamlet is not simply giving us an aristocratic version of this, his reaching out for the New Testament image (Matthew 10.29), his equivocation with 'now' and 'to come', his grasping at the Stoic 'the readiness is all' in the next phrase, and his ending on a question, all testify to the effort such a statement is costing him and to his less than full confidence in what he is saying.

It may be helpful, in assessing Hamlet's attitude at this crucial juncture, to turn once again to Christopher Clark's splendid book on the events that led up to the First World War. He writes of 'the tendency we can discern in the reasoning of so many of the actors in this crisis, to perceive oneself as operating under irresistible external constraints while placing the responsibility for deciding between peace and war firmly on the shoulders of the opponent'. That is why Clark entitles his book *The Sleepwalkers*. And his sensitive exploration of the way in which men react to crisis has, I would suggest, implications for the understanding of individuals as well as for courts and chancelleries. It certainly helps us understand the strange feeling of being at once put upon and resigned to fate which comes to grip Hamlet and, indeed, everyone else at the Danish court, in these final folds.

The passage should not be looked at in isolation, anyway, but as the culmination of the conversation about what life means that Hamlet has been having with himself right through the play, and the conversation about what a good and meaningful life is, one whose end is fulfilment rather than mere cessation, that Hamlet had been having with Horatio just before the appearance of Osric. In the light of that, and of Hamlet's repeated hints of his misgivings and his heavy heart, this stands out clearly as yet another example of Eliot's point about Shakespeare's heroes at moments of crisis using commonplaces (a famous passage from St Paul here rather than anything from Seneca) to cheer themselves up, though my quote from Clark suggests that this is a natural human response to impending calamity rather than a specifically Stoic one. 'Cheer themselves up' is far too dismissive, typical of Eliot in the manner in which it homes in on a real issue and then fails to deal with it. What is important is that we in the audience, as we see and hear Hamlet here, cannot quite believe him and at the same time cannot stop our hearts going out to him.

16.3 (V. 2. 220–355)

And with this, the climactic scene is upon us. The most elaborate stage direction in the play informs us: 'Enter King, Queene, Laertes and Lords, with other attendants with Foyles, and Gauntlets, a Table and flagons of Wine on it.' (Q2. F replicates this in a slightly different order.) In a show of reconciliation Claudius takes Laertes's hand and puts it in Hamlet's. Hamlet has been preparing for this moment. 'Give me your pardon, sir,' he says to Laertes. 'I have done you wrong.' Is he referring to the murder of his father or to his behaviour in the graveyard? It is not clear, since Hamlet does not elaborate but instead goes on to excuse himself by claiming his madness was to blame: 'What I have done . . . I here proclaim was madness.' Disingenuously, but in keeping with what I have called the bad faith of his stabbing of the supposed King behind the arras, he dissociates himself from any deed he has committed:

> If Hamlet from himself be ta'en away,
> And when he's not himself does wrong Laertes,
> Hamlet does it not, Hamlet denies it.
> Who does it then? His madness. (230–3)

In fact, he goes on, in acting as he did he not only wronged others, he wronged himself, so that 'his madness is poor Hamlet's enemy'.

Laertes, however, though acknowledging himself satisfied by this apology 'in nature', insists in rather convoluted language that 'in my terms of honour/ I stand aloof'. His honour, in other words, calls for some satisfaction, though he himself as a human being accepts the apology. This stark division, this need to abide by a code of honour despite what his heart tells him, only serves to characterise Laertes as someone who belongs neither in the courtly world of intrigue nor in the foggy and confused world in which Hamlet finds himself living, but in an older culture which, the play appears to suggest, has had its day, for all its fine features. Not only that, of course. We know all too well that in a sense Laertes is 'playing himself', acting the part of such a person because he and Claudius have plotted Hamlet's death by means of a fencing contest, and that not only will his own blade be without the protective button on the tip, but that tip will be smeared with a deadly poison. Yet though he has completely fallen in with the culture of deceit that permeates the court, Laertes would surely claim that he is doing what he is doing to avenge his father and sister, and that it is therefore inherently noble.

Hamlet, of course, accepts what he says and calls for the foils. The complex relationship between the two young men is brought out by the next exchange:

> *Ham.* I'll be your foil, Laertes. In mine ignorance
> Your skill shall like a star i'th' darkest night
> Stick fiery off indeed.   [stand out conspicuously]
> *Laer.*   You mock me, sir.
> *Ham.* No, by this hand. (252–5)

But Claudius is keen for them to get on with it. 'Give them the foils, young Osric,' he commands, then asks them if they have understood the rules of the wager. Laertes, with the excuse that the foil he has been given is too heavy, chooses another, presumably the poisoned one without the button on the tip, as he had planned with the King.

But before they get down to the contest Claudius has to have the other element of his plot in place:

> Set me the stoups of wine upon that table.
> If Hamlet give the first or second hit,
> Or quit in answer of the third exchange,
> Let all the battlements their ordnance fire:
> The King shall drink to Hamlet's better breath,
> And in the cup an union shall he throw
> Richer than that which four successive kings
> In Denmark's crown have worn – give me the cups –
> And let the kettle to the trumpets speak,
> The trumpet to the cannoneer without,
> The cannons to the heavens, the heaven to earth,
> 'Now the King drinks to Hamlet.' Come, begin. (264–75)

We are back to the very start of the play, when from the darkened battlements is heard the sound of the King carousing with his companions accompanied by celebratory cannon shot, much to Hamlet's disgust. But also back to Claudius's first unctuous words to the court and to Hamlet – it is as if, in the hour of his triumph, he loses all his doubts and radiates kindly self-confidence. There is also the horror, which is a constant in this play where everything the court says and does means something other than at first appears, of a toast to his nephew being nothing other than a toast to his demise. The 'union' thrown into the cup, furthermore, literally means a pearl of 'unique' quality – except of course that in this instance it will be nothing of the sort but a dose of poison designed to finish Hamlet off should Laertes fail in his task. But the poison, in Claudius's mind, also signifies Hamlet's union with death and possibly his own union with Gertrude and with Denmark, now free of the dangers that Hamlet poses to both.

And so to the duel which is not a duel since the set-up has been rigged, like Hamlet's encounter with Ophelia and the journey to England. As they watch, Claudius and Gertrude exchange comments in a way that repeats all the choric commentaries on plays performed or letters read which have been a constant feature of the play. 'Our son shall win,' says Claudius, for the first time since the start daring to assert his implicit paternity. If Gertrude notices this she does not comment. 'He's fat and scant of breath' is her comment as they break between bouts. She follows this comment, which can be taken either as a mother's anxiety for her son or as instruction to the actor and casting director, with 'Here, Hamlet, take my napkin, rub thy brows.' And, no doubt to show her faith in him: 'The Queen carouses to thy fortune, Hamlet.' She calls herself the Queen and not his mother, perhaps to lend weight to her support for him by echoing Claudius's earlier: 'Now the King drinks to Hamlet.'

But Claudius had drunk *before* he dropped the poison/union into the wine. Shakespeare has so played his cards that he can put before us the most naked melodrama even as he distances himself from the over-obvious plotting of the genre. 'Gertrude, do not drink,' cries Claudius, but she is insistent: 'I will, my lord, I pray you pardon me.' And she drinks.

As Claudius mutters: 'It is the poison'd cup. It is too late', Hamlet refuses the cup which she now offers him, saying he will have it 'by and by'. At the same time Laertes gears himself up to deliver the fatal blow, though he too suddenly finds delivering it is not so easy: 'And yet it is almost against my conscience.' However, in the next exchange, he succeeds in wounding Hamlet, they scuffle and each picks up his rapier again, except that, in good melodramatic fashion, each picks up the other's, and now Hamlet wounds Laertes as the Queen falls and Osric calls out: 'Look to the Queen there, ho!'

Horatio cannot understand what he is seeing: 'They bleed on both sides. How is it, my lord?' Osric, meanwhile is asking the same question of Laertes, who now, seeing what has happened, blurts out:

Why, as a woodcock to mine own springe, Osric.
I am justly kill'd with mine own treachery. (312–13)

It is the moment of truth for him. As one who is a man of honour, his treachery had gone as much against the grain as Hamlet's attempt to ape his ranting. There is a huge element of relief, one feels, in his acknowledgement that he has been killed through his own treachery – relief because it means that even though he dies, the code of honour to which he hitched his life is very much intact and blessed by Providence.

Hamlet suddenly becomes aware that something is wrong with his mother: 'How does the Queen?' Claudius tries to keep up the pretence: 'She swoons to see them bleed.' But she is still conscious enough to speak, and, like Laertes, in the moment of death, blurts out the damning truth: 'No, no, the drink, the drink! O my dear Hamlet! . . . I am poison'd.' And with that she dies.

Hamlet is confused: 'O villainy! Ho! Let the door be lock'd./ Treachery! Seek it out.' But Laertes provides the explanation:

> It is here, Hamlet. Hamlet, thou art slain.
> No medicine in the world can do thee good;
> In thee there is not half an hour's life.
> The treacherous instrument is in thy hand,
> Unbated and envenom'd. The foul practice
> Hath turn'd itself on me. Lo, here I lie,
> Never to rise again. Thy mother's poison'd.
> I can no more. The King – the King's to blame. (319–26)

Every artist has occasionally known the moment when the struggle to give shape to an intuition, a mere feeling, is coming to an end, and the material, which had so often seemed unyielding, suddenly takes the shape he dreamed of. So here. *Everything* now seems to resonate. For Hamlet treachery has never really been out there, it has always been 'here'. The treacherous instrument has always been 'in his hand'. Hence the strange sense we get from this scene of both watching a melodrama play itself out and watching that which, Hamlet told us at the start, 'passeth show' parade before us.

And the dream-like quality of the scene, the sense that it is both utterly meaningless *and* what has long been ordained, what

we have long known will happen, stems of course not just from
the fact that everyone knows how *Hamlet* ends, but from the fact
that a variant of the scene has occurred twice before in the play,
first in the Ghost's words about his own murder and then in *The
Mousetrap*, where a nephew killed his uncle by means of poison.

The 'thing' unfolds. Hamlet takes in what Laertes is telling
him: 'The point envenomed too!' he exclaims, then turns on the
King: 'Then, venom, to thy work.' He follows this, as Claudius
cries out and 'all' cry 'Treason! treason!' (for, after all, it is the
elected monarch who is being attacked before their eyes), by
forcing Claudius to drink the poisoned wine:

> Here, thou incestuous, murd'rous, damned Dane,
> Drink off this potion. Is thy union here?
> Follow my mother. (330–2)

It is as though he has at last been compelled to take part in the play
the Ghost devised for him, but, unlike Laertes, he seems to have
found no peace in what has occurred. He still sees his uncle as first
of all incestuous and only secondarily as murderous; he still takes
satisfaction in playing with the word 'union' and besmirching the
name of 'mother' by calling the Queen not Claudius's wife, but
his, Hamlet's, mother. As if *this* indeed was Claudius's crime – to
have attempted union with his mother. Action here is not
resolution.

Laertes, in the moment of death, recognises where the true
guilt lies, acknowledges Hamlet's inherent nobility of spirit, and
seeks to absolve him of his father, Polonius's, death:

> He [Claudius] is justly serv'd.
> It is a poison temper'd by himself.
> Exchange forgiveness with me, noble Hamlet.
> Mine and my father's death come not upon thee,
> Nor thine on me. (332–6)

'Heaven make thee free of it,' responds Hamlet. 'I follow thee.'

The play is winding down. The folds are folding in upon each other. The closing, retrospective speeches are tumbling out. We await the speech of the most eloquent actor in the play. Yet Shakespeare has not finished with surprises.

Hamlet, to begin with. He goes on:

> I am dead, Horatio. Wretched [unhappy] Queen, adieu.
> You that look pale and tremble at this chance,
> That are but mutes or audience to this act,
> Had I but time – as this fell sergeant, Death,
> Is strict in his arrest – O, I could tell you –
> But let it be, Horatio, I am dead,
> Thou livest. Report me and my cause aright
> To the unsatisfied. (337–44)

The old rhetoric is still there, the noble pentameters and the aristocrat's awareness of living in public still come quite naturally ('You that look pale . . . audience to this act'), as does the wit in the choice of metaphor (Death as a sergeant come to arrest him), but his time has simply run out: 'But let it be'. Hamlet will never speak 'the truth' that he so longed for – that is perhaps always beyond us. All he can do is lay an injunction on Horatio to tell his story and to tell it right.

But that is to reckon without Horatio, who now insists that, like 'an antique Roman', he has no intention of doing anything other than die here with his friend and master. Hamlet, though, will have none of it. He tries to wrest the cup from him and pleads again that he will only die in peace if he feels there is someone left alive who can tell his story:

> O God, Horatio, what a wounded name,
> Things standing thus unknown, shall I leave behind me.
> If thou didst ever hold me in thy heart,
> Absent thee from felicity awhile,
> And in this harsh world draw thy breath in pain
> To tell my story. (349–54)

242

Not the truth, then, but simply, 'my story'.

Now for one last time there is an interruption and a noise offstage. 'A march afar off, and shout within', says the Folio, though editors prefer to emend to 'and shot within', in order to motivate Hamlet's surprised comment: 'What warlike noise is this?'

It is, Osric enters to explain, 'Young Fortinbras, with conquest come from Poland,/ To the ambassadors of England gives/ This warlike volley.' So this figure, Hamlet's Norwegian double, who has haunted the play from the start, arrives at last, just as Hamlet dies, and with him messengers newly come from England, presumably with the news of the execution of Rosencrantz and Guildenstern. Thus Norway and England (and, in thought, Poland) congregate at this moment in this place.

Even in death Hamlet knows what the arrival of Fortinbras means:

O, I die, Horatio.
The potent poison quite o'ercrows my spirit.
I cannot live to hear the news from England,
But I do prophesy th'election lights
On Fortinbras. He has my dying voice. (357–61)

In this elected monarchy the reigning monarch cannot choose his successor but he can give him his 'voice' or seal of approval. This was what Claudius had promised Hamlet, and now Hamlet, with Claudius dead, takes it upon himself to speak as monarch. The warlike and impetuous Fortinbras, who had only with difficulty been restrained by his father from attacking Denmark and reclaiming the land his uncle had once ceded to Old Hamlet, appears as a cleansing angel to sweep away the corruption of the Danish court and take over the country, and he does so, Hamlet here tells us, with his blessing. Thus, as Margreta de Grazia and others have noted, the personal feuds and private sorrows of the Hamlet family and those who depend on them are subsumed within the wider geopolitical context – one that has of course been there from the start, though only in the background. But this does not mean that the private gives way to the public, only that the final moments of the play show the two in dialogue.

Hamlet, having done his royal duty, finally reaches his end, still anxious that Horatio lay out in public all that has happened:

> So tell him, with th'occurrents more and less
> Which have solicited – the rest is silence. (362–3)

The Folio has: 'the rest is silence. O, o, o, o', but the editorial tradition appears to be to end with the word and leave any dying sounds to actorly initiative or directorial discretion. Horatio, the man of few but always apt words, is on hand to close off this moment in the play:

> Now cracks a noble heart. Good night, sweet prince,
> And flights of angels sing thee to thy rest. (364–5)

It is worth comparing this with another dirge, spoken to another heroic warrior as he dies before us in an earlier play of Shakespeare's. For Shakespeare, as we have often seen, is both the most fertile and inventive of writers and one who seems to recycle earlier material almost infinitely and usually for the better, more like Bach and Mozart in this than like any other writer. At the end of *1 Henry IV* the two young rivals, both Harolds, the one known as Hal (Harry Bolingbroke) and the other as Hotspur (Harry Percy), finally get the chance to fight it out in single combat, as they meet on the battlefield at Shrewsbury. Hotspur is wounded and falls. His last words run like this:

> O, Harry, thou has robbed me of my youth!
> I better brook the loss of brittle life
> Than those proud titles thou hast won of me.
> They wound my thoughts worse than thy sword my flesh.
> …

> O, I could prophesy,
> But that the earthy and cold hand of death
> Lies on my tongue: no, Percy, thou art dust,
> And food for –

Like Hamlet, he dies before he can say all he wants to say. Hal's dirge for him begins by completing his unfinished sentence:

> For worms, brave Percy. Fare thee well, great heart!
> Ill-weaved ambition, how much art thou shrunk!
> When that this body did contain a spirit,
> A kingdom for it was too small a bound,
> But now two paces of the vilest earth
> Is room enough. This earth, that bears thee dead,
> Bears not alive so stout a gentleman.
> …
> Adieu, and take thy praise with thee to heaven!
> Thy ignominy sleep with thee in the grave,
> But not remembered in thy epitaph!
>
> (*1 Hen. IV*, V. 4. 77–101)

This is wonderful in the way its precise appraisal of Percy's defects is allowed to sit quite easily with admiration for his qualities. Surely this too falls under the rubric of Eliot's pre-modern 'unified sensibility', for today we find it almost impossible to achieve such balance in our assessment of men. Hal begins by cruelly (to us) completing Hotspur's phrase – food . . . for worms. But in the same sentence he brings in quite a different perspective, '*brave* Percy'. This leads to 'Fare thee well, great heart', but that in turn is qualified by what follows about Percy's 'ill-weaved ambition', with a hint of what dangers it posed for the country. And he brings his dirge to a conclusion with a similarly balanced view: 'Adieu, and take thy praise with thee to heaven!/ Thy ignominy [Hotspur was after all a traitor] sleep with thee in the grave,/ But not remembered in thy epitaph!'

And just as this tells us as much about the speaker as about the subject, so Horatio's much briefer dirge for Hamlet. For here there is no qualification and the very brevity of the dirge, after so many words, so much confused and confusing action, comes as a kind of release, as we too join him in wishing for Hamlet, the 'sweet prince', that 'flights of angels sing thee to thy rest'.

16.4 (V. 2. 366–408)

But the sound of a procession approaching causes him to break off with: 'Why does the drum come hither?' just as Hamlet had broken off moments earlier to ask: 'What warlike noise is this?' Or rather, Shakespeare inserts these cues to guide the production as economically as possible. And then, the stage direction tells us, 'Enter Fortinbras and the English Ambassadors, and Soldiers with drum, and colours [and Attendants].' And in one of those devastatingly simple sentences which, in this play, shine out at key moments from the linguistic pyrotechnics, the parodies and 'essays of wit' that predominate, Fortinbras merely says: 'Where is this sight?' And Horatio answers: 'What is it you would see?/ If aught of woe or wonder, cease your search.'

Jenkins forbears to comment on that 'where?' but surely it is vital. Shakespeare could so easily have written, 'What is this sight?', having Fortinbras ask for an explanation of the carnage he beholds. But instead he writes 'where?' and the clear implication is that what he has come upon is some unearthly scene, an image of some sort of Last Judgement. The implication of 'where' is thus: not anywhere on earth. (Arden 3 suggests Fortinbras has been told of the carnage and now looks round for it, which is plausible but banal.) And Horatio, the final 'chorus' in this play of many and varied choruses, asks, almost equally strangely, 'What is it you would see?' And then he stands back, so to speak, and for one last time frames and comments on a scene that appears before us: 'If aught of woe or wonder, cease your search.' Jenkins wants us to take 'wonder' in an archaic sense as 'calamity, extreme wretchedness', but surely the phrase needs no historicising: like the Last Judgement, this is a scene which not only brings one to tears but also fills one with a sense of witnessing something that passes understanding, more a natural disaster than a merely human calamity – not the liberation of Belsen so much as the aftermath of a tsunami.

Fortinbras is no Hamlet; his natural and verbal responses always run on well-worn tracks, emotional and rhetorical, and that, no doubt, is what will make him a firm and reliable ruler:

> This quarry cries on havoc. O proud Death,
> What feast is toward in thine eternal cell,
> That thou so many princes at a shot
> So bloodily has struck? (369–72)

The English Ambassador is no less predictable and even less imaginative:

> The sight is dismal;
> And our affairs from England come too late.
> The ears are senseless that should give us hearing
> To tell him his commandment is fulfill'd.
> That Rosencrantz and Guildenstern are dead.
> Where should we have our thanks? (373–7)

They have arrived too late in every sense. But then everything in this play was always too late – Hamlet feels he lives too late, too late he realises he has killed the wrong man, Laertes returns too late to save his sister, and then, too late, sees the folly of his actions. At the same time there is the eerie feeling throughout that the real play has not yet started, that it is perpetually deferred. Time is indeed out of joint.

The play is rushing now towards its end, and Horatio is ready to fulfil Hamlet's injunction. Since, he tells the new arrivals, you have come, 'jump upon this bloody question', at the precise moment when this terrible denouement took place, 'You from the Polack wars and you from England',

> give order that these bodies
> High on a stage [platform] be placed to the view,

And let me speak to th'yet unknowing world
How these things came about. So shall you hear
Of carnal, bloody, and unnatural acts,
Of accidental judgments, casual slaughters,
Of deaths put on by cunning and forc'd cause,
And, in this upshot, purposes mistook
Fall'n on the inventors' heads. All this can I
Truly deliver. (382–91)

He begins ceremoniously enough, with the injunction to place the bodies on a raised platform in full view. But then, instead of clarifying, highlighting the important and relegating the rest to oblivion, so as to report Hamlet's 'cause' aright and set the story straight, what he does is to tell it as it was, confused, accidental, crooked in every way. It is difficult to overestimate the shock to the audience, who have been waiting for this moment when all will be made clear. But this is more Raymond Chandler than Agatha Christie: there may be a thread of sorts running through it, but in the main it consists of *unnatural* acts, *accidental* judgements, *casual* slaughters, purposes *mistook* and falling on the heads of those who thought them up.

Is this then what the play we have been watching has been? Is it, we want to say, *all* that it has been?

The *Iliad* closes with Hector's death, followed by the laments of the three women with whom his life was bound: his mother Hecuba, his wife Andromache, and the woman who was the cause of it all, Helen. *Oedipus at Colonus* ends with Antigone's marvellous: 'He died in the foreign land as he desired; and he occupies a bed shady for ever, nor did he fail to leave behind mourning with tears.' *Beowulf* closes with a dirge for the great leader as twelve warriors circle round his funeral pyre. It seems that epic and tragedy naturally end not with the death of the protagonist, but with a lament by those who are left behind. And *Hamlet* is no exception. Horatio's lament for Hamlet, however, is not to be found in these lines, but in those he uttered a moment before, as his friend and prince expired:

> Now cracks a noble heart. Good night, sweet prince,
> And flights of angels sing thee to thy rest.

As Hamlet, on being told the provenance of the skull he is holding, suddenly recalls the jester Yorick: 'Alas, poor Yorick. I knew him, Horatio, a fellow of infinite jest, of most excellent fancy. He hath bore me on his back a thousand times' – so Horatio recalls Hamlet. As what remained of Yorick for Hamlet was his 'infinite jest' and carrying him on his back, so what remains of Hamlet for Horatio is his noble heart, his sweetness, his princely spirit.

We in the audience know Horatio is saying something important, just as we come to accept that he is saying something important when he describes what we have witnessed in the past three or four hours as a series of horrible mishaps and confusions, without much rhyme or reason.

Hamlet had, after his initial response, mistaken Yorick's skull for the ultimate reality, trumping, as it were, his memories of the living man. Horatio makes no such mistake: both are equally valid, the skull and the living man, there is not the one without the other. And so with Hamlet. Hamlet, who spent his short life desperately searching for some sort of meaning, does not find that meaning in death, as religiously minded commentators tend to say, but in life – in his life. Or rather, he *finds* nothing, the meaning just *is* his life. Just as Yorick's essential being, his *quiddity*, emerged in his jesting and in his joyful carrying of the child prince upon his back, so Hamlet's own quiddity emerges in his very refusal to take full part in any of the plays offered him and in the confusion and anguish this caused him. Unlike everyone else in the play, apart from Ophelia and Horatio, he alone retains his integrity, remains through it all a noble heart, a sweet prince – not the fallen Renaissance Humanist prince of Ophelia's imagination, but a naturally confused and inherently noble spirit, one who caused much harm and gave much pleasure, and suffered for that, but who has earned the right, in death, to be called 'noble' and 'sweet prince'.

That, of course, is not how he saw himself; but it is how *we* see him. It is how Shakespeare's play of intrigue, botched revenge and confused allegiances allows him to emerge. That is why Romantic views of *Hamlet* as being essentially about Hamlet's interiority are as misguided as modern views of it as not being about his interiority at all. Hamlet imagines that what he feels is what he is, and is fierce in protecting this, when all along what he is is something more like the sum of his feelings and acts, the sum of his words and his way of moving and of speaking. And in that he is, of course, like us. 'These', he had said dismissively at the start, 'are the actions a man might play', the mere outward trappings of an ineffable inner being. It sounded persuasive, but the play goes on to show us that the division he makes here between inner and outer is too sharp: just as Yorick *is* his actions, whether making a joke pouring wine on the clown's head or carrying the young prince on his back, so Hamlet *is* the actions he plays/performs: he *is* his witty retorts and his impassioned speeches. He of course can never see it, but, after his death, we, the audience, can and do.

Mallarmé was much preoccupied with this question of what a person truly is. He sensed that it is only after death, and only in the memories of others, that we become fully ourselves. He put it memorably in his 'tombeau' for Edgar Allan Poe: 'Tel qu'en Lui-même enfin l'éternité le change' – as into himself eternity finally transforms him. And this we experience as *Hamlet* ends.

The play, though, is not yet quite done. We have had Horatio's dirge, which speaks for us of what we feel, and his account of what has occurred, which speaks for us of what we have to acknowledge we have witnessed. Now, to conclude, we need another voice, untainted by the intrigues of the Court of Elsinore, the voice of Fortinbras, the outsider who is to take over the kingdom:

> Let four captains
> Bear Hamlet like a soldier to the stage,
> For he was likely, had he been put on [tested],
> To have prov'd most royal; and for his passage,
> The soldier's music and the rite of war

> Speak loudly for him.
> Take up the bodies. Such a sight as this
> Becomes the field, but here shows much amiss.
> Go, bid the soldiers shoot. (400–8)

Fortinbras the soldier can think only in terms of war and hunting, but it is surely right that this play, which so consummately respects the rules of its genre even as it totally subverts them, which questions every utterance by making us recognise the (usually narrow) world view from which it emanates, should end in so rousing and emphatic a fashion. It only throws into greater relief Hamlet's own last words: 'The rest is silence.'

BY WAY OF CONCLUSION

'Fundamental to any idea of theatre is a notion of precisely how the theatre is to relate to reality,' V. A. Kolve wisely says at the start of his great book on the Middle English religious drama. Scholars of the Elizabethan theatre, and of Shakespeare's theatre in particular, have been far readier than their medievalist colleagues to take up the challenge, and from Anne Righter to Robert Weimann we have had a series of splendid explorations of this central topic. *Hamlet*, though, asks the much stranger question of precisely how reality relates to theatre.

There was, of course, a generalised Renaissance answer to this question, voiced by Jaques in *As You Like It*, that

> All the world's a stage
> And all the men and women merely players;
> They have their exits and their entrances,
> And one man in his time plays many parts,
> His acts being seven ages. (II. 7. 139–43)

But this, like Calderón's 'life is a dream', lacks bite. It is too general. We register it, shrug and move on. The question *Hamlet* (and Hamlet) asks is: What is my part in life and how do I play it? For while once it might have been possible to follow one's father through the seven ages of life, now, in the new, confusing, socially mobile world of the Renaissance and the Reformation, choices have to be made, decisions taken: What faith do I believe in? What ruler do I support? What career should I choose? And with these come those other, modern questions: Am I up to it? (Up to facing death for my convictions, to facing exile for supporting a defeated claimant, to becoming an actor or a lawyer or a writer?) And if I feel I am not, is that my fault or the fault of circumstances, and can I overcome this by an exercise of will? If I can't, where does that leave me?

Such questions do not trouble Hal, the future Henry V. As Part I of *Henry IV* opens we learn that, much as Hamlet seems to be disappointing the King his father, so Hal is disappointing his: 'Yea, there thou mak'st me sad,' says the King to his councillor Westmorland,

> And mak'st me sin
> In envy that my Lord Northumberland
> Should be the father to so blest a son –
> A son who is the theme of honour's tongue,
> Amongst a grove the very straightest plant;
> Who is sweet fortune's minion and her pride;
> Whilst I, by looking on the praise of him,
> See riot and dishonour stain the brow
> Of my young Harry. (*1 Hen. IV*, I. 1. 78–86)

Much like Laertes and Fortinbras, the young Northumberland, another Harry, known as Hotspur, is a man with few doubts and a strong sense of his own military worth. Hal, on the other hand, seems to be consorting with rabble and neglecting his princely duties. Yet, after we have indeed seen him in such company, when he is left alone on stage to utter his first soliloquy, all is made clear:

> I know you all, and will a while uphold
> The unyoked humour of your idleness.
> Yet herein will I imitate the sun,

Who doth permit the base contagious clouds
To smother up his beauty from the world,
That, when he please again to be himself,
Being wanted, he may be more wonder'd at
...
So, when this loose behaviour I throw off
And pay the debt I never promised,
By how much better than my word I am,
By so much shall I falsify men's hopes,
And, like bright metal on a sullen ground,
My reformation, glitt'ring o'er my fault,
Shall show more goodly and attract more eyes
Than that which hath no foil to set it off.
I'll so offend to make offence a skill,
Redeeming time when men think least I will. (I. 2. 188–210)

He knows men and he knows himself. He knows exactly what he is doing and has no doubt that when the moment is right he will 'redeem the time' and appear to be a reformed character so as to enhance his reputation all the more. And Hal never wavers in what follows, telling Falstaff to his face (albeit while they are play-acting) that he will reject him when the time comes, and showing himself to be truly his father's son when he fights with him against the rebels at the Battle of Shrewsbury and kills his rival Hotspur in single combat.

While Hal's soliloquies, like those of Richard III and Iago, merely inform the audience of what he is up to, Hamlet's show him struggling to understand himself. Hal can play many parts with ease because he is clear about the boundaries that lie between them, but Hamlet seems half-heartedly to try out one role after another, part of the trouble being that they flow into and contaminate one another. He cannot take part in the play of the court because he is deeply suspicious of the new King, his uncle Claudius, and he senses that all at court are frightened toadies, desperate to please whoever is in power and terrified of the consequences if they do not. He cannot take part in the Revenge Tragedy his father wants him to act in because, first of all, he is not sure if the Ghost really is the spirit of his dead father and not a spirit out of Hell sent to lead him to destruction, and secondly because the whole notion of Revenge Tragedy strikes him as out of date and no longer relevant, what the French call *pompier*. Because he loved, or imagines he loved, his father, and loathes his uncle, he would dearly like reassurance on the authenticity of the Ghost, and because he deeply admires the old revenge ethos he is deeply troubled by his inability to embrace it wholeheartedly. And he cannot take the part of the *meneur de jeu* for very long because he is unclear about the nature or the goal of the *jeu*. Each of these roles seems open to him yet he cannot persuade himself to enter any of them totally, unlike those around him, who appear to have no such problem.

To grasp Hamlet's relation to Revenge Tragedy it may be helpful to keep in mind an episode from a modern novel much concerned with the issues *Hamlet* puts before us. At the start of Camus's *L'Étranger* the hero, Meursault, looks out of his apartment window and watches the crowds streaming away from the local cinema. On first coming out, he notices, people hold themselves more upright, make large gestures and speak loudly. But as they move away and the magic of the cinema starts to fade they gradually assume their normal mode of walking, lower their voices, gesticulate less amply. Briefly while watching the film they were transformed, heroic, participants in some great adventure, but very soon they are back to their old unheroic, ordinary selves, struggling with lives that never make much sense and without a whiff of adventure in them. Meursault himself, as we discover, is almost pathologically incapable of responding not only to the magic of the cinema but to the debased magic (or so the novel implies) that subsists in our society under the name of morality and law, with fatal consequences for others and for himself.

Hamlet, too, though at times he works himself up to a state in which he can both mouth the appropriate words and even imagine himself performing the appropriate deeds, cannot keep this up for long. Scepticism keeps breaking through, a feeling that all forms of action and all interpretation depend on the assumptions we bring to them and the frames we place around them, and this reinforces his doubts about playing the parts expected of him by his uncle and by his father.

Simon Palfrey and Tiffany Stern, in their fascinating book, *Shakespeare in Parts*, quote a mid-seventeenth-century writer, Thomas Randolph, who said of his friend Thomas Riley, who performed the lead role in his own plays, that he was

> [A] Proteus that [could] take
> What shape he please, and in an instant make
> Himself to anything: be that, or this,
> By voluntary metamorphosis.

'The word "Proteus" – the god of shape-shifting –', they explain, 'gives the clue. The term is used here not to imply an ability to change character so much as an ability to "become" whatever character they are playing. Riley can make himself be whoever he has been given to perform.' The same praise was, it seems, bestowed on Richard Burbage, Shakespeare's leading actor and almost certainly the first Hamlet. Palfrey and Stern quote a contemporary comment that he was 'a delightful Proteus . . . wholly transforming himself into his Part, and putting off himself with his Cloathes'. This is almost precisely the opposite of Hamlet. He cannot 'wholly transform himself' into any of the parts he is offered, feeling, as he says at the very beginning, that to do so would be merely to act a part and not be truly himself. As we see from his comments about the Player's speech, he would dearly love to be able to do so.

But what is this 'true self' Hamlet says he cannot utter? In an entry in his diary for 19 September 1917 Kafka writes:

> Have never understood how it is possible for almost everyone who writes to objectify his sufferings in the midst of under-going them; thus I, for example, in the midst of my unhappi-ness, in all likelihood with my head still smarting from unhappiness, sit down and write to someone: I am unhappy.

Yes, I can even go beyond that and with as many flourishes as
I have the talent for, all of which seem to have nothing to do
with my unhappiness, ring simple, or contrapuntal, or a whole
orchestration of changes on my theme. And it is not a lie, and
it does not still my pain; it is simply a merciful surplus of
strength at a moment when suffering has raked me to the
bottom of my being and plainly exhausted all my strength.
But then what kind of a surplus is it?

Kafka is always compelling because he looks at himself as he looks
at others, with complete honesty and objectivity. Writing was his
life, was, he was convinced, the way to the truth, the way to a real
understanding of the world and his own place in it; yet was it not
also, he often wondered, taking him further and further away
from the world, further and further away from a real understanding of himself? Here he comes at the problem via the question of rhetoric. All writing involves rhetoric, the ability to use
words, yet rhetoric seems to be nothing but the decoration of a
theme which forms its ground base and which, silent, obdurate,
remains there unchanged no matter how many words he deploys
to express it, a theme that can actually be expressed in a single
word: unhappiness. Yet as he deploys words to give it voice he
finds that this does give him a kind of pleasure – but is it the false
pleasure of covering a silent, obdurate pain with words, or the
glorious expression of a merciful surplus of strength? Hamlet feels
a surge of pleasure when he hears of the arrival of the players, and
clearly enjoys giving the Player the lead in the Hecuba speech – yet
in the end finds he cannot emulate him. Is the ability to speak as
the Player speaks the result of a 'merciful surplus of strength'? Or
is Hamlet's inability to emulate him the recognition that to do so
would take him away from his own self? Does writing down 'I am
unhappy' bring about a blessed momentary release from unhappiness or start one down the path of self-pity and self-deception?
Wisely, Kafka ends on a question: 'What kind of a surplus is it?'
    Hamlet too has no answers, only questions. Why does he feel
as he does when his contemporaries so obviously don't? On the

one side Rosencrantz and Guildenstern seem to have no qualms about taking part in courtly play; on the other Laertes, who is, like him, both noble and idealistic, seems to have no qualms about taking part in a Revenge play when he learns that *his* father has been murdered; while Young Fortinbras, his Norwegian mirror image, seems to think nothing of taking a large company of fighting men off to conquer a miserable and useless piece of land. The explanation given at the start, by Hamlet himself, is that he is afflicted with melancholy. But this, demonstrated by his black clothes and gloomy demeanour, is, in a sense, merely another kind of play-acting, as both his mother and his uncle tell him. However, it is a form of play-acting with which he feels more comfortable than with either of the two parts he is offered, that of dutiful heir and courtier, and that of avenging son. Partly this is because it fits in better with his sceptical frame of mind, but partly too because he has a genuine reason for it in his father's recent death and his mother's over-hasty marriage to a man he loathes and despises, his father's brother. He tries to justify his feelings by referring both to her haste in remarrying and to the nature and appearance of the person she has chosen to marry, but his sharp differentiation of his father and his uncle, the one a god the other a demon, one noble the other base, one chaste and respectful to his wife, the other a vile seducer whose hold on Gertrude depends entirely on sensuality and lust – all this would have made Shakespeare's audience, no less than a post-Freudian one, feel that part of the problem at least may lie with Hamlet himself. And they would have had no difficulty in intuiting that what Hamlet cannot bear about his mother's remarriage is the idea that she is a person in her own right, with her own feelings and desires, which have nothing to do with her son.

Proust is of more help here than Freud. What the young Marcel discovers on the traumatic day on which his mother first refuses to leave her dinner party to come upstairs to kiss him goodnight, and then, when he waylays her on the stairs as she is finally going to bed and she, realising his overwrought state, agrees to read him to sleep – what he discovers that day is that his mother is manipulable, just like any other human being. But if this is the case it means that, like other human beings, she is mortal. Suddenly, paradoxically, he understands that just as she had come to him that night so she will one day leave him for ever. It is his induction to adulthood; though, such is human nature, it is a discovery he will have to keep remaking with every woman with whom he becomes involved.

So with Hamlet. The discovery of his mother as a sexual being and therefore as a sexual being even with his father, brings with it an awareness of his own contingency. There is nothing necessary or inevitable about his existence; like Tristram Shandy's, it is an existence with a chance beginning in a bed, the result of a moment of desire uniting two people whose thoughts might have been very far from united even as he was being conceived. There is thus nothing necessary about his relation to his parents, and so to his past. Unlike St Jerome, contentedly transmitting the ancient scriptures to future generations, he is, like the Melancolia, alone with his imagination, his energy and his confused desires, and with nothing meaningful to engage them. The notion is too painful to be accepted, and Hamlet will go on idealising his father and desperately trying to do the same with his mother, imagining her not as a desiring being in her own right but as the victim of a villain's blandishments. This idealisation is reinforced by the Ghost, for the story he has to tell is precisely the one Hamlet has been telling himself, except that it is more extreme. The Ghost's brother seems not only to have seduced his wife (though whether before or after his death is a mystery Shakespeare deliberately leaves unsolved, and in a sense it seems not to matter to either the father or the son), but also to have murdered him. The two merge into one in the Ghost's account, as they do in Hamlet's mind, and the one is never mentioned without the other: Claudius, in the minds of both father and son, is always both murderer and adulterer/seducer.

The Ghost's story resonates with Hamlet because it is precisely the one he has been telling himself. However, for just that reason it is to be doubted. For is it not *too much* like the one he has been telling himself to be true?

Hamlet's attempt to get at the truth is thus the attempt to exorcise something within himself that he cannot come to terms with and which, for that reason, is poisoning his whole life. The mime and play he puts on 'to catch the conscience of the King', is at the same time an attempt to catch his own conscience, to put to bed his own obsessions. Finding Claudius guilty would mean exorcising his own guilty sense that there is no meaning to his existence and that he should not exist at all. Instead of a psychodrama we would then (only) have a melodrama. But, inevitably, his ruse succeeds in neither of these aims. It is still unclear when Claudius stomps out in anger whether he is guilty of murder or not, and therefore whether Hamlet is justified in his feelings or not. His subsequent actions are half-hearted at best, done in bad faith at worst. Unable to act in any of the plays on offer, he nevertheless senses that he cannot stand on the margins for ever. If the only parts on offer are in plays in which he cannot wholly believe he senses that he will nevertheless have to take part in one or other of them whether he likes it or not. In such circumstances he is unable to act except by shutting out that part of himself which refuses to believe in or to assent to such action/acting. The desire to be free of the unresolvable knot at the centre of his being has been with him from the start and has been expressed by him as the desire to melt and merge into the universe, to let go, to cease to be. Yet suicide is exactly the kind of grand gesture ('Roman', he calls it when Horatio at the end threatens to make it) that he cannot find it in himself to make, and so, like Ophelia, he comes to it half-heartedly and in bad faith, trying to manoeuvre himself into a position where all decision is taken from him, and in the end he succeeds.

Just as Hamlet does not feel able to inhabit naturally any of the roles on offer, so the play *Hamlet* does not feel able to inhabit naturally any of the theatrical models on offer. It is not a comedy, though it has many of the elements of Shakespeare's comedies; it is not a history, though it has many of the elements of Shakespeare's histories. Is it then a tragedy? Rather than worrying about nomenclature it is better to focus on what it is: a vast collage of different forms and styles, many presented in conjunction with comments on them by other voices within the play. At its heart, as at the heart of the great prose works of Rabelais and Sterne, which are similarly made up of a bewildering array of styles and forms collaged together, lies a silence which longs to erupt into speech but which knows that all existing forms of speech will betray what is crying out to be said. All three works are driven by the desperate desire to speak, allied to the implacable sense that all speech is only the product of its cultural and social moment and, as such, can never express the whole person, let alone the whole society, as Homer and Dante do, in their different ways. Paradoxically, though, it is this very tension, this very awareness, that makes them feel so representative of modernity, as Homer and Dante were representative of earlier, pre-modern cultures.

Part of our pleasure in *Hamlet*, as well as our critical frustration with it, lies in the fact that it is obsessed with performance. Not only does it contain, like many of Shakespeare's comedies, a play within a play, it also contains a mime to which Hamlet acts as chorus/explainer. The Ghost appears in circumstances which Shakespeare is at great pains to make as realistic and as melodramatic as possible, but then this is undercut by having the Ghost move about in the understage area with the audience's attention specifically drawn to this, with the implication that he is some kind of comic stage devil. We are given information about the theatre wars of the day and about the visit of English actors to the Court of Elsinore. We are entertained by long disquisitions on the nature of plays and acting by both Polonius and Hamlet, and by in-jokes about the recent production at the Globe of another play of Shakespeare's, *Julius Caesar*, and the performance in that play of two of the actors who also play key roles in *Hamlet*. In the light of all this, Hamlet's sense of being outside all the plays on offer, and so in a way outside this very play we are watching (until the very end, when he can say, with total conviction, 'I die, Horatio'), marks him out as playing a role the Elizabethans would have been very familiar with – not the melancholic we are prepared for at the start, but the Clown.

The Clown, as modern theatre historians like Robert Weimann and David Wiles have shown, was an integral part of late medieval and early Renaissance drama, a figure with roots in the Vice of morality plays like *Mankind*, who acted as a a link between the audience and the play, his role emphasised by the fact that he was usually stationed on the same level, inhabiting the same space, as the audience, talking to them and engaging with them, while the play proper, as it were, took place on an elevated platform behind him. As medieval drama, both religious and secular, gave way to Renaissance plays with complex self-contained plots, sealed off more and more from the audience, the role of the Clown declined or mutated and eventually disappeared.

Theatre historians, though, like all specialists, have, while providing us with many new insights, also perhaps been too obsessed with the history they are examining, which, for them, seems at last to explain everything. Since we know that Shakespeare's company included the famous clown William Kemp, and that Kemp left the company in 1599, just before the writing of *Hamlet*, to be replaced by a very different kind of comic actor, Robert Armin, and that this coincided with the building of the Globe and the establishment of a group of actors, of whom Shakespeare was one, with a quite new relationship to the theatre in that they were not only company members but shareholders in their own building, these historians wish to argue that after that date Shakespeare's theatre changed utterly. Some argue that it finally freed itself from its medieval and sixteenth-century roots and that at that moment Shakespeare found his true self at last and became a proper Renaissance playwright, constructing self-contained works that held up the mirror to their audience, as Hamlet recommends; others argue that when it turned away from its popular roots it lost that rich relationship with its audience which was the wellspring of the extraordinary achievement of Elizabethan drama. What both overlook or downplay is that, though 1599 was indeed a watershed in many ways for Shakespeare and for the theatre, a viewer or reader who knew nothing of this would find it difficult to spot any hiatus here or anywhere else in the dense mass of

Shakespeare's *oeuvre*, produced in a hectic twenty-year period from the early 1590s to the early 1610s, and whose precise chronology is still (and is likely to remain) unclear.

The work of these recent theatre historians does, though, shed interesting light on *Hamlet*, but only if taken in the right way. What if *Hamlet*, far from being the play in which Shakespeare put the Kemp Clown behind him, or rather relegated him to just one scene at the start of Act V, were to be seen as the play in which Shakespeare most fully exploited the possibilities and limits of the Clown? For it seems to me obvious, if one attends to the play with care, that Hamlet, who feels himself outside every play on offer, who so often comes downstage to comment on what is going on behind him or to talk to himself in the hearing of the audience, occupies exactly the position of the Clown. And the speed of his repartee and the shafts of his wit suggest that this is a role he recognises himself to be playing.

But to leave it at that is to stop too soon.

David Wiles, one of the most critically astute of the recent theatre historians, has written well about the Clown. Quoting the anthropologist Victor Turner, he remarks that 'Clowns are the prime example of figures who, "representing the poor and the deformed, appear to symbolise the moral value of *communitas* as against the coercive power of supreme political rulers."' He also reminds us of Bakhtin's comments, in his work on Rabelais, about the body as open and fluid, not closed and self-contained, and of Sancho Panza's *panza* or paunch as expressing the carnivalesque spirit, which, he suggests, clashes in *Don Quixote* with the new emphasis on private and self-enclosed bodies and systems. Bakhtin, he goes on,

> clarifies the point that the clown's task in performance is precisely *not* to create a character. His task is to project himself bodily, exploiting the grotesqueness of his 'scurvy' face and his stunted or lumpish anatomy. The clown's gaping mouth can be seen as part of a system of meanings: there is no bodily closure for the clown, just as there is no narrative closure.

Through images of incompleteness or non-containment, the language of laughter signifies something akin to what Turner calls *communitas*.

Wiles brings this anthropological perspective to bear, to excellent effect, on his study of Shakespeare's clowns, but it is on his discussion of Falstaff I want to focus. 'The Falstaff of the two Henry IV plays', he writes, 'is structurally the clown's part, with significant modifications.' Like other clowns, he points out, Falstaff introduces himself as a melancholic, 'the better to offset his later mirth': ' 'Sblood, I am as melancholy as a gib cat or a lugged bear' (*1 Hen. IV,* I. 2. 72–3). Hal thinks of him as a Vice from the old moral interludes, calling him 'devil', 'vice', 'iniquity', 'ruffian' and 'Satan' (*1 Hen. IV,* I. 2. 244–57). Like the Vice's, his weapons are mock-weapons, a 'leaden' dagger and a pistol that turns out to be a bottle of sack (V. 3. 54, s. d.). He uses a stave or short staff (from which he may derive his name), and which, explains Wiles, 'signifies low rank, in contrast to the rapier, which was the international mark of the gentleman'. At the end of Part I Falstaff is apparently killed, but then he rises up again, fully alive, 'and pronounces himself to be no counterfeit because only dead men are truly counterfeit'.

In his splendid essay on Falstaff, 'The Prince's Dog' (in *The Dyer's Hand*), Auden long ago noted that, like all clowns, he belongs essentially outside time, his first words being, 'Now, Hal, what time of day is it, lad?' (*1 Hen. IV,* I. 2. 1), but that Shakespeare placed him within a history play and not a comedy, and therefore within a structure where time rules. That is why, though at the end of Part I he is indeed 'resurrected', like any clown (and like the medieval St George of the mummers' plays), at the end of Part II he has to be banished, for in the 'real time' of the histories those who imagine they live outside time are in the end fooling only themselves.

All this is of course highly pertinent to *Hamlet*. For of Hamlet too we might say that his is 'structurally the clown's part, with significant modifications', the chief of which being that, like

Falstaff, he does not exist within a comedy, though, unlike Falstaff, he is a prince and the likely heir to the throne. He feels that the time is out of joint, but he knows that he and no other 'was born to set it right'. This means that even the role of the Clown is not one he can naturally inhabit. Though he feels, like the Clown, that he inhabits infinite space, he knows that this is only in his imagination, and that in reality he lives in the prison that is Denmark. Though he desires nothing more than to shed the burden of his being and melt and dissolve, let his body merge with the world, he knows that he is a bounded and enclosed being who can never really shed his sorrows and anxieties. His tragedy, we might say, is that he is both Falstaff and Hal, lacking the purity, the single-mindedness, of both. Interestingly, in the light of Wiles's remark about Falstaff and his mock sword, Hamlet enters the world of time first by stabbing through the arras with his sword and accidentally killing Polonius, and then, at the end, by agreeing to fight a duel with rapiers, 'the international mark of the gentleman', and dying in the process.

Hamlet dies and, unlike the Falstaff of *1 Henry IV*, he does not rise again.

Or does he?

There is one obvious way he does, and that is when the actors take their final bow. But there is a more profound and vital way in which he does so, and to find this we need to return to Yorick.

For Hamlet, the encounter with the old jester's skull leads to the conclusion that all that life, all that *joie de vivre*, only ends in the grinning mass of bone, and is therefore worth nothing from the start. But, I argued, this was to draw the wrong conclusion from the encounter. What it really shows is that the mere mention of Yorick, who, we surmise, had not been in Hamlet's thoughts for a long time, is enough to trigger one of his most spontaneous outbursts, as spontaneous as his 'I loved Ophelia'. 'I knew him, Horatio,' he says to his friend, 'a fellow of infinite jest, of most excellent fancy.' And what he recalls, specifically, is this: 'He hath bore me on his back a thousand times.' But 'recalls' is the wrong word here. For in that moment time is momentarily abolished. It is a Proustian moment, when Hamlet experiences again what it felt like to be carried on the old jester's back, and he conveys this to us in the very lilt and rhythm of his own words: 'Where be your gibes now, your gambols, your songs, your flashes of merriment, that were wont to set the table on a roar?' The implied answer is: 'They are nothing but dust and bones.' But, as with the 'For O, for O, the hobby-horse is forgot', the ostensible meaning is contradicted by the utterance of the sentence itself. Just as in that moment the hobby-horse is, precisely, not forgotten but recalled, so the gambols, the songs, the flashes of merriment of the old jester are not subsumed into and rendered meaningless by the grinning skull, but on the contrary, brought to life by it. Hamlet's question, 'where be they now?' is not a rhetorical one. It is one that is capable of an answer: they be here, now, in the theatre, at this moment.

And in just the same way, while Hamlet is borne from the stage to martial music at the end, he comes to life again, for us, as we allow what we have been experiencing in the past few hours to flood through our minds and bodies. We realise then that what has stayed with us is not the series of 'carnal, bloody, and unnatural acts,/ Of accidental judgements, casual slaughters' which make up the plot of the play, but the sweet prince of Horatio's elegy, his nobility of spirit, his questing and troubled mind, his wonderful way with words and all that happened to him in the course of his brief and troubled life.

This brings us to a final reflection. Theatre historians and other recent scholars, as I have pointed out, have been divided as to whether *Hamlet*, a new play for a new theatre with a new clown, should be seen as the start of a new phase in Shakespeare's work and in the dramaturgy of the Renaissance, or whether, in fact, the persistent identification of Hamlet with the old Vice should not make us see it as very much a part of a Tudor or even a medieval world. Looking at the play in the way I have suggested we see that Shakespeare, as always, manages to have it both ways. Hamlet is not a Clown or a Vice. He is a Renaissance prince, and he is embedded in a new kind of self-contained and perfectly plotted play. But what the play shows us is a man who cannot believe in the plots of any of the plays offered to him and yet cannot, like the Clown, remain forever aloof from them. It is that concatenation of circumstances which makes of him a modern man, with all the doubts and hesitations, all the awareness of possibilities that leads to the dizzying sense that his life lacks necessity and therefore meaning. But what Shakespeare demonstrates is that such a man can have a life which is meaningful and also, in a sense, exemplary, a life and death with its own distinctive shape, to which we can return again and again, 'with awe and wonder'. But – and it is a big but – that shape cannot be seen by the one who lives it but only by those who come in contact with him and only after he is dead. The miracle of art – of Shakespeare's art, in this instance – is that we can, as we participate in the play by attending a performance or even reading it, live both inside Hamlet and his tortured search for meaning and for freedom from the anguish that plagues him, and outside him, within the play called *Hamlet*, living again and again, as we fold and unfold it in our imaginations, the way events conspired both to make and to unmake him, as they do with us all.

NOTES

page viii. 'Long been fascinated by an image' – plates 29 and 30 in Robertson's study.

page 6. 'Rowe worked on the neoclassical assumption' – Emrys Jones, *Scenic Art in Shakespeare*, 66.

page 9. 'When we see them performed' – Emrys Jones, *ibid.,* 28.

page 12. 'A Bulgarian historian . . .' – Christopher Clark, *The Sleepwalkers,* xxvii–xxviii.

page 23. As Emrys Jones rightly says' – *Scenic Art,* 12.

page 23. As another Oxford scholar . . . – John Jones, *On Aristotle and Greek Tragedy*, Section Three, *passim.*

page 27. 'The grossest part of our blood' – *Nashe,* 217.

page 28. 'Like the great spectre . . .' – Victor Hugo, *William Shakespeare,* 218.

page 28. As Erwin Panofsky tells us – *The Life and Art of Albrecht Dürer,* 156. (The following paragraphs take up a passage from *What Ever Happened to Modernism?*, 24–6.)

page 28. Panofsky – *ibid.,* 169–70.

page 30. 'Tolstoy had noted' – Robert Pippin, *Modernism as a Philosophical Problem,* 155.

page 30. Robert Weimann – this is the substance of Weimann's remarkable *Shakespeare and the Popular Tradition in the Theater.*

page 34. 'Now goth sonne' – *Medieval English Lyrics,* 54.

page 35. 'I do not care for anything.' – This and the subsequent quotes from *Either/Or,* I.

page 37. 'Søren Kierkegaard' – W.H. Auden, *Collected Poems,* 513.

page 38. 'Claudius's isocolonic style' – Margaret Ferguson, '*Hamlet*: Letters and Spirits', in *Shakespeare and the Question of Theory,* 293.

page 40. 'Hamlet', Ferguson goes on – *ibid.,* 294.

page 43. 'I understand Hamlet's "I know not seems" ' – Stanley Cavell, 'Hamlet's Burden of Proof', in *Disowning Knowledge,* 185–6.

page 50. As Stephen Greenblatt has noted – *Hamlet in Purgatory,* 242.

page 58. Stephen Greenblatt reminds us – *ibid.,* Chapter Three.

page 69. 'The ghost asks initially' – Cavell, 'Hamlet's Burden of Proof', 188.

page 74. Empson draws the right conclusion – '*Hamlet*', in *Essays on Shakespeare*, 84.

page 76. Vladimir – Samuel Beckett, *Waiting for Godot*, Act II.

page 78. Margreta de Grazia has observed – Hamlet *Without Hamlet*, 177.

page 81. As Stoppard understood so well – Tom Stoppard, *Rosencrantz and Guildenstern are Dead.*

page 91. 'He walks out to the audience' – Empson, '*Hamlet*', 104.

page 95. Panofsky, in the book on Dürer – *Dürer*, 165–71.

page 107. 'Seneca,' he suggests – T.S. Eliot, 'Shakespeare and the Stoicism of Seneca', in *Selected Essays*, 131–2. To be fair to Eliot he provides a far more nuanced view in 'Seneca in Elizabethan Translation'.

page 111. 'Would not a man have thought . . .' – John Dryden, Preface to *Troilus & Cressida or Truth Found Too Late.*

page 113. Harry Levin has made the intriguing suggestion – Harry Levin, *The Question of Hamlet*, 156.

page 116. So Margreta de Grazia's at first startling suggestion – Hamlet *Without Hamlet, passim.*

page 131. I have a DVD of John Barton – *Playing Shakespeare.*

page 135. As Weimann has shown – *Shakespeare and the Popular Tradition in the Theater*, Ch.VI.

page 135. For James Shapiro – James Shapiro, *1599*, 43.

page 141. 'When Hamlet describes himself' – Stephen Wiles, *Shakespeare's Clown*, 57.

page 142. A.D. Nuttall pointed out – '*Hamlet*: Conversations with the Dead,' in *Proceedings of the British Academy* LXXIV, 58.

page 154. Wiles suggests – David Wiles, *Shakespeare's Clown*, 58–9.

page 157. By breaking up the stream of continuity – Benjamin, *Illuminations*, 152–3.

page 157. 'Universal history', – Benjamin, 'Theses on History', Thesis xvii, in *Illuminations.*

page 161. ''Her hands were certainly small and delicate' – Kafka, *The Castle*, Chapter Two, 39.

page 173. The last time we see the Ghost – Barbara Everett, *Young Hamlet*, 126.

page 179. 'Michal, for example, is described' – e.g. in *2 Samuel* 6.20, *1 Samuel* 19.11.

page 186. What Margreta de Grazia has . . . noted – Hamlet *Without Hamlet, passim.*

page 210. As Margreta de Grazia has shown – it is a major strand of her argument in Hamlet *Without Hamlet.*

page 217. To which John Jones has drawn our attention – *Shakespeare at Work*, 79ff. On 'soft' *see* 120.

page 226. 'The Chester *Expositor*' – Kolve, *The Play Called Corpus Christi*, 27.

page 228. 'It is a classic example' – Simon Palfrey ad Tiffany Stern, *Shakespeare in Parts*, 152.

page 234. 'the tendency we can discern' – Clark, *Sleepwalkers*, 529.

page 251. 'Fundamental to any idea of theatre' – Kolve, *Play called Corpus Christi* 11.

page 255. 'The word "Proteus"' – Palfrey and Stern, 45.

page 262. 'Clowns are the prime example' – Wiles, *Shakespeare's Clown*, 176.

page 263. 'The Falstaff of the two Henry IV plays' – *ibid.*, 116.

page 263. 'He uses a stave' – *ibid.*, 122.

BIBLIOGRAPHY OF WORKS CITED

W.H. Auden, *Collected Poems*, ed. Edward Mendelson, Faber and Faber, London, 1976.

—— 'The Prince's Dog' in *The Dyer's Hand*, Faber and Faber, London, 1962.

Walter Benjamin, *Illuminations,* edited by Hannah Arendt, tr. Harry Zohn, Jonathan Cape, London, 1970.

Stanley Cavell, 'Hamlet's Burden of Proof' in Cavell's *Disowning Knowledge In Six Plays of Shakespeare*, Cambridge University Press, 1987.

Christopher Clark, *The Sleepwalkers: How Europe Went to War in 1914*, Penguin, London, 2013.

Dante Alighieri, *The Divine Comedy of Dante Alighieri*, vol. II, *Purgatorio*, ed. and trans. by Robert M. Durling, Oxford University Press, 2003.

R.T. Davies, ed., *Medieval English Lyrics: A Critical Anthology*, Faber and Faber, London, 1976.

John Dryden, *Troilus & Cressida, or, Truth Found Too Late. A Tragedy as Acted at the Dukes Theatre To Which is Prefix'd, A Preface Containing the Grounds of Critcism.* The British Library, London, 2010.

T.S. Eliot, '*Hamlet*' and 'Shakespeare and the Stoicism of Seneca', in Eliot's *Selected Essays*, Faber and Faber, London, 1951.

William Empson, '*Hamlet*' in Empson's *Essays on Shakespeare*, Cambridge University Press, 1986.

Barbara Everett, *Young Hamlet*, Oxford University Press, 1989.

Margaret W. Ferguson, '*Hamlet*: letters and spirits', in *Shakespeare and the Question Of Theory*, ed. Patricia Parker and Geoffrey Hartman, Methuen, London, 1985.

Margreta de Grazia, Hamlet *without Hamlet*, Cambridge University Press, 2007.

Stephen Greenblatt, *Hamlet in Purgatory*, Princeton University Press, 2001.

Victor Hugo, *William Shakespeare*, ed. Dominique Peyrache-Leborgne, Flammarion, Paris 2014.

Emrys Jones, *Scenic Art in Shakespeare*, Oxford University Press, 1985

John Jones, *On Aristotle and Greek Tragedy*, Chatto & Windus, London 1962.

—— *Shakespeare At Work*, Oxford University Press, 1995.

Gabriel Josipovici, *What Ever Happened to Modernism?* Yale University Press, New Haven, CT and London, 2012.

Franz Kafka, *The Castle*, tr. by Willa and Edwin Muir, Everyman's Library reprint, London, 1992.

—— *The Diaries of Franz Kafka*, ed. Max Brod, Penguin, Harmondsworth, 1964.

Søren Kierkegaard, *Either/Or*, tr. David F. Swenson and Lillian Marvin Swenson, Anchor Books, Doubleday, New York, 1959.

—— *Fear and Trembling*, tr. by Walter Lowrie, Princeton University Press, 1954.

—— *On Authority and Revelation*, tr. by Walter Lowrie, Princeton University Press, 1955.

V.A. Kolve, *The Play Called Corpus Christi*, Stanford University Press, 1966.

Harry Levin, *The Question of Hamlet*, Oxford University Press, 1959.

Heiner Müller, *Hamletmachine and Other Texts for the Stage*, ed. and tr. by Carl Weber, Performing Arts Journal Publications, New York, 1984.

A.D. Nuttall, '*Hamlet*: Conversations with the Dead', in *Proceedings of the British Academy* LXXIV, 1988, pp. 153–69.

Simon Palfrey and Tiffany Stern, *Shakespeare in Parts*, Oxford University Press, 2007.

Erwin Panofsky, *The Life and Art of Albrecht Dürer*, Princeton University Press, 1955.

Patricia Parker, *Shakespeare from the Margins*, Chicago University Press, 1996.

Robert Pippin, *Modernism as a Philosophical Problem*, Oxford University Press, 1999.

D.W. Robertson, Jr, *A Preface to Chaucer: Studies in Medieval Perspective*, Princeton University Press, 1962.

András Schiff, www.wigmore-hall.org.uk/podcastdras-schiff-beethoven

William Shakespeare, *The Complete Works*, General Editor Alfred Harbage, Viking, New York, 1969.

James Shapiro, *1599: A Year in the Life of William Shakespeare*, Faber and Faber, London, 2005.

Edward Snow, *Inside Bruegel: The Play of Images in* Children's Games, North Point Press, New York, 1997.

Tom Stoppard, *Rosencrantz and Guildenstern Are Dead*, Faber and Faber, London, 1973.

Bart van Es, *Shakespeare in Company*, Oxford University Press, 2015.

Robert Weimann, *Shakespeare and the Popular Tradition in the Theatre*, Johns Hopkins University Press, Baltimore, MD, 1978.

Glynne Wickham, ed., *Mankind*, in *English Moral Interludes*, J.M. Dent and Sons, London, 1984.

David Wiles, *Shakespeare's Clown*, Cambridge University Press, 1987.

INDEX

Works by Shakespeare are indexed under their titles, those by other authors under the authors' names